WHERE TO MOUNTAIN BIKE IN BRITAIN

Compiled by Nicky Crowther

Open Air Books

Edition 2004, published by Open Air Books (31 Winnock Rd, West Drayton, Middx UB7 7RH, tel 01895 441145). Printed by
es Limited, Sparkford nr Yeovil. No part of this publication may be reproduced, stored in a retrieval system or transmitted in any
or by any means, electronic, mechanical, photocopying, recording or otherwise, without the permission of the publisher and
pyright owner. To the best of the publisher's knowledge the information in this book was correct at time of press.
sponsibility can be accepted for any error or their consequences. ISBN 0-9547041-0-X.

WHERE TO MOUNTAIN BIKE IN BRITAIN is a nationwide review of the best biking in the country. You can use it to plan trips in your backyard and further afield for memorable days and holidays off-road. You can use the outline directions to plot hundreds of routes on the map, or explore an area from a suggested base. Local bike shops and clubs are included, where you can ask for route advice, and possibly find riding buddies.

It's boom-time in British mountain biking! The Forestry Commission is extending trail-building in its woodlands, with new venues due. If there's a volunteer group in your area, get along, get digging and add a new dimension to your biking.

Wherever you go, particularly in those Forestry Commission woods, ride responsibly. Be friendly to other people on the trails, stop for horses, and go elsewhere if you know your tyres are damaging the ground beyond recovery.

This is the book I've always wanted to have, and the book I've always wanted to write. I hope it opens up new riding for you, as it has for me!

Happy trails
Nicky Crowther

FEEDBACK WANTED: Info on good routes and places to ride, or on poor routes and places which close, is gratefully received. Information used in the second edition may earn you a free copy. Please email comments to the publisher via the website www.wheretoMTB.com.

Adamthwaite in the lovely Howgills.

Acknowledgements
The book has been compiled with the help of a number of mountain bikers. For their knowledgeable written contributions I tha Mark Alker, Katie Dixon, Kieran Foster, Ben Haworth, Katie Jarvis, Clive Powell, Derek Purdy, Neil Simpson, Andy Stephenson a Steve Thomas. For their lovely shots, I thank the photographers (see the back page for who took what, and where to get more Simon Barnes, Steve Behr/Stockfile, Steve Bennett, Chipps Chippendale, Robert Hamilton-Smith, Ben Haworth, Ian Linton, Bob Love, Andy McCandlish, Steve Makin and Neil Simpson.
Thanks also to Steven Price (steven.price25@btinternet.com), for his slick eye in creating the design and layout.
Disclaimer
Ride safely, within your limits and wear a helmet. The author and publisher have done their best to ensure the accuracy and cur of the information in *Where to Mountain Bike in Britain*, however, they can accept no responsibility for any loss, injury or inconvenience sustained by any user of this guide as a result of information or advice contained in the guide.

CONTENTS

TRAIL-RIDING
Get sussed, get legal, get home...

DON'T LEAVE HOME WITHOUT...
- Puncture kit and working pump that fits the valves on your inner tubes (stored in a bag if it's muddy, to keep the seals clean).
- Inner tubes (preferably two good ones, in case of multiple punctures, or someone in the group has come out with nothing).
- Tools (multi-tool, 4, 5, 6mm allen keys, chain tool)
- Warm and waterproof clothing (for colder/wetter/longer rides than expected).
- The map (laminated or in a case if rain is expected) and a compass.
- First Aid Kit and helmet.
- Drink (full water-bottles, or a bladder pack which has a larger capacity).
- Food (snacks, energy foods, sweets, dried fruit).
- Money and phone (for emergencies, fully-charged).

BIKE-LEGAL TRAILS
These are;   Waymark colour
Bridleways   Blue
Byways Open to All Traffic (BOATs)   Red
Roads used as Public Paths (RUPPs)
(being renamed restricted byways)   Not decided
Other routes with public access (ORPAs)

Note: You may not ride on footpaths   (yellow)

MORE ON 'WHITE ROADS' (ORPAS)
Coloured white rather than yellow on Ordnance Surv maps, these are 'other routes with public access' also called 'green lanes' because they are often grassy. You may also hear them mentioned as UUCRs, 'unsurface unclassified roads'. If they have dots you are in the cle However, some are private tracks which we have no right to use.

You may also ride on:
- Forestry Commission stoned tracks
- Some unsurfaced Forestry Commission tracks
- Forestry Commission MTB trails
- Cyclepaths and cycletracks
- Some canal towpaths (download a permit from britishwaterways.co.uk)
- Unsurfaced council roads (called routes with othe public access on Ordnance Survey maps)

HOW TO PLOT A SELF-NAVIGATED ROUTE USING OUTLINE DIRECTIONS
1
- Get the Ordnance Survey or OS-based map (off t shelf or order from book shops, also online at ordnance survey.co.uk).
- The pink Landranger series (1:50,000, 2cm to 1kr 1km gridlines) is sufficiently detailed for navigating.
- The orange Explorer (1:25,000, 4cm to 1km, 1kr gridlines, formerly Outdoor Leisure/Pathfinder) gc into greater detail, showing useful navigating mark such as dry-stone walls.

2 Find the start/finish point. Plot the route on cycle r of way (see above, use a highlighter pen if you want Compass directions may be abbreviated (N - north,

3 Map references show two letters then six figures (SK 897 673), which pinpoints a place to within 100r
- The letters refer to the OS National Grid 100km square.
- The first three figures are the easting (left to right) made up of the two numbers of the kilometre sq (see the top/bottom edges of the map), then the tenth/s of the square.

The second three refer to the northing (side edges of
he map), same applies.

~ERTAKING OTHERS

~w to overtake a horse and rider
~ British Horse Society recommends 'hail a horse', where
~ shout 'hello' or 'passing' and await acknowledgement
~re slowly overtaking. If the horse is approaching it is best
~ismount and get off the trail. If the trail is narrow then put
~bike between you and the horse!

~w to overtake walkers
~Ber are required by law to give way to walkers, so
~rtaking can be problematic. The best thing is to slow
~t down and say 'Hello, may I come past?', which
~ally has the desired effect.

HTS OF WAY TIPS

~nhappy farmers complaining that you shouldn't
~e there
~w the farmer the map and ask if you are in the right
~e. If you are, politely say that you are allowed to ride
~~ bike, cite the 1968 Countryside Act or the 1980
~ways Act, and thank him for his interest before

continuing. If you have strayed from the legal route, ask if
you may continue, and if not, which way should you go.

● Gates
If they are shut - close them again
If they are swinging open - close them
If they are tied open - leave them open
If they are 'grounded' but not tied open, it may be best
to close them

● The local council rights of way department
These deal with issues, such as obstructions or disputes.
Landowners are responsible for keeping rights of way
clear of vegetation, such as hedges or trees.

● Which cattle may graze fields crossed by rights of way.
All cows are OK, but be wary of cows with calves. All
beef bulls such as Herefords or Aberdeen Angus are
okay, as they are normally quite placid. But it is illegal
to have a dairy bull such as a Jersey, Guernsey or
Fresian in a field with a right of way, because they can
be very aggressive. There are no restrictions on
horses or sheep.

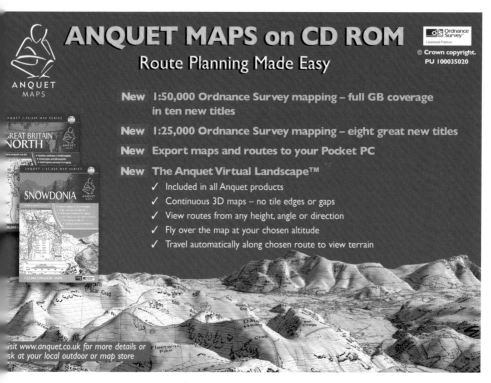

JOIN IMBA

IMBA, the International Mountain Bike Association, was formed in the USA in 1988 to promote new and improved trails and to defend mountain biking against closures or restrictions. IMBA has been involved in Britain since 1998, and the highly successful partnership with the Forestry Commission has led to many purpose-built MTB trails, with more planned. It promotes environmentally-sound and socially-responsible biking, and works to keep trails open and maximum access for mountain biking.

So the UK needs IMBA UK, and IMBA UK needs you! Join via the website. www.IMBA-UK.com. Send a cheque (£12 per adult per annum) to IMBA UK, PO Box 305, Harrogate. HG2 7WU.

Trail-building and IMBA

- If you want to start trail-building, first find out who the landowner is and approach them.
- Explain what you'd like to do, that you'd like their permission and that you'll build the trail to known specifications.
- If and only if they agree, get something in writing.
- Walk the area to identify both good and bad control points. Decide on the type of trail - either open and flowing or tight and technical - and join the good control points with trail. Mark the trail alignment and show it to the land owner. If they agree, you can start building using the tools described by IMBA.
- Take a look at IMBA *Building Better Trails* manual, on sale on the US IMBA website, or download it from the IMBA-UK.com website.

Leading the way in trail-building: Coed y Brenin

e~Cycle
ing Poverty by taking Used Bikes
w Territories
rity no. 1063570

E-CYCLE - THE BICYCLE CHARITY

ou know someone thrilled to be getting a new bike, re is someone in a less developed country who uld be very, very happy to receive an old one. Cycle does simple and extremely effective work. It es unwanted bikes lying around in the UK and ships m to a country where they're really needed.

003, the charity shipped over 1,750 bikes in five 40ft tainers to South Africa. Bikes of all shapes and sizes nt, also spare and new parts donated by bike shops manufacturers; tyres, lights and tools for new work- ps. Also shipped out were a set of wonderful red t bikes kindly donated by the Royal Mail (for further ures, see the Re-Cycle website).

002, Daniel James opened a Re-Cycle collecting re on the Isle of Wight. He soon had over 100 s, but getting them delivered to the charity's barn in

Essex proved a problem. This was neatly resolved when Mercy Ships, a charity that operates hospital ships around the coast of Africa, contacted Re-Cycle requesting bikes to take out to Africa. Their ship, the MV Anastasis, was docking in Avonmouth and, with the generous help of Somerfield Stores on the Isle of Wight, the bikes were transported to the ship free of charge. Unfortunately, the IoW collecting point had to close, but they hope it will open again in the future.

If you want to help Re-Cycle, you can donate your bike, form a local group, identify garage space for collecting, or organise a sponsored fund-raising ride.

Contact Re-Cycle at; the Loft, 110 Coast Road, West Mersea, Essex, tel 0845 458 0854, mob 0797 073 15 30, www.re-cycle.org.

Children outside a workshop in Africa with bikes shipped out from the UK by Re-Cycle.

A GUIDE TO HORSE-RIDING, FOR MOUNTAIN BIKERS

Catriona Cooke of the British Horse Society analyses horse – and horse-rider – behaviour

Like people, horses come in a variety of characters and their behaviour is also be affected by their rider.

The horse is a fright-and-flight animal, which means that in the wild it survived by galloping away from danger and thinking about it later! This is why some horses, especially young or highly-strung ones, may spin round ready to gallop away if they are startled by cyclists. So please call out if you come up behind a rider, because probably the horse and definitely the rider are unlikely to have heard you. Remember that if you pass too close and fast to a horse, it is liable to kick out in fear.

Heavy, cobby horses, which tend to plod along, are generally less flappable than showy, flighty types. And while horses can get used to anything, unfortunately, if they have a bad experience they never forget it. Riders' abilities also vary, so a child, an inexperienced or a nervous rider will not cope with a startled horse as well as a competent rider. A nervous rider can transmit their fear to the horse, so always do what a rider asks of yo because they know their horse and their capabilities.

Unfortunately, like lads with sports cars, many a young girl is over-horsed (maybe she thinks she need the extra horse-power for competitions). This means she is probably nervous of her horse when it plays up and has to concentrate hard to keep things together. if a rider appears haughty, it is more likely they are concentrating than cutting you dead! If a rider puts the hand up or calls out for you to stop, then please do s

Many families combine riding bikes and horses wi great success. Often the father and son are on moun bikes and end up as official gate-openers, while the mother and daughter ride horses. A trick we had to the biker up the hills was this; the cyclist would grab of the crest of the horse's neck and get the horse to them up the hill. But only try this once your horse is accustomed to the bike!

end in sight: chasing down the Lakes

Welcome to Wales,
especially if you like mountain biking

Explore the mountain trails of Snowdonia, the Brecon Beacon
Powys and the Preselis. Ride specialist singletrack in five
headline forestry sites; Coed y Brenin, Gwydyr Forest,
Afan Argoed, Cwmcarn and Nant yr Arian.

SOME CLASSICS...
- *Snowdon*
  **(the highest mountain in England &
  Wales is bridleway all the way to the
  top) (p36)**
- *Karrimor trail at Coed y Brenin*
  **(mountains of climbing, volumes of
  singletrack descending) (p22)**
- *White's Level Trail at Afan Argoed*
  (steep, exciting specialist trail) (p12)
- *The Gap in the Brecon Beacons*
  **(no frights, but a steady climb with
  views) (p17)**
- *The Wayfarers trail in the Berwyns*
  (a cycling pioneer's high pass) (p15)

Route websites
Mbwales.com, Mtb-wales.com,
Mtbroutes.com, also Forestry.gov.uk
(go to Recreation, then Cycling, and enter
a forest name)

Route Literature
- *Mountain Bike Guide - North Wales*
  (Pete Bursnall, Ernest Press, £8.25)
- *Mountain Bike Guide - Mid Wales and the
  Marches* (Jon Dixon, Ernest Press, £8.25)
- *Philip's Cycle Tours - South Wales* (£8.99)

Rights of way
In Wales and England, the main legal tracks f
mountain biking are bridleways, byways, 'ro:
used as public paths' (RUPPS) and 'other ro:
with public access' (ORPAs).

WHERE TO RIDE

Snowdon
Gwydyr Forest
Betws y Coed area
Coed y Brenin
Clocaenog
Clwydians
Berwyn Mountains
Lake Vyrnwy
Cader Idris
Machynlleth
Nant yr Arian/Plynlimon
Radnor
Rhayader
Builth Wells
Llanwrtyd Wells
Preseli Hills
Canaston Woods
Brechfa Forest
Brecon Beacons &
 Black Mountains
Afan Argoed
Cwm Darren
Sirhowy Valley
Cwmcarn
Gower Peninsula

▶ AFAN ARGOED
Afan Forest Park, south Wales

For experienced riders, the White's Level Trail at Afan Argoed (say *avan ar-goyd*) and Skyline Tra
are a must, given the juicy drops from the top to the bottom of the steep-sided valleys. All
combined, Afan's four testing MTB trails, its valley rail trail, forest roads and family route make t
former coal-mining area one of the nation's top 10 MTB sites.
Also known as Little Switzerland, the valleysides have a mixture of trees (not just pines), and the
hill-tops have been felled for views to the Gower and Brecon Beacons.

Where to ride
Guided and supported Contact holiday companies
Lets Offroad (tel 020 8402 6652, www.letsoffroaduk.
com) and Saddle Skedaddle (tel 0191 265 1110, www.
skedaddle.co.uk) for individual and combined trips to
Afan; also Afan Valley Bike Hire (see below)
Dedicated trails The Penhydd and Wall trails start from
the Afan Forest Park Centre, the White's Level and
Skyline trails start from Glyncorrwg (but you can ride to
Glyncorrwg (10km) from the visitor centre along the rail
trail.
White's Level Trail (difficult, purple markers), the tough
one, with outstanding singletrack using rocky outcrops
down the steep valley sides (runs close to Glyncorrwg
Ponds centre)
Skyline Trail (57km, difficult) Another top route, in
construction at time of writing, runs close to Glyncorrwg
Ponds centre)
Penhydd Trail (20km, difficult, orange) testing, starts Afan
Forest Park Centre
Wall Trail (24km, difficult, red) singletrack, views and
descents, starts Afan Forest Park Centre
Celtic High Level Scenic Route (40km) part of the
Sustrans Celtic Trail, this is non-technical linear forest
route through the forest park between Pontypridd and
Neath (an alternative to the parallel road route via
Bridgend, map from Sustrans tel 0117 929 0888)
Mapping OS Landranger 170 171; see www.
mbwales.com; *Philip's Cycle Tours - South Wales* (one
Afan route, £8.99)

Location From M4 J40 (Port Talbot) take the A4107
north for 8km, the Countryside Centre is signposted
the right
Visitor facilities
Afan Forest Park Centre (tel 01639 850564,
www.mbwales.com). Park here and ride along the rai
trail to:
Glyncorrwg Ponds Visitor Centre (and Afan Valley Bike
Hire), turn N off the A4107 at Cymer on little road.
Bike facilities Afan Valley Bike Hire, Glyncorrwg
(10km up at the top end of Afan Valley, next to the
Glyncorrwg Ponds visitor centre (guiding, spares, tel
07952 577316, www.afan-valley-bike-hire.co.uk)
Where to eat Cafes at the both park centres
Where to stay See *Guided and supported*;
Independent Hostels HoBo Backpackers, Tredegar (s
Sirhowy Valley entry), Glyncornel Environmental
Centre, Llwynypia (say *cloin-a-pia*), Rhondda Valley
(25mins drive from Afan, for groups (min six) and ind
uals if already open, book (and avoid school parties),
01443 431727); *Self-catering lodges* L&A Holiday/R
Centre, Goytre (Afan Valley, tel 01639 885509,
www.lariding.co.uk); Fferm Ty Canol, Cynonville (Afa
Forest Park, tel 01639 851907, mary.raymond@btir
ternet.com); *B&B* Bryn Teg House, Cymer (Afan Val
tel 01639 851820); Llynfi House, Cynonville (Afan
Valley, tel 01639 851692); Ty'n-y-Coed, Ten Acre
Wood, Margam (tel 01639 885500)

The Berwyns: remote, dramatic and little ric

ERWYN MOUNTAINS
owys-Wrexham-Gwynedd
ee also Lake Vyrnwy)

 7

e dramatic, rugged Berwyn range, peaking at Moel Sych (827m), has miles of remote mountain
d forest trails, often by-passed in favour of Snowdonia by cyclists and walkers alike. The remote
:ure of the area, which lies south the A5 and Llangollen, lends itself to the more adventurous
d experienced mountain biker. There's fantastic riding as long you're armed with food, water
d map skills to make the most of it. This is the least populated area in Britain, so it's great for
ting away from It all. Riding around Lake Vyrnwy to the southwest, is close enough for
nbined visits and rides.

ere to ride

-navigating The Berwyn trump card is splendid
ation. Long, hard climbs are rewarded by fast and
nical descents, wonderful views, lakes, waterfalls and
else. The distance can be adapted, but the climbs
descents are nigh on impossible to escape

farer classic route (57km), this climbs and descends
580m mountain pass (non-technical but high and
osed) between Llandrillo and Pentre/Llanarmon
ryn Ceiriog. A summit stone commemorates
farer, a cyclist from the pioneering Rough Stuff
wship. The map on www.nwmba. demon.co.uk
ws a challenging double-pass circuit, that returns on
higher Bwlch Maen Gwynedd (700m) to the south.

ller trails of 35km and 20km take you up from
rhaeadr-ym-Mochnant to the Pistyll Rhaeadr water-
nd Llangynog - all good, tough riding. You can create
ute from **Llangollen** itself, but this isn't a popular a
point with those in the know.

ded and supported Trajectory Outdoors, rides and
B courses for all levels (Tony Griffiths, tel 07941
881, www.trajectoryoutdoors.com)

ping OS Landranger 125 Bala & Lake Vyrnwy;
brers 255 Llangollen & Berwyn. **Location**
haeadr-ym-Mochnant lies on the B4580 24km from
estry and the A5. The village of Llangynog lies
m out of Llanrhaeadr, with Pistyll Rhaeadr 6.5km
the centre of the village.

e Shops Stuart Barkley Cycles, Oswestry (17km

away, tel 01691 658705); Alf Jones Cycles, Chester
Street, Wrexham (tel 01978 261580, www.everything-
butthebike.com). **Stations** Welshpool 23km from Lake
Vyrnwy. **Where to stay** Camping Pistyll Rhaeadr Falls
(basic, tel 01691 780392); **YHA hostels** Cynwyd (self-
catering only, tel 0870 7705786), Llangollen (meals, tel
0870 7705932); **B&Bs** New Inn, Llangynog (tel 01691
860229). In the Llanrhaeadr area - Llyf Morgan (tel
01691 780365), Bron Heulog (tel 01691 780521). Tan-
y-Pistyll (Waterfall House) at Pistyll Rhaeadr (Rhaeadr
Waterfall) has a restaurant, B&B and self-catering cottage
(tel 01691 780392); **Hotels/Inns** Wynnstay Arms,
Llanrhaeadr (tel 01691 780210), Hand Hotel,
Llanarmon Dyffren Ceriog (tel 01691 600666), West
Arms, Llanarmon (tel 01691 600665)

Where to eat & drink Restaurant/tearooms at Pistyll
Rhaeadr (the waterfall, at the head of the road out of
Llanrhaeadr-ym-Mochnant); Llanrhaeadr has two cafes,
a small shop and three pubs, the Hand Inn, the Three
Tuns and the Wynnstay Arms. Llanarmon has two typical
Welsh country pubs, The Hand and the West Arms,
which do tea and cake as well as pub fare. Two more
pubs in Llangynog at the south of the range; the New
Inn and the Tanat. Lake Vyrnwy has a visitor centre with
cafe (and the cleanest toilets in Britain). The Lake Vyrnwy
hotel has a pub attached and a nice tea shop. Llanwdyn,
near the lake has a small shop and petrol station.
Tourist offices Lake Vyrnwy (tel 01691 870346),
Oswestry (tel 01691 662488)

BRECHFA FOREST
Carmarthenshire

Brechfa Forest, in southwest Wales northeast of Carmarthen, has a testing 14km route that show
off the best of Brechfa's plateau-like top and deep-cut river valleys on a combination of forest
road and singletrack. Combine this with the Preselis further west, for three or four day's riding.

Where to ride

Red route (red/difficult, 14km), steep gradients, track narrower than 1m in places on rough tracks. See the signboard in Abergorlech car park, and follow the red arrows.

Also *medium* and *easy* trails.

Location Brechfa lies eight miles northeast of Carmarthen: the place to start is the car park (grid ref SN586337) in Abergorlech beside the forest on the B4310. Coming from the east (mid Wales and England) head for Llandovery (A40/A483), then follow the A482 (Lampeter road) as far as the turnoff for Llansawel (B4302). In Llansawel follow signs for Abergorlech.

Stations Carmarthen, Llandeilo

Venue details Brechfa is a Forestry Commission fore (ranger: Emma Felkin, 01550 720394, email emma.felkin@forestry.gsi.gov.uk, www.forestry.gov.uk open year round, free car park and picnic site

Mapping OS Landranger 146, Explorer 186

Where to stay *B&Bs* Black Lion (01558 685365); Forest Arms (01267 202339), Glasfryn, Brechfa (tel 01267 202306)

Tourist offices Carmarthen (tel 01267 231557), Llandovery (tel 01550 720693)

BRECON BEACONS & BLACK MOUNTAINS
(see also Sirhowy Valley)

The brown Beacons of South Wales offer enough riding to keep you busy for over a week without repeats. The classic route is the very rideable Gap pass across the main ridgeline, with the Sarn Helen Roman road another well-known traverse. However, there are bikers who reckon the high, steep bridleways of the Black Mountains to the east are best, featured largely on the notorious MBR Killer Loop, while the south Merthyr Tydfil/Tredegar side of the range also has memorable riding, including the Tri Chwm trail (see Sirhowy Valley). 15 quality MTB routes have been mapped by the National Park (at time of press intended for a leaflet and waymarking); ride the reds and blacks (including the Black Mountains) for the challenge; the blues, greens and yellows for a relatively easier time. Brecon town is a good base for the north side of the Beacons, also Sennybridge; Abergavenny and Crickhowell for the Black Mountains, and Tredegar and Ystradfellte for the south side and adjacent valleys.

Where to ride

Guided and supported Holiday company Saddle Skedaddle (tel 0191 265 1110, www.skedaddle.co.uk); Brecon Cycle Centre (see bike shops), Bikes & Hikes (see Where to stay)

Self-navigating

Use OS Brecon Beacon Explorers OL12, OL13.

Sarn Helen, Roman Road between Ystradfellte (S side) and Penpont (N side, A40 7km west of Brecon), traverses ridgeline (to 470m on Bryn Melyn). The southerly one is shallower, better for climbing)

circuits from **Ystradfellte and Pontneddfechan around the Mellte and Upper Neath river valleys** (including in-and-out bridleway into Sgwd yr Eira waterfall - ride with utmost care around the waterfall, there have been fatalities among visitors to the waterfalls).

National Park self-navigating routes;

Brecon red (classic, difficult, see pics this and next page), Brecon, Llanfrynach, Talybont, S on Taff Trail 2km, left to Bore Tramway 4km (to top of forest), R DH forest boundary, SO Taff Trail onto metalled road, L road 4km (a climb), R forest Taff Trail 2km, fork R road edge of forest, SO the Gap, 7km down, metalled road back to Brecon (for track last 2km into Brecon, 2km down lane R past Cefn Cantref Farm, 450m L on to track).

Talgarth red (difficult, start also Llangorse), Talgarth S, via

nr Trefeca,, W round bottom Mynydd Troed, from Cockit Hill contour W side Mynydd Llangorse, up to Cefn Moel, S down to Bwlch, NW via Allt yr Esgair to Pennorth, to Llanfihangel Tal y Llyn and Llangorse.

Black Mountains Killer Loop (very similar to Nat Pk **Talgarth black**) (40km, clockwise, plotted (see map) by mtb-wales.com for **MBR** magazine). Talgarth/ Pengenffordd to RUPP (map ref 188 333), SE up over Y Das down Grwyne Fawr valley. SE into Mynydd Du Forest,climbing to exit at the high southern tip (Disgwylfa), SW up Crug Mawr over Blaen-yr-henbant N road via Milaid, Blaenau, Hermitage Bridge (**Talgarth Black** stays lower in forest, S lanes round Crug Mawr/Blaen-yr-henbant to Llanbedr, up W side of valley), NW track up to Mynydd Llysiau, descend notorious Rhiw Trumau and return.

Talybont red (difficult), Talybont, S bridleway above reservoir, bdw over Waun Rydd down to Pontsticill, W side reservoir, E Dolygaer, RUPP Bryniau Gleision, retrace, divert E Tor y Foel, Cwmcrawnon, back.

Sennybridge red 1 (difficult, 33km), Sennybridge, S thru Defynnog, public access road S to Wern-ddu Weir, lane to Brychgoed Fm, bdw to Heol Senni, NE road to before A4215, SE 1km to crosstracks, SW Sarn Helen 8km to road, N 5km to Heol Senni, W road 1.5km, N RUPP/lane/bdw 4km back to Defynnog.

BRECON BEACONS (continued)

Sennybridge red 2 (difficult), Sennybridge to summit of Bryn Melin (473m) anticlockwise.

Crickhowell red 1 (difficult) From Crickhowell northeast to Llanbedr, east into the valley that runs NNW, to the head of the valley below Bwlch Bach, returning on the west side, on forest trails in the Mynydd Du Forest, up and over Crug Maw, Blaen-yr-henbant, and down to Llanbedr.

Mapping and literature

National Park routes pamphlet (green to black) available from bike shops and tourist offices in the park; downloadable routes on www.mtb-wales.com; OS Explorer OL 12, 13 (western and eastern); *Philip's Cycle Tours-South Wales* (£8.99, mapped Gap)

Location

The Brecon Beacons range in south Wales comprises the Black Mountain (singular) in the west, the Beacons in the middle and the Black Mountains to the east, and caps the top of the old coal-mining valleys. The M40 runs through the park, accessible from the Midlands via the M50 and Ross on Wye, and from southern England via Newport and the M4/A4042 junction. Abergavenny has the nearest train station.

Bike shops and hire Brecon Cycle Centre (guiding if arranged, tel 01874 622651, wwwbreconcycles. com); Bikes and Hikes (10 The Struet, Brecon, tel 01874 610071, www.bikesandhikes.co.uk); Bikebase, Abergavenny (tel 01873 855999). Pedalaway, Hopyard Farm, Govilon (nr Abergavenny, tel 01873 830219)

Where to get ice cream and drink Italian coffee

The Ice Cream bar in Brecon (Lion Yard, tel 01874 624911), local Llanfaes ice cream and a fresh brew.

Where to stay

(For *B&Bs* go to www.visitwales.com, click on Places to Stay, find the search page, and enter town name, eg, Brecon, for list of nearest)

Camping

Pencelli Castle Caravn & Camping, on Taff Trail/canal (5km SE of Brecon, bike friendly, shop, 5* shower bloc pitches year round, tel 01874 665451); Brynich Carav Park (2km east of Brecon, tel 01874 623325); Llynfi Holiday Park, Llangorse (Black Mountains, tel 01874 658283); Pyscodlyn Camping, Llanwenarth Citra (Black Mountains, tel 01873 853271, www.pyscodlyncaravanpark.com)

Independent hostels

Bikes and Hikes (10 The Struet, Brecon, tel 01874 610071, www.bikesandhikes.co.uk), Clyngwyn Bunkhouse, Clyngwyn Organic Farm, Pontneddfechan (Brecons south side, tel 01639 72293 email bunkhouse@just-organic.com), The Held (modern barn conversion, north side of Cantref, tel 01874 624646), Upper Cantref Farm (tel 01874 665223)

YHA hostels

Brecon - Ty'n-y-caeau (meals, tel 01870 770 5718), Llwyn-y-celyn (on A470 west of the main summits, meals, tel 0870 770 5936), Capel-y-ffin (Black Mountains, in the Vale of Ewyas, meals, tel 0870 770 5748), Ystradfellte (south side of the ridge, self-caterin only, tel 0870 770 6106)

Self-catering cottages

Brecon Beacons Holiday Cottages (Talybont, tel 0870 754 0999, www.breconcottages .com), Upper Bettws Farm (near Abergavenny, tel 01874 890141, bettwsbron@ talk21.com)

Tourist offices

Brecon (tel 01874 622485)
Abergavenny (tel 01873 857588)
Llandovery (tel 01550 720693)

BUILTH WELLS, Powys

`14`

ne of the half-dozen mid-Wales and border towns surrounded by good rights of way over green
d rolling hills. Builth Wells Cycles does guided rides.

Where to ride
If-navigating
uth is *Mynydd Eppynt* (north of the Beacons), an army
ea now being opened for public access.
ortheast is *Radnorshire* (see also Radnor); rolling hills
ch great views and singletrack
uthwest is *Llangammarch Wells/Llanwrtyd Wells*, and

the *Cambrian Mountains*
Location On the junction of the A470 and A483, in the
heart of Wales **Station** Builth Road 3km northwest
Bike shop Builth Wells Cycles (hire, guide, sales,
repairs, tel 01982 552923, www.midwalesonline.
co.uk/bwcycles)
Tourist office Builth Wells (tel 01982 553307)

CADER IDRIS, Snowdonia

`9`

en more than Snowdon, the ascent of Cader Idris (893m) is trophy ride.

7km (14km return), the distance is short but the
ent is massive. Climb from the SW on the Tywyn Path
ony Path). The contouring singletrack alongside Rhiw
redydd (map ref 685 127) makes an entertaining
ak (ie, has hidden pedal-banging rocks and dips) from

the farmroad and rockfest of the mountain proper.
Descend the way you climbed, with a lot more care.
Carry full mountain gear and know the forecast. **Map**
OS Landranger 124. **S/F** Llanfihangel y Pennant (toilets,
car park). **Bases** Dolgellau (N side), or Machynlleth (S).

CANASTON WOODS
Pembrokeshire

`17`

southwest Wales, an easy trail and some bridleways in semi-ancient natural woodland at the tip
the Eastern Cleddau river estuary.

Where to ride
en trail (easy, 5km), surfaced route on forest roads
f-navigating on a small number of bridleways.
cuit possible on lanes and RoW; around Narberth,
naston, Landsker Border Trail
pping OS Landranger 158, Explorer OL36
cation In Pembrokeshire, southwest Wales. From

the A40 8mi east of Haverfordwest, turn south on to the
A4075. The entrance and car park is a short distance
along here, grid reference SN074140.
Where to stay Lawrenny YHA hostel (tel 0870 770
5914) lies 5mi southwest near the banks of the lovely
Cleddau river
Tourist office Haverfordwest (tel 01437 763110)

5 ▶ CLOCAENOG FOREST
Denbighshire/Conwy

Comisiwn Coedwigaeth Cym
Forestry Commission Wales

Just east of Snowdonia, the Clocaenog Forest is a large area that's hardly visited due to its remoteness. The riding is on gravel-surfaced forest roads on a few hills (the peak is 501m) and around the glistening Brenig reservoir.

The Llyn Brenig visitor centre on the southwest shore does refreshments. The forest has a reputation as the venue of rounds of the RAC rally, also as one of the last homes of the black grouse and red squirrel. Base towns are Ruthin (see Clwydian Range) and Denbigh

Where to ride

Self-navigating Start from the car park at north end of Llyn Brenig or the Llyn Brenig visitor centre for general forest road riding

Up to the Lake (40km, moderate-beginner), this lengthy but not technical route is detailed on www.ridethe-clwyds.com, and ends up circumnavigating the entire lake, via the visitor centre for a cuppa

Location From Denbigh take the B4501 (single track road!) for about 11km. Where the road widens to two lanes there is an obvious road down to a signed car pa next to Llyn Brenig. An idyllic spot to leave the family f the afternoon!

Mapping OS Landranger 116; www.ridetheclwyds.com

Tourist office Ruthin (tel 01824 703992)

CLWYDIANS
Northeast Wales

6

...ne of Wales' best-kept upland secrets, the rolling Clwydian Hills lie between Merseyside and ...owdonia with views to both. Ride on hundreds of kilometres of bridleways, on lung-busting ...mbs and spectacular descents, including an **MBR** Killer Loop. An ideal getaway, with some ...sier trails too, the Clwyds are also precious for having a good-quality dedicated MTB website ...ich includes all information plus ride-through route movies and 3D. Base town is Ruthin.

...here to ride
...e best riding in the Clwydians are on routes down-...dable from the excellent www.ridetheclwyds.com; *Over the Top, Almost the Delyn* and, if you haven't ...d enough, the *MBR Killer Loop.*
...pping OS Landranger 265;
...w.ridetheclwyds. com
...cation Head for Ruthin, on the southwestern side of ...hills, the car park opposite the craft centre (grid ...rence SJ128586, near the tourist office). From here ...easy to access the range by MTB. At Loggerheads ...untry Park (tel 01352 810614) you can get informa-...n on local facilities and activities
...e shops
...ones Cycles in Wrexham (tel 01978 261580)

Cellar Cycles in Ruthin (tel 01824 707133)
Graffiti Cycles in Mold (tel 01352 759878)
Venue details Open year round. Run by the Denbighshire Countryside Service
Where to stay
Camping Three Pigeons Inn, Graigfechan (tel 01824 703178).
B&Bs Clwyd Gate Motel in Llanbedre (tel 01824 704444), Griffin Inn in Llanbedre (tel 01824 702792), Bryn Tirion Cottage in Maeshafn (tel 01353 810444), Hafan Deg in Maeshafn (tel 01352 810465)
Events Merida 100 MTB marathon
Tourist offices Ruthin (tel 01824 703992)

4

COED Y BRENIN
Snowdonia

Home of frothing home-brewed singletrack, the notorious **Mantrap** and the **Root of All Evil**, Coed y Brenin, one of the first dedicated MTB sites, must not be missed. Four of its five MTB pistes, including the long headlining **Karrimor**, are for experienced riders. The site is irresistible, particularly given the cafe, bike facilities and stupendous mountain scenery of Snowdonia. No mountain biker has won their spurs til they've spent a weekend here. Base town is Dolgellau, 13km south.

Where to ride

Guided and supported Contact Saddle Skedaddle (guided trips/hols, tel 0191 265 1110, www. skedaddle.co.uk); Trajectory Outdoors (guided trips/courses, tel 017941 970381, ww.cismbiking.com)
Dedicated trails all signed, all starting from the Maesgym/Coed y Brenin visitor centre (car park £1-£3)
Karrimor (38km red/difficult, featuring Morticia and Gomez downhill, ascent 1100m, 2-4hrs, mountain-height climbs and descents)
MBR (22km red/difficult, featuring the Cain & Able and flowing Pink Heifer descents, ascent 300m, 1.5-3hrs, climbs and technical singletrack)
Red Bull (11km red/difficult, 330m ascent, 1-2hrs, some rough 'n' tumble tracks, and Root of All Evil for finale) 15km Sport (red/difficult, combination route of best bits of other trails, including Flightpath descent, ascent 170m, 1.5-2hrs)
Fun (11km medium/yellow, 200m climb, suitable for novices but not Under-10s, with a short cut to reduce riding time from 1.5-2hours to 3/4hour)
Mapping free five-trail map from the visitor centre (tel 01341 440666); see www.mbwales.com; OS Landranger 124 125, Outdoor Leisure 18 23
Location Cyb lies 13km north of Dolgellau on the A470. Clearly signposted after Ganllwyd village
Bike facilities Bikewash; Beics Coed y Brenin (spares, repairs, tel 01341 440666, www.parcnet.com)
Bike shop Dragons Bikes, Dolgellau (hire, guides, sales, repairs tel 01341 423008)

Visitor facilities Coed y Brenin/Maesgwym visitor centre (tel 01341 440666)
Sustrans Cyb lies on NCN8, the Lon Las Cymru
Where to stay (see also **Guided and supported**); Sel catering Plas Isa, run by Coed y Brenin pioneers Dafy and Sian (ideal for groups, sleeps up to 24, with room let individually, Dolgellau central, tel 01766 540569). Brynygwin Isaf, The Tower, Brynygwin Isaf, Dolgellau (simple, tel 01341 423481, www.holidaysinwales. fsnet.co.uk), Farchynys Hall, Bontddu, near Barmouth (studio and self-catering, tel 01341 430693; **B&B** Abe Cottage, Dolgellau (made-to-measure breakfasts and 'departure lounge' for left luggage, cleaning up and going-home snacks, tel 01341 422460, gmullin1@ compuserve.com); Trem Hyfryd, Barmouth Road, Dolgellau (MTB- and motorbiker-friendly, route advic on CyB and around, washdown, secure indoor stora drying facilities for clothing/shoes, free laundry service time for next day's ride, licence and evening meals, te 01341 423192, email enquiries@Bikers-Retreat.com
Where to eat Cafe on site; in Dolgellau - Dylanwad Da is the top restaurant in town, cooking with fresh lo produce (opening days/times vary, ring ahead, tel 013 422870)
Where to buy food Popty-r Dref bakery deli selling delicious Welsh produce, Dolgellau
Events Fat Tyre Festival at Coed y Brenin
Tourist office Dolgellau (tel 01341 422888)

CWM DARREN
Caerphilly

andscaped valleyside country park with a degree of satisfying riding, views of the Brecon acons central massif and a cafe.

here to ride

a short **5km circuit** with great downhill, a BMX track hone your jumping skills) and a cafe.
www.hobo-backpackers.co.uk

Location In the Rhymney Valley, beside the A469 2km northwest of New Tredegar.
Park office (tel 01443 875557)
Where to stay Hobo Backpackers (see Sirhowy Valley)

WMCARN
bbw Vale, south Wales

outstanding single singletrack trail awaits at Cwmcarn in the Valleys. It's named after the rch, a ferocious beast of Welsh legend, and features 'Vertigo', a section of trail that's right on edge. It is the solo track here at the moment, but it's worth the trip, especially if combined h riding at Afan Argoed or in the Sirhowy Valley and Beacons. There's year-round camping on , and it's only 15 minutes off the M4 motorway.

ere to ride

ded and supported Contact holiday company Lets oad (www.letsoffroaduk.com, ring 020 8402 6652).
icated trail Starting from Cwmcarn visitor centre, marked, is the **(Whyte Bikes) Twrch Trail** (15km, ult, 450m climb) 98% natural singletrack through ods and to the ridge tops, named after the wild boar e Mabinogion legend! Start on 'Take-off', leading to challenging 'Mabinogion' singletrack climb through valley (up 300m). On top it's fast and flowing, leading /ertigo', hugging the side of a steep slope. After 'the of Death' it's down to the 'Landing Strip' and back.
oping OS Landranger 117 (map ref 230 935); see download from www.mbwales.com
e facilities MTB-friendly cafe, bikewash, clean ts, some spares sold on site. **Visitor facilities** ncarn visitor centre (tel 01495 272001)
ation Very accessible from south Wales and and; M4 J28, NW A467 (towards Abercarn) 12km,

to just after Crosskeys. Follow signs 'Cwmcarn Forest Drive' to visitor centre. **Sustrans** NCN 47, Celtic Trail, passes through Crosskeys. **Station** Newport, then cycle up the Monmouthshire & Brecon Canal to Crosskeys! **Bike shops** Risca - Martyn Ashfield Cycles (3km south, tel 01633 601040), Newport - Beserk Bikes (tel 01633 855019). **Where to eat** Visitor centre cafe, or Cardiff's restaurants and excellent nightlife.
Where to stay (see *Guided and supported*) *Camping* Cwmcarn visitor centre (open year round, tel 01495 272001); *Independent hostels* Glyncornel Environmental Centre (see Afan Argoed); Basecamp Bunkhouse, the Welsh International Climbing Centre, Trelewis (near Treharris 16km west, tel 01443 710749); *B&B* Wyrloed Lodge, Manmoel (Victorian farmhouse 15km north, tel 01495 371198, www.btinternet.com/ ~norma.james); Ty Shon Jacob Farm, Tranch, Pontypool (300m with views, 15km northeast, tel 01495 757536)
Tourist office Newport (tel 01633 842962)

The Betws y Coed surrounds in Snowdonia in autumn: beat that!

24 ▶ GOWER PENINSULA
Swansea

An Area of Outstanding Natural Beauty where the pleasant if hilly biking of Rhossili Down and Cefn Bryn is boosted by the distraction of the Atlantic beaches, castles, dunes and nature reserves. The Gower is a compact peninsula that you can ride around in a day, but is really too pretty to hurry - you could happily play on Rhossili Down for an hour or two alone. Take your beach toys, and ride as part of a general trip to what is one of Wales' top holiday spots. Mumble and Swansea have all facilities. The villages have scattered shops and pubs. Port Eynon is the fan venue, with plenty of fish and chips.

Where to ride
Self navigating
Circuit In good weather, see most of the peninsula and do most of the riding on a circuit that covers the west, centre, Oxwich and Scurlage (see below)

West The west end of the peninsula is laced with bridleways. Don't miss the climbs/descents and coastal views of *Rhossili Down* (193m, the summit bridleway is very steep, the lower bridleways are easier, great fun for two hours), also *Hardings Down, Llanmadoc Hill* (186m) and little *Ryer's Down* (start/finish either end of Rhossili Down: Worm's Head visitor centre or Hillend Burrows).

Central Long climbs/descents on the linear bridleway runs through the central upland, *Cefn Bryn*, from northwest of Reynoldston via the 167m and 188m summits and Arthur's Stone burial chamber, to a fine descent at Penmaen.

Others Mumbles to Southgate, Oxwich to Scurlage
Bike shops Swansea Cycle Centre, Wyndham St (tel 01792 410710)
Mapping and literature OS Landranger 159; Explorer 164
Location From M4 J47 (avoids central Swansea) wo through the Swansea suburbs to the A4118 road to t Gower
Where to stay
Camping Oxwich Camping Park (tel 01792 390777); *YHA hostel* Port Eynon (self-catering, tel 0870 770 5998)
Tourist office Swansea (open year round tel 01792 468321), Mumbles (seasonal, tel 01792 361302)

GWYDYR FOREST PARK AND BETWS AREA
nowdonia
ee also Coed y Brenin)

ings are stirring in the steep, secretive forests of Snowdonia around base town Betws-y-Coed. e purpose-built trail is in at Gwydyr Forest Park, but there's far more to be had with canny ding of the OS maps, and there are more signature Welsh trails being planned to the south und Penmachno. Check out links to the high Carneddau, also the course of the Sarn Helen man Road, and the RUPP to Capel Curig and through Dolwyddelan. A destination for pure untain trails and cut routes that's only at the beginning...

ere to ride

ded and supported Contact Saddle Skedaddle ded trips/hols, tel 0191 265 1110, www. daddle.co.uk)

dicated route Starting from the trailhead car parks Location), waymarked (new trails are planned for area).

in Gwydyr Trail (25km, difficult, 450m climbing) a ly cross-country course for experienced riders, with technical singletrack connected by forest road. This appeal to downhillers in part.

ydd Cribau and Penmachno At time of writing, three class trails are planned for south of the A5/Betws in ydd Cribau and further south in Gwydyr Forest (as osed to Gwydyr Forest Park) around Penmachno, promised to show the latest in Welsh trail-building wledge in a wonderful setting/

-navigating There are links from Gwydyr Forest to high neighbouring **Carneddau mountains** (ribbon s along the top); also miles of forest roads to re; **Sarn Helen** there is a section of the once-paved man Road that runs through Dolwyddelan to the n; **old RUPP** from A5 to Capel Curig.

ping Get the Gwydyr Forest Park route leaflet Beics Betws (see below) or Betws tourist office; and download map from www.mbwales.com; andranger 115 116, Outdoor Leisure 17

e shop Beics Betws, Betws y Coed (route informa- sales, hire, repairs, by the tourist office, tel 01690

710829)

Location From Betws-y-Coed (on the A5), head north on the A470 (toward Conwy) to Llanrwst. Go left and immediately right at Cwydyr Castle towards Llyn Geirionydd. 100m up this track are two signposted trail-head car parks (£1).

Stations Betws-y-Coed, Llanrwst

Visitor facilities Forest Centre (tel 01341 422289)

Where to stay

Camping Riverside Camping & Caravan Site (open Mar-Dec, near Betws railway station, tel 01690 710310)

Bunkhouses Tyddyn Bychan, Cerrigydrudion (on A5 20km southeast, tel 01490 420680); Glen Aber Hotel Bunkhouse

YHA hostels Betws y Coed (self-catering only, tel 0870 770 5732), Capel Curig (meals, tel 0870 770 5746)

Self-catering cottage Nant Cottage, Trefriw (300-yr-old woodland cottage nearby, tel 01690 710760, www.betws-y-coed.co.uk/acc/nant/)

B&Bs Bryn Llewellyn (centre of Betws, tel 01690 710601, www.brynllewellyn.com); Llannerch Goch, Capel Garmon (17thC, 4 acres garden, 6km southeast, tel 01690 710261, www.betwsycoed. co.uk/acc); Tyddyn Du Farm, Nant y Rhiw, Llanrwst (working farm, tel 01492 640189)

Tourist office Betws-y-Coed (tel 01690 710426)

8 ▸ LAKE VYRNWY
Powys
(see also Berwyn Mountains)

Lying at the southern end of the Berwyn range, huge Lake Vyrnwy occupies a remote and beautiful spot, with tough, steep riding nearby and good lakeside visitor facilities. Combine your riding here with elevated trails in the Berwyns, and you're in for a treat.
If you enjoy the highs and lows of lactic acid burn – and of course you do!

Where to ride
Self-navigating
Find excellent forest riding with stiff climbs, great views and stonking descents NE from the visitor centre at Llanwddyn at the eastern end of the lake. The round-the-lake road also gives access to riding in other directions.
You are unlikely to meet many others out on the trails!
Mapping
OS Landranger 125 Bala & Lake Vyrnwy, Explorer 239 Lake Vyrnwy
Location Approach via Llanfyllin, accessed from the south via Welshpool/from the north the A5 past Oswestry/ from the Midlands cross-country from Shrewsbury.
Parking is easy at the visitor centre, or one of many lakeside car parks just out from the centre (good for picnics). These make for great picnic spots.
Station Welshpool, 23km east

Lake Vyrnwy visitor centre (tel 01691 870346) h a cafe, a souvenir shop and, officially, the cleanest toile in Britain!
Where to eat/drink At the cafe at the lake visitor centre; at the decent pub and nice teashop at the Lak Vyrnwy Hotel up the hill from the lake; or at the lakes tearoom 5km from visitor centre.
Llanwdyn, the closest village, has just a tiny shop and one-pump petrol station.
Where to stay See *Berwyn Mountains*
Bike hire You can hire basic non-MTB bikes at the visitor centre
Bike shops
Stuart Barkley Cycles, Oswestry (tel 01691 658705)
Alf Jones Cycles, Chester Street, Wrexham (tel 0197 261580, www.everythingbutthebike.com)
Tourist offices
Lake Vyrnwy (tel 01691 870346)
Oswestry (tel 01691 662488)

LANWRTYD WELLS
owys

me of those nutty events, the MTB Bog-Snorkelling and Bog-Leaping world championships,
the relatively sane Real Ale Wobble, Llanwrtyd Wells has become a playful place for mountain
ing, rather than a site for gritted-teeth singletracking. Set near the Cambrian Mountains, with
Vale of Tywi and Llyn Brianne to the north, surrounded by 500m peaks, the town has a good
e shop, civilised hostel, city-standard restaurant and the Neuadd Arms, the town inn which first
anised the Man vs Horse event. It's somewhere to enjoy MTB get-togethers, as much for
ng the waymarked forest and rights of way network.

ere to ride
ded and supported
Kite Mountain Bike Centre, Neaudd Arms Hotel (tel
91 610236)
e Powell Mountain Bikes, Rhayader (tel 01597
343, www.clivepowell-mtb.co.uk)
icated trails
outes start from town;
ginners (13km), gentle, through forest
oderate (17km), some long climbs and technical
ents
oderate (23km), great scenery and moderate climbs
oderate (19km), fine views, long forest climbs and
nical descents
oderate, great views over Llyn Brianne Lake,
ilating route
allwm Trails link to route 4, purpose-built trails on
te land
e shop
Cycles (tel 01591 610710, www.cyclesirfon.co.uk)

Mapping and literature
See www.llanwrtyd-wells.Powys.org.uk
Also www.mbwales.com
Guidebook to the routes from Powys CC (tel 01874
612278, £4.99)
OS Landranger 147 160, Outdoor Leisure 11, 12, 13
Location
Llanwrtyd Wells lies north of the Brecon Beacons, 20km
as the crow flies from Brecon, on the River Irfon
Station Llanwrtyd Wells, 1km from town
Where to eat
The Stonecroft Inn (tel 01591 610327)
The Drover's Rest (high-class country restaurant with
serious chefs, tel 01591 610264)
Where to stay
Independent hostel Stonecroft Hostel & House (indi-
vidual rooms, tel 01591 610327)
B&Bs Neuadd Arms (tel 01591 610236), Drovers Rest
(upmarket, tel 01591 610264);
Tourist office Llanwrtyd Wells (tel 01591 610666)

10 ▶ MACHYNLLETH AND DYFI FOREST
Powys

There are three waymarked MTB routes at Machynlleth at present, with more being built. Rout cover a wide variety of terrain and include singletrack and mountain trails, also quiet country lan and river valleys. For those who prefer the independent approach, you can self-navigate the bridleways in the surrounding mountains and the northeastern Dyfi Forest to suit all abilities. Machynlleth is a cool little host town, 16km in from the coast at the head of the lovely Dyfi estuary. There's a switched-on bike shop which hires out bikes, plus cafes, bike-friendly accommodation and several hotels.

The Centre for Alternative Technology (5km north heading up to Corris, tel 01654 705950), is a glad-I-went place that wields a strong green influence on the local culture.

Where to ride
Guided and supported MTB Cymru does hols and wilderness weekends, DH days with shuttle, guiding and hire. They are local to Machynlleth but cover all Welsh sites (tel 01974 241714, mob 07815 202012, ian@mtbcymru.com); also RedBikeHire (with prior booking, www.redbike.co.uk)

Dedicated routes
All trails start from the main street in Machynlleth.
Mach 1 (16km), a good introduction to the riding here
Mach 2 (23km), steep ups, steep downs and not to be under-estimated
Mach 3 (30km), the big one, with breathtaking scenery, great climbs and technical descents including the infamous Chute!

Self-Navigating
Tan-y-Coed forest (3.2km from Machynlleth) has scenic mountain trails full of tight twisty steep singletrack.
Dyfi Forest (6km northeast of town) has ample singletrack to explore.

Mapping and literature Get the Mach routes leaflet from Machynlleth tourist office (see later) or Greenstiles (see Bike Shops).OS Landranger 135 Aberystwyth & Machynlleth, 124 Porthmadog & Dolgellau. Explorer OL23 Cadair Idris & Llyn Tegid;

Location On the A487 between Dolgellau and Aberystwyth. Park in the town council car park in the centre of town (around £1 per day)

Bike shops Greenstiles Cycles (route info, spares, h and workshop, Maengwyn St, tel 01654 703543); RedBikeHire (Ty-Joyo Graigfach, 3mins from station, 01654 703622)

Mountain Bike Club
No obvious club at time of writing, but Greenstiles Cycles may help with ride buddies

Stations Machynlleth

Where to stay *YHA hostel* Corris, 10km north of Machynlleth (self-catering only, tel 0870 770 5778); *B&B* Maenlwyd Guesthouse (tel 01654 702928). *Self-catering/B&B* Hafod Wen, Prentrelly, Llanilar (sit MTB Cymru accommodation (see *Guided and supported*); *Hotel* Wynnstay Hotel, bike-friendly and great desse (tel 01654 702941).

Where to eat and drink
The Quarry Cafe in the centre of town is recommended. The Wynnstay Hotel has a good reputatior too. There are lots of other good cafes and pubs

Events
Greenstiles Cycles organises the annual Raw Dyfi Enduro, which takes place in May

Tourist office Machynlleth (tel 01654 702401)

ANT YR ARIAN AND PLYNLIMON
eredigion-Powys

11

nt-yr-Arian Forest sits in high hinterland in from coastal Aberystwyth, and offers an epic
derness ride, the Syfydrin Trail, also excellent all-weather, cut singletrack carved into steep
eys and ridges in the forest. The most remote of the developed Welsh sites, the big riding is
ged and for experienced riders, and there's a biker-friendly caff.
erystwyth, nearby, is a buzzing town, full of good eateries and nightlife.

ere to ride
ded and supported MTB Cymru (hols/wilderness
kends, DH days with shuttle, guiding, hire, local but
rs all Welsh sites, tel 01974 241714, mob 07815
012, ian@mtbcymru.com).
ding also by Summit Cycles, Aberystwyth
below)
icated trails All start from the visitor centre,
ned
tinental Tyres) Syfydrin Trail (35km, epic) A long
trail that takes you out into the hills with amazing
s, follows technical doubletrack, and includes all the
etrack on the Summit and Pendam trails
mit trail (16km, hard) Maximum singletrack
ring the Mark of Zorro, High as a Kite and the
urner climb.
am trail (9km, moderate) Short but full of single-
, the easiest on site
navigating
of options on the rights of way network in the area
ing towards the Plynlimon Hills, source of the
n and the Wye Rivers (which meet again at their
hs at Chepstow)
ping and literature OS Landranger 135,
rer 213; see and download map from
.mbwales.com; display board on site, route leaflet
visitor centre
tion 13km east of Aberystwyth, off the A44 4km

east of Goginan (map ref SN 718 814). Car park £1.
Bike/visitor facilities bike-friendly cafe, visitor centre
(tel 01970 890694), basic bike bits in stock, toilets
Bike shop Summit Cycles, 65 North Parade,
Aberystwyth (guiding too, tel 01970 626061,
www.summitcycles.co.uk)
Where to eat
Cafe at visitor centre
In Aberystwyth - the Oasis Cafe Bar (on the high road,
trendy/delicious, tel 01970 626040)
In Aberystwyth - the Treehouse Organic Restaurant
(tel 01970 615791)
Where to stay
Camping Aberystwyth Holiday Village (in town, open
Mar-Oct, tel 01970 624211)
Woodlands Caravan Park, Devil's Bridge (near falls,
11km southeast, tel 01970 890233)
Self-catering/B&B Hafod Wen, Prentrelly, Llanilar (apart-
ment sleeps four, MTB Cymru accommodation, tel
01974 241714, mob 07815 202012,
ianl@mtbcymru.com)
Hostel and B&B Y Gelli/Plas Dolau (superior hostel,
restored farmhouse, 3km in from the coast in the
Rheidol Valley, tel 01970 617834, www.dolau-
holidays.co.uk)
Hotel George Borrow Hotel (Ponterwyd 2km east, tel
01970 890230)
Tourist office Aberystwyth (tel 01970 612125)

16 ▶

PRESELI HILLS
Pembrokeshire

Although little biked, there are enough low and high-level bridleways on the lovely Preselis in the western tip of south Wales for two to three day's exploration, best combined with a Pembrokeshire beach holiday.

The attraction of the hills is their high emptiness and the fact they overlook the gorgeous coastline, so you can do a ridge ride at noon, and be on the beach for tea-time ice-cream. Being holiday destination and national park, the area has lots of places to stay, eat and enjoy off the bike

Where to ride

Most rides include a major climb, so the tops are for fitter riders rather than beginners. Being moorland bog and liable to erosion, the park wardens ask that you only ride in the summer. But don't bother after wet weather anyway, you'll be pushing more than riding.

Self-navigating

The semi-classic *Preseli Ridge Ride* runs on bridleways about 8km along the spine of the range: start from the car park at the top of the B4329 pass, and head east, along the ridge but north of Foel Cwmcerwyn (the high-point in the range, 536m). At the end, either descend to lanes to the north and return via Pontyglasier and Crosswell then up the B4329, or stay high and retrace your pedalstrokes.

Explore other bridleways around the massif of *Mynydd Melyn and Carn Ingli* (347m) SW of Newport, and on the south side of *Foel Cwmcerwyn*, around *Rosebush* Easy riding is found in the lanes of the pretty *Gwaun Valley* (which runs into Fishguard) on the *Sustrans Celtic route* (one of Sustrans' nicest).

Location The Preselis are part of the Pembrokeshire Coast National Park, and accessible from the south from the A40 (turn north at Narberth on the B4313, then B4329 for the main road pass and Newport)

Bike shop Newport Cycle Hire (and repairs), Llysmeddyg, East St, Newport (tel 01239 820008). The hardware store on the north side of the main street sells small items such as inner tubes and lube.

Mapping and literature OS Landranger 157, 145,

Explorer OL35; two mapped Preseli routes in Mountain Biking in West Wales (£6.95, Dave & Barbara Palmer, see www.mtb-wales.com).

Station Fishguard, at the hills' western end

Where to stay

Camping Morawelon Caravan and Camping Park (towards the beach from Newport, tel 01239 82056

Camping/Bunkhouse Brithdir Mawr, an organic farm, welcomes cyclists (in the hills behind Newport, 6 be tel 01239 820164)

Independent hostel Hamilton Backpackers Lodge, Fishguard (small dorms and double rooms, tel 01348 874797, www.fishguard-backpackers.com)

YHA hostel Trefdraeth, near Newport (overlooking beach, north of the hills, used by coast path walkers, catering only, tel 0870 770 5996)

B&Bs Soar Hill, Newport (Cilgwyn Rd, 800m south centre, tel 01348 820506), Hafan Deg (Long St, tel 01348 820301)

Where to eat Newport has a selection of quality cafe/restaurants on or just up from the main street; the Fronlas Cafe. There's also a cafe above Parrog Beach.

For something special (not a budget option), go to th Manor Town House (also a B&B) in Fishguard for high quality home-cooked food in very civilized surround

Tourist offices Newport/Trefdraeth (tel 01239 820912), Fishguard (tel 01348 873484)

ADNOR
adnorshire

uperb destination in the Welsh/English borderlands, an achingly green and peaceful landscape
ere the hills are big but not too big, and the real ale pubs are irresistible. The most famous
up here is Hergest Ridge, which also acts as the start/finish for the popular annual Marin Rough
e enduro. Route information for the whole area is unbeatably organized into one website.

ere to ride

website www.roughrides.co.uk has mapped and
ed the rideable trails into the following areas for you
make up your own routes;

gest Ridge
y Traylow
scastle
or Forest and
emely English (huh?)

t/finish towns

ton, Gladestry, New Radnor and Painscastle.

ping and literature

andranger 147, 148
site: www.roughrides.co.uk (the OS maps are
nloadable cos they're out of copyright!)
ebook: *Philip's Cycle Tours - South Wales* (route in
or Forest, £8.99)

Bike shops

The petfood shop opposite the Kington Post Office
carries inner tubes, patch kits and pumps;
Slim Willys Cycles 2, Broad Street Leominster (tel 01568
614052) (20km east of Kington);
Dave Pearce Cycles, Fishmore Road, Ludlow (tel 01584
876016, www.pearcecycles.co.uk)
Coombes Cycles, Hereford.

Station Leominster (20km from Kington), Builth Road
Station (1.5km from Builth Wells)

Where to eat/drink and stay

Beg, steal or borrow a computer, to see
roughrides.co.uk's full lists for the above, including real
ale pubs (with specialities), trail grub and named accommodation (which includes *camping*, the new *Kington
YHA hostel* and *B&Bs*). Give this site a prize!

Tourist office

Kington (tel 01544 230778, www.kingtontourist.info)

13 ▶ RHAYADER AND THE ELAN VALLEY
Powys

There's excellent riding in verdant, hilly mid-Wales around the great reservoirs and dams of the Elan Valley where the summits rise to around 550m. Using Rhayader as a base, you can make u rides on the fine rights of way network from easy round-the-water routes to rides with technic – but not scary – climbs and descents . The views are spectacular, with a feeling of isolation. M of the mountain biking focuses around Clive Powell Mountain Bikes, the local enthusiast and operator. The region is known as Red Kite Country, after the number of these raptors that whe about the skies, courtesy of a 100-year-old conservation and feeding programme.

Where to ride
Guided and supported
Clive Powell Mountain Bikes (Cwmdauddwr Arms, West St, Rhayader, tel 01597 811343, www.clivepowell-mtb.co.uk), Saddle Skedaddle (guided trips/hols, tel 0191 265 1110, www. skedaddle.co.uk)

Self-navigating
Rhayader is the start point for nearly all rides.For advice on routes, enquire at the Clive Powell MTB centre. Favourites (identify them from the OS Explorer) include;
'Golf Links' (starts 1.6km NW from Rhayader, continues NW as byway, with a standing stone at the start of main descent, marked Maen-Serth ancient monument),
'Bonk Hill' (Esgair Perfedd),
the Roman Camp,
Rhydoldog Hill,
the Miner's Trail (Pant Dolfolau),
'Puke Hill' (about 5km SW of Rhayader),
the 'Submerged Track' (follows the river and is slightly below the level, so it frequently floods but remains ride-able and fun with a hard surface, NW to the base of Claerwen Dam),
and *Nant Gwyllt* (the Black Run, named after the chapel at the base, summit is Cefn Llanerchi).
During drier periods the *Monks Trod* is a great long-distance route over desolate hill country.

Go also W over to Strata Florida Abbey (excellent st trails around Claerwen outward, forest trails home-ward), as detailed on www.tracklogs.co.uk.
Dedicated route
Elan Valley Trail, 15km past the dams on roads
Mapping and literature
OS Explorer 200; see www.tracklogs.co.uk;
Guidebook: *Philip's Cycle Tours - South Wales* (route south of Rhayader)
Location
Rhayader lies on the junction of the A470 (Builth Wells/Brecon) and A44 (Leominster/Worcester) roa 15km northwest from Llandrindod Wells.
The Elan Valley and reservoirs lie 8km west of Rhaya at the end of the minor road to Elan Village.
Bike shop
Clive Powell Cycles, Rhayader (tel 01597 811343)
Where to stay Elan Hotel (tel 01594 810109), Be Head Inn (tel 01597 810289)
Where to eat Eagles Inn (tel 01598 810400), Cro Inn (tel 01597 811099).
Events
Venue of the Merida 100 (www.mtb-marathon.co.u
Tourist office Rhayader (tel 01597 810898)

RHOWY VALLEY AND THE SOUTH
RECON BEACONS
ee also Brecon Beacons)

ething knobbly's happening around the Sirhowy Valley and the southern Brecon Beacons. re's an impressive number of long, short, tough or easy rides, running from bottom to etop, including the new 64km classic, Y Tri Chwm. The specialist local base is the Hobo kpackers hostel in Tredegar (see picture) at the head of the Sirhowy Valley, 30km north of diff, where owner Horace is an MTB guide and beacon.

ere to ride

Chwm (hard 64km, climb 1600m), new long nce route in the Valleys with something for yone, from the floors to the tops, smaller sections ble over a number of days

and info see www.ytrichwm.co.uk).

l of the Sirhowy (easy 19km, 130m climb), ride y and play or put your head down and go! Nice hill finish through the St James forestry.

wy Valley (medium/hard 30km, 340m climb), mix en hills, disused railway, singletrack, couple of stiff s, technical decent. Route and pub options.

Gap (hard 51km, climb 620m), the classic Brecon ns trail: long climbs some technical, two fast tech-descents, great views from the highest legal point in Wales.

Reservoirs of the Beacons (moderate/hard m, climb 590m), best tracks in the National Park est scenery. Similar to the Gap trail with more track technical descending.

distance route (130km), from Hobo on the Coed annwg Way to Neath, overnight stay at Campthir. n on the Sarn Helen across the Beacons and back bo.

icill Reservoir (easy 14.5km, climb 75m), start/finish steam railway station), great reservoir views and icky bit to test/stretch beginners, plus one gentle Cafe at the steam railway station is usually open all with parking for a few cars.

wm Darren (easy/moderate); selection of routes MX track! 5km family route around lake. Or *22km*

moderate from the visitor centre with stiff climb to the ridgeway, reward is great panoramic views of the Beacons and a Celtic stone cross in secluded cemetery.

Sustrans routes near Tredegar
NCN8 (Taff Trail, 6mi north); NCN46 (Heads of the Valleys, 0.25mi); NCN47 (Celtic Trail, 4mi south)

Mapping
OS Explorer 152 & 166, Outdoor Leisure 12 & 13

Where to stay
Camping Park Cwm Darren (OS Explorer 166, map ref 113036, in the Darren Valley between Rhymney and Merthyr, tel 01495 711816);

MTB hostel Hobo Backpackers, Morgan St, Tredegar (tel 01495 718422, www.hobo-backpackers.co.uk, self-catering, groups, pick-up, bike hire, guided rides, routes from the door, ride/drive to Afan Argoed and Cwmcarn MTB centres, Black Mountains 30mins drive)

Independent hostel Black Sheep Backpackers, Abergavenny (tel 01873 859125);

B&Bs Roselands, Dukestown, Tredegar (tel Susie 01495 722040, email susanroseland@aol.com); Tynewydd Farm, Nantybwch, Tredegar (tel 01495 724155)

Events Beacons Beast, Iron Lemming, Dragon Downhill and Enduros (email Jason at dragondh@dsl.pipex.com)

Tourist offices Caerphilly (tel 02920 880011), Blaenavon Ironworks (tel 01495 792615), Abergavenny (tel 01873 857588)

SNOWDOWN
Gwynedd
(see also Coed y Brenin, Gwydyr Forest)

The highest mountain in Wales and England (1085m), Snowdon (Yr Wyddfa in Welsh) is unusual having a bridleway that climbs nearly 1000m up to the summit. This makes it a classic MTB trophy ride, except for problems caused by over-popularity. To contain the crowds, let alone the erosion, voluntary ban on mountain biking operates 10am-5pm daily June to September, when you are asked not to go up. However, while there's better all-round riding at Gwydyr Forest and Coed y Brenin not far away, Snowdon can be considered a summit bikers should bag before they die. Note, this is a total exposed mountain ride, so carry all contingency gear (clothing, food and emergency kit). It gets proper parky in winter.

Where to ride
Self-navigating
Observe the 'opening hours' (see above). The main bridleway, the *Llanberis Path*, begins from Llanberis village to the north, and simply climbs and climbs for 7.5km up 1000m beside the rack-and-pinion summit railway. The much-trampled track is broad and rocky in places, and often filled with walkers. Take care coming back down (the same way), and check you have full brake-power beforehand.

Another summit bridleway, the Rhyd-Ddu path, approaches from the southwest, but you'll be carrying your bike most of the way on that. The path is quieter outside the summertime voluntary-ban hours and in the winter (when snow and ice are common hazards).

Mapping and literature
OS Landranger 115, Explorer OL17; Guidebook *Mountain Bike Guide - North Wales* (Snowdon route, Pete Bursnall, Ernest Press, £8.25)

Location
Llanberis, in northwest Wales, lies on the A4086,

reached from most of the country via the A5 through Llangollen, turning left on to the A4086 at Capel Curig

Bike shop
Beics Betws, Betws y Coed (sales and hire, tel 01690 710829)

Where to stay
YHA hostel Llanberis (tel 0870 770 5928, catering) *Independent hostel* Jesse James Bunkhouse, 5km north on the Bangor road (tel 01690 870521, dorms, self-catering) *B&B* The Heights Hotel, 74 High St, Llanberis (a buzzy in-town place with dorms/rooms, tel 01690 871179) And Llanberis has lots, lots more...

Where to eat
The Snowdon summit cafe is a 'carbuncle' and scheduled for appropriately sensitive demolition and reconstruction.

In Llanberis go to Pete's Eats on the high street, for hearty over-flowing platters of food.

Tourist office Llanberis (tel 01690 870765)

ke your bike to the highest point in
gland and Wales (and we will know if you
de up on the Snowdon mountain railway).

The Marin Trail, Gwydyr Forest, Snowdonia

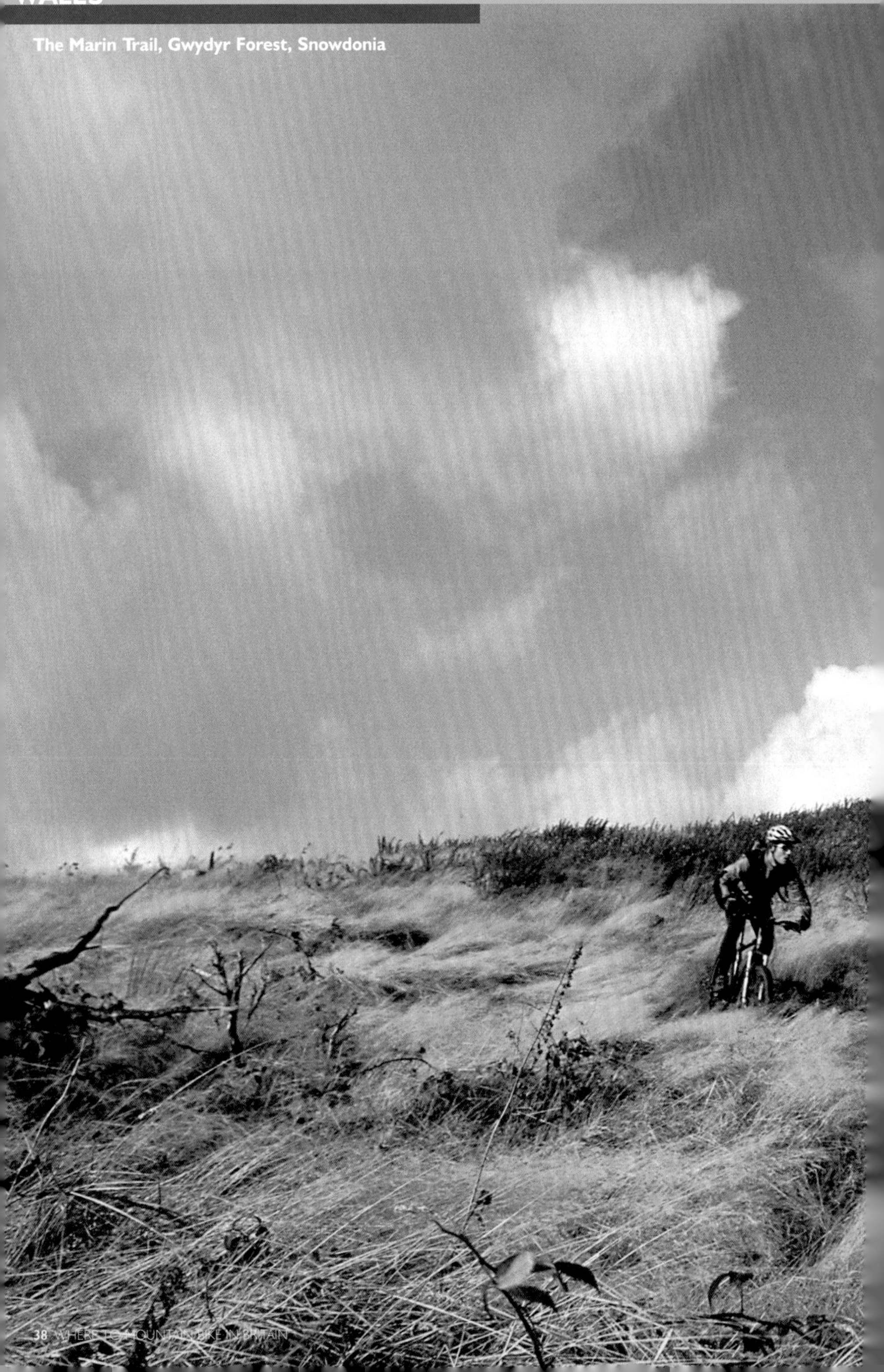

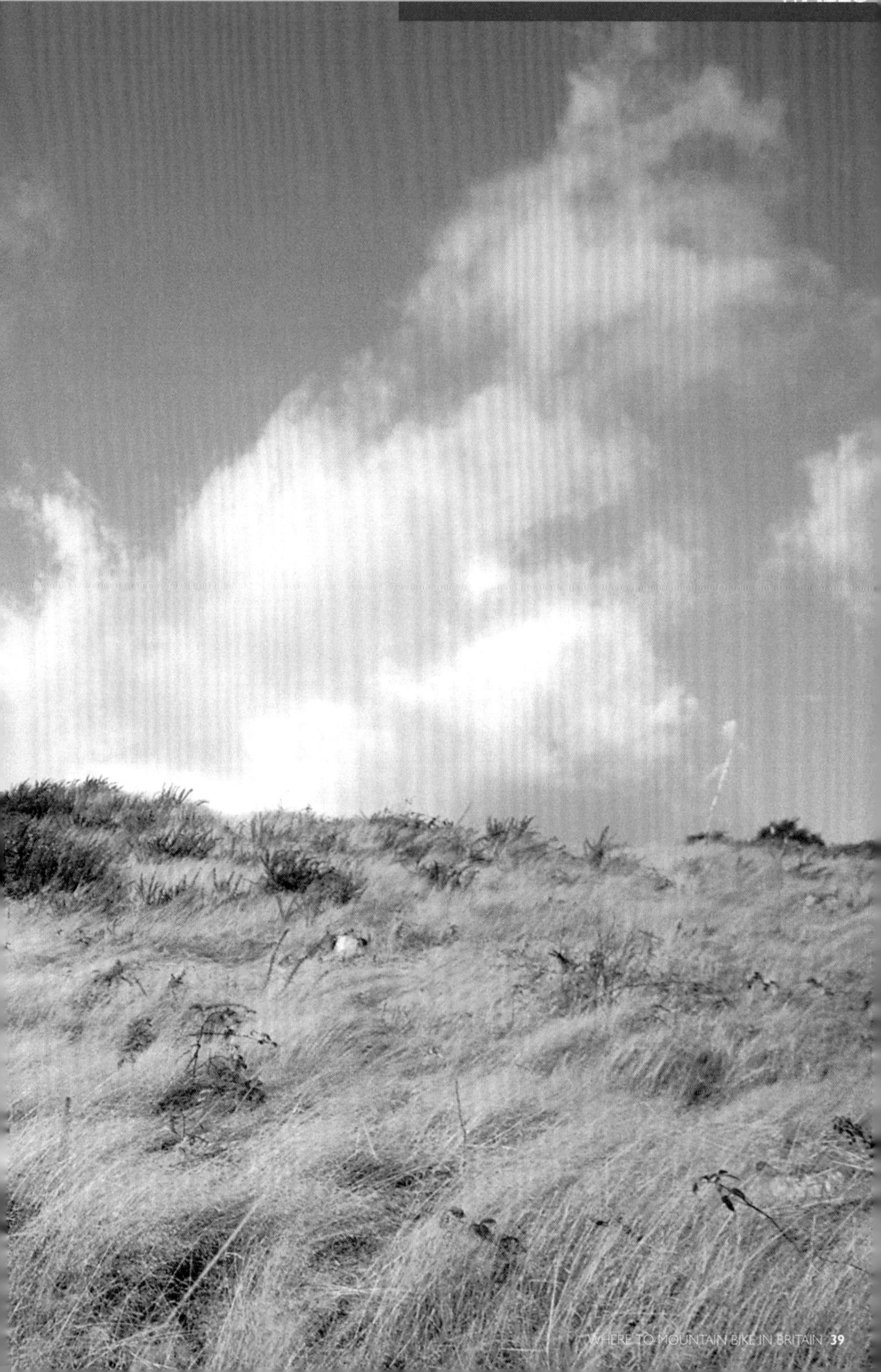

Scotland rising

The mountain land of Britain was born to mountain bike.

Go remote in the Highlands and Islands. Ride the gondola and world cup trails at the Nevis Range. Then peer down the Slab at Dalbeattie, and become a Stanes-bagger...

SOME CLASSICS...
- Innerleithen and Nevis Range/Fort William Downhills (p63 and p55)
- Dalbeattie's the Slab trail (p53)
- Crossing Rannoch Moor (Central Highlands) (p47)
- Devil's Staircase to Kinlochleven (Central Highlands) (p47)
- Cross-Border Trail (Newcastleton to Kielder) (p69)

Literature
- *101 Mountain Bike Routes in Scotland* (by Harry Henniker, Mainstream Publishing, £14.99)
- *Mountain Bike Guide - Inverness and the Cairngorms* (by Timothy King, The Ernest Press, £6.95)
- *Exploring Scottish Hill Tracks* (for MTBers and walkers, by Ralph Storer, David & Charles £12.99)

Websites
Mtbroutes.com
7Stanes.gov.uk
Forestry.gov.uk (go to Recreation, then Cycling, and enter a forest name)

Seven Stanes - specialist MTB venues
These seven forestry sites (stane means 'sto are all in development as specialist MTB venues. The leading ones are Dalbeattie For ('the Slab'), Mabie Forest (near Dumfries) an Glentress (Tweed Valley).
Ae Forest, Galloway Forest/Glen Trool, Kirroughtree and Newcastleton have existin forest routes with handbuilt trails and better bike facilities being added.

WHERE TO RIDE

Lochabers
The Islands
Glenlivet
Glenurquhart & Cannich
Farigaig Forest
Glen Garry
Auchterawe Forest
Corrieyairack Pass
Aviemore
Rothiemurchus
Cairngorms
Bunzeach Forest
Pitfichie Forest
Glen Loy
Great Glen
Laggan (Strath Mashie)
Drumtochty Forest
Fort William
Glenachulish
Central Highlands
Rannoch Moor
Loch Aline and Savary
Glen Dubh
Glen Orchy
Craigvinean Forest
Trossachs
Ardgartan Forest
Argyll Forest Park
Glentress – Tweed Valley
Innerleithen
Kintyre Peninsula
Craik Forest
Ae Forest
Galloway Forest Park
Kirroughtree Forest
Mabie Forest
Newcastleton
Dalbeattie Forest

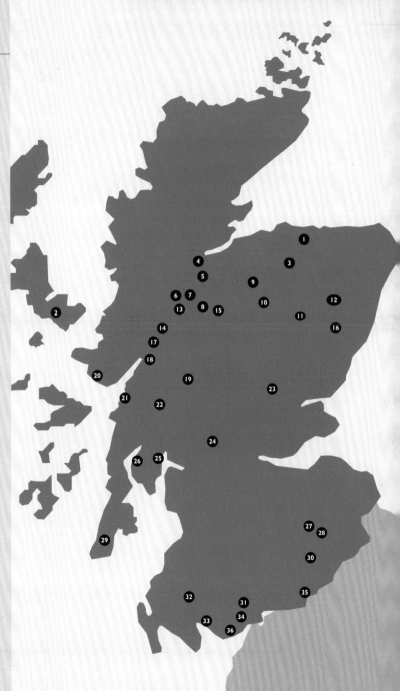

AE FOREST
Dumfries and Galloway

Forestry Commission

Lying 16km north of Dumfries, the Forest of Ae has long been a DH and cross-country venue, with plenty of both stiff and easy forest riding. One of the 7 Stanes projects, the main feature is long-distance trail with singletrack sections. The nearest sizeable towns are Lockerbie and Moffat where you'll find accommodation and food. For an idea of the downhilling, see www.Scottish-downhill.co.uk. PS. Ae is the shortest place name in Britain.

Where to ride
Long-distance cross-country trail, including winding ascents and smooth descending switchbacks
Downhill course
Easy and intermediate trails on forest roads for families and beginners
Location 16km N of Dumfries on the A701 (to Moffat and A74(M)), take the minor road signposted 'Forest of Ae'. Follow for 3km. At Ae village go right at the cross-roads and follow signs.
Station Dumfries (18km south)
Bike shop Both in Dumfries -
Mike's Bikes and Boards, Dumfries (tel 01387 255325), Kirkpatrick Cycling (tel 01387 254011)
Information Free parking, open all year, run by the Forestry Commission Scotland, Ae Forest District office

Mapping and literature Route leaflet available from Ae Forest District office (tel 01387 860247) in Ae villa from local bike shops, and on www.7stanes.gov.uk.
Where to stay *Camping* Barnsoul Farm, Shawhead, Dumfries (7km W Dumfries, tel 01387 730249), Hammerlands Camping and Caravan Club Site, Moffa (tel 01683 220436).
Farm B&Bs Low Kirkbride Farmhouse, Auldgirth, Dumfries (14km W of forest, 3* tel 01387 820258), Branetrigg Farm, Torthorwald (7km E of Dumfries, 3* 01387 750650).
B&Bs Scaurbridge House, Thornhill (12km W of fore tel 01848 331052), Hollybank, Dumfries (10km S of forest, tel 01387 264076), Blair Drummond House, Moffat (15km NE of forest, tel 01683 221240).
Tourist office Dumfries (seasonal, tel 01387 25386

RDGARTAN FOREST
rgyll Forest Park, Argyll and Bute

ing along the shores of Loch Long, Ardgartan Forest is surrounded by the magnificent mountain
nery of the Argyll Forest Park. The nearest village is Arrochar at the northeast end of the loch.

here to ride
gartan Peninsula trail (forest-road-red, 30km, clock-
e), a grand and technically unchallenging forest-road
r of the rugged, remote peninsula with excellent
ws of the Clyde and mountains. Mostly forest roads
some tarmac, and off-road between Corran
han and Stuckbeg at the south end of the Peninsula.
e clockwise from the visitor centre, which is one of
e starting points.
ation From Glasgow A82 N along the W shore of
h Lomond through Tarbet, entering the Park at

Arrochar, then A83 5km to Ardgartan (map ref NN 271
032) and the visitor centre.
Ardgartan Visitor Centre
Cafe, toilets and parking (tel 01877 382383)
Where to eat
Cafe at the visitor centre, the Cottage Inn in Arrochar
Where to stay
Camping Ardgartan Caravan and Camping site
(3km W of Arrochar on the A83, map ref NN 275 030,
tel in season 01301 702 293/360, tel out of season
0131 314 6505)

ARGYLL FOREST PARK
Argyll and Bute

West Argyll in the coastal mid-west of Scotland has a growing mountain bike scene. Some singletrack is being etched through stunning forest scenery, and a 40km epic ride includes the 10km crossing of Leckan Muir. The other routes listed however are on forest roads, so for local knowledge on the (bike-legal) unmapped singletrack trails contact Crinan Cycles in Lochgilphead

Where to ride

Knapdale Forest (Barnluasgan) lies near the coast at Loch Crinan 8km NW of Lochgilphead, and has two forest-road-red routes (and one green) with some stunning views. Start from the Barnluasgan Visitor Centre (on singletrack road SW from nr Bellanoch on B841).

Faery Isles trail (forest-road-green, 10km, out-and-back ride), go SW through oakwoods to Starfish Bay on the edge of stunning Loch Sween, and return the same way.

Lochan Buic trail (forest-road-red, 15-18km), start at Dunardry car park near Cairnbaan on the B841 (or Barnluasgan visitor centre), ride clockwise via Achnamara, returning on the road.

Ardnoe trail (forest-road-red, 21km), a route with a seaview, from Barnluasgan Visitor Centre, head SW for 900m, then N for 1km to the parking spot. Ride on forest roads to Crinan Harbour, then Ardnoe Point and SW down the western seaboard (views to Islay, the Paps of Jura and others), to open hill ground at Carsaig and Tayvallich, and back beside the sea loch of Caol Scotnish.

Loch Awe has two forest-road routes, the red Two Lochs Trail and green Loch Avich trail. Both start at the Barnaline car par NE of Dalavich on the very minor road NE from the A816 (turn-off 3km N of Kilmartin)

Two Lochs Trail (15km, forest-road-red), along the shores of Loch Awe and Loch Avich into Inverninan Forest (home to the rare capercaillie), returning to Barnaline along the River Avich past the Avich waterfalls.

Loch Avich Trail (20km, forest-road-green), longer but easier, this route runs through the forest of Barnaline rising to look out over the Loch, then riding round it.

Leckan Muir Trail: (muir is moor in English, 41km, very hard exposed backwoods route), start/finish car park at Auchindrain Farm Museum (see Location), a seriously big clockwise route via Carron and across the exposed Leckan Muir road, to Loch Awe, returning through the Eredine Forest (see literature)

Mapping and literature OS Landranger 55; leaflet showing all routres available free from the Forestry Commission (tel 01546 602518); copies of Leckan M route (featured in **What MTB?**) from Crinan Cycles.

Location Lochgilphead lies on the A83 on Loch Fyne (50km W as the crow flies from Glasgow). From Glasgow, A82 N, to A83 (near Tarbet). Go left (W) o the A83 and continue 70km to Lochgilphead. Auchindrain Folk Museum, the start of the Leckan Mu Trail, lies on the A83 23km earlier.

Mountain bike club Mid Argyll Cycling Club is a ne venture. Contact the club through Crinan Cycles.

Bike shops Crinan Cycles, Lochgilphead (Kevin's yo man, tel 01546 603511)

Where to stay

Camping Ardgartan C&C site, Arrochar (open Mar-N tel in season: 01301 702293, out of season: 0131 3 6505), Lochgilphead Caravan Pk (tel 01546 602003)

SYHA hostel Inveraray (tel 01499 302454)

B&B Empire Travel Lodge, Lochgilphead (tel 01546 602381), Kilmory Guest House, Lochgilphead (tel 01546 602003)

Hotel Kilmartin Hotel (tel 01546 510250)

Tourist offices Lochgilphead (open Apr-Oct, tel 01546 602344), Inveraray (tel 01499 302454)

VIEMORE AND ROTHIEMURCHUS
airngorm Mountains

e Cairngorms' reputation for tough and exposed routes with lots of walking is based on truth, there are also plenty of bikeable and enjoyable routes to be had, including superb forest trails. emore is now an excellent centre for mountain biking.

ere to ride - *all self-navigating*

eral rides start from Coylumbridge (NH 915 107), ably the remote **Gleann Einich** (through NH 925), while Loch Morlich (965 095) is the focus for the ern part of the renowned **Rothiemurchus Estate** s, including the **Ryvoan Pass** (summit 411m at NJ 118).

the west side of the A9, **the Burma Road** reigns eme. A continuous climb takes you steeply to the mit (698m, NH 846 129) from where a big loop be made via Slochd (at 847 238), while a downhill rn provides an incredible descent on gritty estate d. Pressing on NW then NNE gets you about 20% e downhill distance - some highly spectacular - so take your choice. The best way to return is by eral Wade's Road or Sustrans Route 7 from Insharn 223), then the Speyside Way back to Aviemore.

Lairig Ghru (running from map ref NH 940 071 SSE O 984 960), despite its reputation as a 'must-do' -distance route, is over-rated as far as bikes are erned, due to the very high percentage of enforced der walking. Bikers wanting to ride through the ngorms should go via **Glen Feshie** (perhaps the ngorms' prettiest) or the **Lairig An Laoigh** (quite re in places).

ation Aviemore (map ref NH 895 125) is on the A9 Perth-Inverness road. **Station** Aviemore **r stalking** Stalking is the main business of estates in area, and the culling season is something you must ware of in case your route is closed in places. The

season for culling red deer stags is 1 July-20 Oct, and for hinds from 21 Oct-15 Feb. However, the most critical time is generally mid-August to mid-October. Notices of shooting are often posted and updated on a daily basis. The Aviemore area is particularly good for this, but don't rely on it. *Heading for the Scottish Hills* (see Literature) has all the relevant stalker telephone numbers.

Bike shop Aviemore - Bothy Bikes (route advice, hire, tel 01479 810111), Inverdruie MTBs (hire, tel 01479 810787).

Mapping and literature OS Landranger 35 (Corrieyairack and Aviemore); 36 (Aviemore, Cairngorms & Glentlivet). There's not the density of tracks for Explorers. Guidebooks: *Mountain Bike Guide - Inverness, Cairngorms & the Great Glen* (Tim King and Derek Purdy, The Ernest Press, www.ernest-press.co.uk, tel 0141 637 5492); Stalking information, *Heading for the Scottish Hills* (info on all Scotland estate closures, Scottish Mountaineering Trust, £6.95).

Where to stay *Camping* Rothiemurchus Caravan park, Coylumbridge (great sites in the pine forest, NN 915 106, tel 01479 812800), Glenmore Caravan & Camping Site (part-open 2004, fully 2005+, in-season tel 01479 861 271, out of season tel 0131 314 6505); *SYHA hostels* Aviemore (NN 893 119, tel 01479 810345), Loch Morlich, north side of the loch, Glen More Forest Park (fab views, pre-booking essential, tel 01479 861238); *B&B and self-catering cottages* Ian Bishop, Slochd (NH 848 237, tel 01479 841666) *Hotel* Corrour House (NN 897 111, tel 01479 810220)

Where to eat Modern bar meals at Café Mambo (Grampian Rd, tel 01479 811670). Traditional at the Old Bridge Inn (near the tourist office, tel 01479 811137) **Tourist office** Aviemore (tel 01479 810363).

11 ▶ BUNZEACH FOREST
Strathdon, Aberdeenshire

Ride the 15km red route in this small forest on the south side of Strathdon on the eastern edge the Grampian Mountains (60km west of Aberdeen).

The western section climbs on to open hillside with super views of Morven and the Strathdon countryside and mountains. The eastern section follows the forest road with views of the surrounding countryside.

Parts of the trail may be shut during the nesting season to try to increase the small numbers of capercaillie and black grouse.

Start from the Semeil (say se-meel) car park just east the village of Heugh-head, off the A944.

Strathdon and Bellabeg villages lie to the west.

10 ▶ CAIRNGORM & MONADHLIATH MOUNTAIN
(see Aviemore, Corrieyairack Pass, Glenlivet, Great Glen)

Winter wonderland in the Cairngorms

CENTRAL HIGHLANDS - RANNOCH MOOR

19

ee also Kinlochleven)

e Central Highlands is a vast area, and all the classic riding involves Rannoch Moor: Rannoch
tion to Kinlochleven/Fort William; Rannoch Station to Spean Bridge; the Black Mount (Military)
ad; the Devil's Staircase; and a gem in the shape of Lairig Ghallabhaich (say *galla-vaig*, aka the
k Road), little used, but a useful link.

boundaries of the area are generally accepted as the
at Glen to the west, the A9 road on the east and a
roughly west to east from the mouth of Glen Etive
annoch Station and then east to the A9. (The
hadhliaths are also here, see Corrieyairack Pass).
fact only one road traverses Rannoch Moor gives
cation of the conditions - soft and rocky, or rocky and
The most useful lifeline is the West Highland
way, which during construction had to deal with peat
o 5m deep in places.

cally, what is drawn on the OS Landranger as an
nced white road will be eminently rideable, often
a stony base and probably regularly used by
oting parties. Those tracks shown only as a black
ed line can vary enormously from grassy twin tracks
l by stalkers, to rock-strewn singletrack demanding
and strength, because some of them go on some
nce. Above all, any route can be wet, very wet!
rain any track may have a residue of peat, from a
ole of centimetres to half-metre stoppers, swept
n off the hillside. Don't take any pool for granted!

ere to ride - *all self-navigating*

noch Moor to Fort William or Spean Bridge
ossing of the moor must be high on any serious
's list. West to east is most logical, because you
d a better chance of having the wind at your back,
you start at Rannoch Station you are already at
n, and Fort William sits at sea level! Near Rannoch
on the off-road starts from map ref NN 446 578
le a weathered SP 'Road to the Isles'. Aim for

Corrour Old Lodge (NN407 647), reaching 550m on
the western flank of Sron Leachd a Chaorainn, then
Peter's Rock (at NN 393 670), before the steep downhill to SYHA Loch Ossian (371 670), then again downhill
to Loch Treig.
Tracks diverge after the airy bridge at Creaguaineach
Lodge (309 688), the north route to Spean Bridge
station being 19km, while the south route to Fort
William is 38km via Luibeilt (map ref NN 263 683), Carn
Dearg col 373m, Mamore Lodge (186 630) and Tigh-
na-sleubhaich (344m, NN 140 640), where begins the
15km downhill (apart from two nasty little climbs from
streams), to reach Fort William (at NN 099 735). One
word of consolation: if you decide to ride the latter
west-east, more than half the climb out of Fort William
on the leg to Mamore Lodge is tarmac, the rest is stony
old military road.

Black Mount (Military) Road/Inveroran to
Kingshouse In 1816, the Road Commissioners
reported, 'from Kingshouse to Inveroran over the Black
Mount (..the road..) is now inferior to none in the
North'. And in all fairness the first part from Victoria
Bridge, Inveroran (NN 270 423) to Ba Bridge (at 277
484), which now also doubles as the West Highland Way
(but has been used for at least 50 years by the old rough-
stuffers on stout touring bikes), is still in excellent
condition. North of Ba Bridge it is lumpier, but still very
good. You can follow the line of the military road, more
or less, all the way to King's House (259 546), via the col
between Ben Chaorach and the monster Meall
a'Bhiuridh, summiting at 449m, then Altnafeadh [CONT]

(at NN 200 560), and over the Devil's Staircase, some 548m above Glen Coe. An impressive spot.

Descent of the Devil's Staircase to Kinlochleven

(187 620) is one of THE highland classics, but beware the pebble washouts in the early part of the descent. The climb up the south side of the Staircase is a carry. Some bits are rideable, but it's quicker to shoulder the bike and walk virtually all the way. Once over the top, much of the route is bedrock. There is a high, broken rock step, but overall the track improves as you descend, especially after joining the 'reservoir road' (at NN 201 604).

Around Kinlochleven, Onich and Ballachulish

Here between Loch Leven and Fort William are adventurous barely-ridden tracks that include traditional fall lines. These villages have small stores, cafes and camping. (See also *Glenachulish*).

Lairig Ghallabhaich, technically just outside our definition of the area, runs from Carie (NN 617 571) on the S side of Loch Rannoch, to Innerwick in Glen Lyon (at 587 475), via the 490m col. It has often been a useful link, and is an impressive bit of countryside on a fine day.

Stations Bridge of Orchy (Inveroran 7km), Rannoch (also hotel), Corrour (also bunkhouse), Spean Bridge, Fort William

Bike shops See Fort William

Mapping and literature Landrangers 41, 42, 50, 5

Tourist offices Ballachulish (open Apr-Oct, tel 0185 811246), Fort William (see entry), Spean Bridge (ope Apr-Oct, tel 01397 712576)

Where to stay *Camping* wild camping possible 500 west of Inveroran Hotel (map ref 269 412), also in G Etive; *Hostel* Alan Kimber, Fort William town (open ye round, drying room, tel 01397 700 451, alan@westcoast-mountainguides.co.uk); *SYHA hostels* Glencoe (open year round, tel 01855 811219), Glen Nevis (open year round, 01397 702 336), Loch Ossian, Corrour (Apr-Oct, tel 01397 732 207); *B&B* Braes Guest House, Spean Bridge (tel 01397 712 437); *Ho* Mamore Lodge, Kinlochleven (food until 8pm, tel 01 831213); Ballachulish Hotel (tel 01855 811606)

CORRIEYAIRACK PASS
Monadhliath Mountains

8

y Corrieyairack Pass to any Scottish mountain biker and they will have a tale to tell. Its zigzags
d situation make it a classic. Built as a military road in 1731, it crosses the Monadhliath
ountains (pronounced *mona-leeah*) between Fort Augustus in the Great Glen to Laggan in
estern Strath Spey (11km southwest of Newtonmore, and not to be confused with Laggan in
e Great Glen). Full suspension is definitely a bonus here - although many bikers rode without
y suspension on their first crossing!
e setting is dramatic, the riding is tough and the weather can be severe. Go well prepared!

here to ride
e off-road section of the pass stretches from the
nor road south of Fort Augustus (at NH 373 071) to
lgarve (NN 468 959), via the col (764m, at NN 419
5) making it the highest motorable road in Britain at
e time.
the western end there is no room to park on the
nor road, so most people start from Fort Augustus
d head S, making the crossing a distance of 24km, a
al of 42km if you choose to ride all the way to Laggan
NN 615 943).
e western side of the pass has the best surface - well-
mpacted stone most of the way - and gentler
dients. The eastern side is much rougher these days,
13 zigzags down through Corrie Yairack itself are
igh and deserve great respect, while much of the
ver section has been ravaged by water leaving a really
npy ride.
cation The pass traverses the mountain range east of
ch Ness. Fort Augustus lies 40km from Fort William
the Great Glen. Laggan lies 11km southwest of

Newtonmore in Strath Spey.
Stations Newtonmore (12km to Laggan), Fort William
(40km to Fort Augustus)
Mapping and literature OS Landranger 34 Fort
Augustus & Glen Albyn, 35 Kingussie & Monadhliath
Mountains. Guidebook: *Mountain Bike Guide -
Inverness, Cairngorms & the Great Glen* (Tim King &
Derek Purdy, the Ernest Press, tel 0141 637 5492);
good write-up and photo of the pass in *Exploring
Scottish Hilltracks* (Ralph Storer, David & Charles)
Deer stalking see Aviemore entry
Bike shops Bothy Bikes, Aviemore (trail advice, hire, tel
01479 810111), Inverdruie MTBs (hire, tel 01479
810787)
Where to eat/drink Lock Inn, Fort Augustus (good
food, NH 378 091, tel 01320 366302)
Where to stay B&B Sue Calcutt, Tigh Na Mairi, Fort
Augustus (map ref NH 373 091, tel 01320 366766)
Tourist offices Fort Augustus (Apr-Oct, tel 01320
366367), Aviemore (open year round, tel 01479
810363), Kingussie (tel 01540 661297).

Take-offs and landings at the Innerleithen and Ae airstrips

23 ▶ CRAIGVINEAN
Tay Forest District, Perthshire

Craigvinean Forest lies in Strath Tay on the main north-south A9. Being good for outdoor activiti
the area has is plenty of accommodation and places to eat.

Where to ride
Waymarked route
One route (20km) climbs steadily on forest track for
16km, to fantastic views of Deuchary Hill and the
surrounding countryside, then descends 4km back to the
car park.
Self-navigate other routes in the region with OS maps.
Mapping OS Landranger 52 Pitlochry & Crieff,
Explorer 379 Dunkeld, Aberfeldy & Glen Almond
Location Craigvinean lies 3km northwest of Dunkeld,
13km south of Pitlochry on the A9. Turn off at the
National Trust Scotland 'Hermitage' sign, follow the
forest road to the free car park.
Bike Shops Dunkeld Cycles, Tay Terrace, Dunkeld

(tel 01350 728744)
Sustrans route NCN 77 2km east of Craigvinean
Station Dunkeld 2km southeast
Where to eat Chattan Tea Room, Perth Road, Birna
(tel 01350 727342); Erigmore House, Birnam (bar
lunches and evening meals, tel 01350 727236), Katie'
Tearoom, Perth Road, Birnam (tel 01350 727223)
Where to stay
Camping Invermill Farm Caravan Park (next to NTS
Hermitage, tel 01350 727477); *Independent hostel*
Wester Caputh hostel (6.5km east of Dunkeld, tel
01738 710449); *Hotel* Birnam House Hotel, Perth
Road, Birnam (01350 727342)
Tourist office Dunkeld (tel 01350 727688)

30 ▶ CRAIK FOREST
Scottish Borders

There's great riding at tranquil Craik near the border, where the main route climbs hard to Crib
Law, and descends harder. The forest was a fixture on the early national XC and DH scene, and
now local riders, based at the Hawick Cycle Centre, are cutting singletrack and building jumps t
balance out the forest road riding. Nevertheless, Craik is a place to enjoy riding alone. Carry all
food and spares (including midge cream in the summer) - the only facilities are toilets.

Red route (18km) The first half is a 250m-up challenge
up forest road to Crib Law, for outstanding valley views.
Singletrack comes on the second half with steep gradients on cut track, also jump section (with by-passes).
Location 18km W of Hawick. Head SW on the A7,
and go right (W) after 3km B711 (to Roberton). After
7km go left (SW) on minor road. Craik lies 13km on.
Mapping OS Landranger 79, Explorer 331

Bike shops/mountain bike clubs Hawick Cycle
Centre (off-road and road section), The Rush (Jedbur;
bike enthusiasts and shop, tel 01835 869643)
Where to stay *Farm B&B* Wiltonburn Farm, Hawick
(3km W of Hawick, tel 0870 240 7060); *B&Bs* Hopel
House, Hawick (tel 01450 375042), Ellistrin, Hawick
01450 374216, eileen@ellistrin.co.uk)
Tourist office Hawick (tel 01450 372547)

DALBEATTIE FOREST
Dumfries & Galloway

...aturing the Slab and the Terrible Twins, the Hardrock Trail in Dalbeattie Forest is an essential ...pert off-road experience. Come here for granite-littered built trails at their best. Two other ...ils in the forest are slightly easier, so you can prepare for the big one. ...e forest lies just outside Dalbeattie town, and is one of the 7 Stanes dedicated sites.

...mbine a trip with riding in Mabie Forest, 18km back ...r Dumfries, or continue to Galloway Forest for more ...icated trails at Kirroughtree and an easy classic ...ough Glen Trool.

...ere to ride
...dicated routes
...drock Trail (27km intermediate-difficult, 2-4 hours, it ...hurt when you fall, but all the tricky bits have easier ...ons), featuring expert swoopy singletrack, the Moby ...k granite hump, the 15m-high granite Slab, followed ...he steeper Terrible Twins! Returning to the car park, ...Volunteer Ridge, a 100m black graded rockfest ...ion. All the difficult sections all have escape routes, ...there's a skills loop at the start to warm up on.

...le Hill Trail (14km easy-intermediate, 2.5-3 hours), ...for newcomers, this route climbs on forest trails ...n the Richorn car park to a great view over the Urr ...y and the Solway coast. There's also easy taster ...etrack if you want it.

...Hash Trail (10.5k easy, 1.5-2 hours), moderate with ...e steep sections, generally easy riding.

...ation Trails start from the Richorn car park, 1.5km S ...albeattie, down the A710 'Solway Coast' road, from ...second Forestry car park on the left

...tion Dumfries (23km NE)

...ping Go to www.7stanes.gov.uk, Dalbeattie section, ...ownload route maps; good route leaflet for the site ...n the garage in Dalbeattie, local bike shops, and the ...stry Commission, tel 01387 860247, email

feae@forestry.gsi.gov.uk).
OS Landranger 84, Explorer 313
Bike shops Mikes Bikes and Boards, Dumfries (tel 01387 255325), Castle Douglas Cycle Centre (12km NW, tel 01556 504542), on-site at Mabie (see entry)
Where to stay
Camping/accommodation
Kippford Holiday Park, Kippford (bike wash, storage, on A710 3km S of car park, tel 01556 620636)
Independent Hostel
Barnsoul Farm, Shawhead, N off A75 10km W of Dumfries (scenic farm, with four heated bothies for 4/5 people (tel 01387 730249, email barnsouldg@aol.com).
Self-catering
Redcastle House, Haugh of Urr 7km from 7 Stanes (tel 01665 660475).
B&Bs
The Cottage, Rockcliffe, 10mins from 7 Stanes (tel 01556 630460)
Bellvue, Port Rd, Dalbeattie, 2mins from 7 Stanes (tel 01556 611833)
Cowans Farm Guesthouse, Kirkgunzeon on the A711 halfway between Dalbeattie and Dumfries (tel 01387 760284, sarah@cowansfarmguesthouse.co.uk).
Hotel Anchor Hotel, Kippford, 5mins from 7 Stanes (run by cyclists, tel 01556 620205).
Tourist offices Dumfries (seasonal, tel 01387 253862), Castle Douglas (tel 01556 502611)

16 ▶ DRUMTOCHTY FOREST
Aberdeenshire

Ride the 25km long **Bervie forest-road** route, which is graded hard due to its remoteness rather than technicality. The start is Drumtochty car park (where there are toilets). The route climbs stiffly from the car park over the watershed into Glen Bervie, encircles Bervie Water and returns the same way. Slow down for walkers on the shared start section. There's also a steady through-route NW to **Fetteresso Forest** where there are easy forest road routes. Drumtochty Forest lies 16km SW of Stonehaven (A90, B966 (13km from Stonehaven), 7km to turn off to Auchenblae, continue from Auchenblae NW to Drumtochty Caste, for the car park).

5 ▶ Farigaig Forest, see Great Glen

1 ▶ FOCHABERS - BEN AIGAN & CRAIGELLACHI
Strathspey, Moray

Ace singletrack, tricky descents and all-ability trails built by the volunteer riders and foresters of Moray make the area around Fochabers an MTB silverlode. Most trails are for experienced ride some are for novices, with a continuous challenging trail from Fochabers to Craigellachie planne The area has a renowned Whisky Trail, so local accommodation and facilities are good.

Where to ride - *Dedicated routes* Two start points: Winding Walks/Fochabers car park, NE of Fochabers on A98, and Ben Aigan, S of Mulben on A95.
Whiteash Loopy (red, 8km), top singletrack descents with the option to include the severe Freeride downhill for expert riders and jumpers
Ordiequish Explorer (green 13km)
Ben Aigan summit trails (blue, 9.5km good singletrack descent or red 7.5km)
Knockmore Blast (red, 1.5km) ride separately or tag on to Ben Aigan: technical singletrack and a twisting climb
Mapping OS Landranger 28 Elgin & Dufftown, Explorer 424 Buckie & Keith. **Location** Ben Aigan lies on the NW side of the A95 between Keith and Craigellachie. Fochabers town is midway between Elgin and Keith with Ordiequish and Whiteash on the S and N sides respectively of the A96. **Bike Shops** *Elgin* - Bikes n Bowls and Junner's, Elgin (tel 01343 542492); *Craigellachie* (for Ben Aigan) - Clark's Cycles (tel 01340 881525)
Mountain Bike Clubs Moray MBC (www.moraymbc.

freeserve.co.uk) is working hard with the Forest Distri (tel 01343 820223) to develop more trails.
Stations Elgin (15km), Keith (13km)
Where to stay *Camping* Burnside Caravan Site, Fochabers (tel 01343 820511); *Bunkhouse* Red Lion Tavern, Fochabers (tel 01343 820455); Swan Bunk House, Drummuir (5km NE Dufftown, tel 01542 810334); *B&Bs* Brackens, Fochabers (tel 01343 820544); Kay's Guest House, Fochabers (tel 01343 820371), Craigellachie Lodge, Craigellachie (tel 013⁴ 881224), Strathspey, Craigellachie (tel 01340 87111 *Hotels* Red Lion Tavern, Fochabers (tel 01343 8204. Gordon Arms Hotel, Fochabers (tel 01343 820508) Highlander Inn, Craigellachie (tel 01340 881446)
Where to eat and drink *Fochabers* - Red Lion Tavern, Gordon Arms Hotel, Quaich Cafe, Mosstodoloch Filling Station; *Craigellachie* - Highland Inn (good pub food), Craigellachie Hotel (tel 01340 861204, 530 malt whiskies to sample!) **Tourist offi** Elgin (tel 01343 542666); Dufftown (tel 01340 820⁵

ORT WILLIAM - NEVIS RANGE
eanachan Forest, Highland

tain's international downhill and cross-country venue is the Nevis Range ski centre in Leanachan
rest near Ben Nevis and Fort William. Key to its DH success is that rider and bike travel in
ndolas to the top of a devilishly long and steep course. There is also plenty of top-class cross-
untry trail, including the world cup course, individual obstacles and more gentle riding.

ere to ride

wnhill course The world cup course is adapted
n the permanent **Off Beat course**, dropping 525m
5m-100m) in 2.6km in one of the longest on the
ld cup circuit. One top feature is the Off Beat Wall
the finish, accessible for spectators. To ride the full
rse you have to take the gondola to access the top,
rating for MTBs during the summer (see below for
s/fees). You can ride the bottom half of the course
-round, but you have to haul your own butt up.

ch's Trails cross-country riding A total of 36km of
s-country trail, from elite to family, but including the
km world cup cross-country course. Ride this loop
ll, or just tackle individual sections such as the
minator, Lazy K, Bomb Hole, the Cackle, Nessie and
Cauld-run. Start from the Nevis Range base station
e Torlundy car park (both on the XC loop)

vis Range Ski Centre facilities (tel 01397
825, www.nevis-range.co.uk, www.visithighlands.
); cafe, bike wash, hire centre, open year round,
parking

dola/DH Open for MTBers to ride the full course
May-mid-Sept 10.30am-3pm; single-trip £9.75/7
r/youth (12-17 yrs); multi-trip/1 day £17.50/13.00
r/youth; season ticket holders £3.50/9.50
e/multi-trip; gondola season pass £37/23
/senior. 15min ride, 6 per gondola.
Snowgoose restaurant/bar is at the top station.
ation 11km northeast of Fort William just off the
to Inverness. Fort William is 2.5hr north of
gow. Leanachan Forest is owned by the Forestry
mission. **Stations** Fort William (11km SW), Spean

Bridge (12km NE)
Bike shops Off Beat Bikes of Fort William has an
outpost at Nevis Range base station in the summer
hiring downhill bikes (ring to confirm openings, main
shop High St, Fort William, tel 01397 704008); Nevis
Cycles, Inverlochy (on the A82 1km out of Fort William,
8km before Nevis Range, bike hire, tel 01397 705555)
Events This is Britain's world cup venue for downhill/4
cross/cross-country, go to www.fortwilliam
worldup.co.uk for dates (probably annual); Scottish and
British national MTB championships.
Where to stay *Camping* Glen Nevis Caravan &
Camping, foot of Ben Nevis, from N of Fort William,
Glen Nevis, 4km (from £3.50 per night, tel 01397
702191, cottages@glen-nevis.co.uk); *SYHA hostel* Glen
Nevis (start of Ben Nevis path, tel 01397 702336);
Hostels Fort William Backpackers (Alma Rd, FW, tel
01397 700711), Alan Kimber, Fort William town (open
year round, tel 01397 700 451); Calluna, Heathercroft,
Fort William (5min ride from Fort William centre,
bedding supplied, tel 01397 700451), Smiddy
Bunkhouse, Corpach (on Great Glen cycle route, 6km
N of FW on A830, tel 01397 772467).
B&B Thistlebank, Cameron Rd, FW (tel 01397 702700)
Where to eat Nevis Range base station cafe and
summit restaurant/bar; in Fort William at the Nevisport
Bar & Restaurant (mountain decor, tasty food, tel 01397
704921); McTavish's Kitchen (regular menu, tel 01397
702406); Crannog Seafood Restaurant (for celebrating
world cup champions - top-notch seafood overlooking
the loch, Town Pier, tel 01397 705589)
Tourist office Fort William (tel 01397 703781)

GALLOWAY FOREST PARK
Dumfries and Galloway
(see also Kirroughtree Forest)

Forestry Commiss

The loch district of Galloway Forest Park, where Glen Trool is one of the 7 Stanes clan, contains southern Scotland's highest peak, Merrick, at 843m, and Loch Dee, which has golden sandy beaches! The lovely Loch & Glens off-road Sustrans route is in place, as are a number of forest-road rides. But cutting singletrack is proving a problem because of the nature of the ground. So, for singletrack, head to Kirroughtree Forest, southeast of base town Newton Stewart.

Where to ride
Lochs and Glens - National Cycle Route 7
Running through Glen Trool in the middle of the forest park, this is a fine 50km Sustrans off-road alternative to their parallel on-road route. From the NW, start at Glen Trool visitor centre (13km north of Newton Stewart, and off right), and go via the N bank of Loch Trool (and Bruce's Stone) to Glenhead (the E bank), through to beautiful Loch Dee, down near the W bank of Clatteringshaws Loch to the Clatteringshaws visitor centre and A712. (NCN route 7 continues S through forest to Gatehouse off Fleet.) To make a circuit, turn back via Black Loch, follow the forest road round Craignell Hill and back to the public road near Craigencallie, and retrace your steps.

Dedicated trails Get the forest-road cycle routes leaflet from the visitor centre. Singletrack is planned, but not decided at time of writing (go to www.7stanes.gov.uk for up-to-date information). Included here are the moderate routes (there are also two easy ones, see leaflet).
Glen Trool route 2: Caldons and Water of Minnoch (16km moderate), undulating at first then flattening out; from Glen Trool visitor centre on the road to Caldons, southwest down the Water of Minnoch down to the public road, then forest road back.
Glen Trool route 3: Garwall Hill (26km moderate), longer and harder with some hills, but nothing technical; north from Glen Trool visitor centre, round Balunton Hill, via Palgowan Farm and back.

Clatteringshaws-Craignell Hill Route 2 (23km moderate), start from Clatteringshaws visitor centre, head anticlockwise, along the A712, on forest road around Craignell Hill, and back on the public road on southwest bank of Clatteringshaws Loch.
Mapping OS Landrangers 77 and 83, Explorer 319; good cycle route leaflet from visitor centre, £1
Visitor facilities *Glen Trool visitor centre* is 13km north of base town Newton Stewart, up the A714, a off to the right (open Apr-Oct, 01671 840302);
Clatteringshaws visitor centre is on A712 New Galloway-Newton Stewart road, opposite Clatteringshaws Loch (tel 01644 420285)
Bike shop Da Prato, 114 Victoria St, Newton Stewa (route advice, sales and hire, tel 01671 402656)
Where to stay *Camping* Glen Trool Holiday Park, Bargrennan (tel 01671 840280), Creebridge Carava Park, Minnigaff/Newton Stewart (tel 01671 402324)
SYHA hostel Minnigaff (open Apr-Sept, tel 0870 004 1142); *B&B* Blair Farm, Bar Hill (tel 01465 821247), Duncree House, King St, Newton Stewart (tel 0167 402792); Hotel Bruce Hotel, Queen St, Newton Stewart (tel 01671 402294)
Where to eat Tearoom at Glen Trool visitor centre base town Newton Stewart; traditional local smoke salmon for sale at the Marrbury smokehouse shop (n Glen Trool, but on the A714, 15km north of Newto Stewart, tel 01671 840241)
Tourist office Newton Stewart (Easter-Oct, tel 01671 402431)

GLEN DUBH
Highland

21

rth of Oban overlooking the Firth of Lorne, the longer of two Glen Dubh forest-road routes
es a steady ride round the reservoir with fantastic views over the National Scenic Area.

ere to ride
n Dubh long route (forest-road-red, 12km), start
utherland's Grove car park, 1km NE of Barcaldine on
A828 (16km N of Oban), map ref NM 966 422.
ow waymarkers for 2km, go right for a short off-road
on, and climb to join the easier route. After sharp
urn, look for a turn to the right by Scots pines,
ing to a high road around Glen Dubh itself. Circle
reservoir and return down the far side of the glen.

Mapping and literature OS Landranger 49.
Free *route leaflet* from Lorne Forest District
(tel 01631 566155). **Bike shops** David Graham, Oban
(tel 01631 562069), Oban Cycles (tel 01631 566966,
www.obancycles. com). **Station** Oban. **Where to
stay** Lodges at Appin slightly north; *Camping* at
Barcaldine Camping/Caravan Park right next door (in
walled garden, bar on site, open Apr-Oct, tel 01631
720348). **Tourist office** Oban (tel 01631 563122).

en Garry, see Great Glen

6

en Loy, see Great Glen

13

GLEN ORCHY
rgyll and Bute
ee also Central Highlands)

22

emanding forestry route through wild Scottish scenery, with burn crossings that need care.

km **forest-road-red route** This parallels the
etrack B8074 (A85-A82 road) through Glen Orchy,
ng halfway up at the Bailey bridge over the Orchy
THE Bridge of Orchy) at map ref NN243 321 (Eas
aidh, limited parking). Follow the forest road up the
of Allt Brioghleachan to the flats where the road
es. Go right across the river with care and take the
to the right. Continue (burn crossings) to Allt Coire
air, a tricky river crossing difficult in spate. Continue
the Leacan Inbhir-bhiocair to the end of the road at
le Face. 2km more forest road lead out of the forest

at Bridge of Orchy (north end, NN 297 396).
Route leaflet from Lorne Foresters (tel 01631
566155). **Mapping** OS Landranger 50, Explorer 377.
Where to stay SYHA hostel Crianlarich (16km SE,
friendly wardens, tel 01838 300260), Tyndrum
Bunkhouse (10km SE, 8 dble rooms, central heating, nr
Invervey Hotel), (camping Tyndrum also); Strathfillan
Wigwams (near Tyndrum, 3 per ww, radiator, cookhouse
but only 4 rings, tel 01838 400251); Bridge of Orchy
Hotel (welcomes cyclists, tel 01838 406208). **Tourist
office** Tyndrum (tel 01838 400246). **Station** Tyndrum.

18 ► GLENACHULISH
Highland

Twiddle round a short steep forest circuit 17km south of Fort William below the horseshoe ridge of Beinn A'Bheithir with views to the Nevis Range.

Where to ride
Glenachulish circuit (6.5km, non-technical but steep), start at the small car park (map ref NN 047 588) at the end of the county road to Glenachulish, 500m W of the Ballachulish bridge on the A82 Oban road (turn off A828 at NN 044 595). Ride up to a road junction by water treatment buildings, continue sharp up to the middle road above Abhainn greadhain, continue round the head of the glen (views). **Route leaflet** from Lorne Forest District (tel 01631 566155). **Map** OS Landranger 41.

Where to stay *Camping* Red Squirrel campsite, Glen Coe (tel 01855 811256), Glen Coe campsite (tel 01855 811397); *SYHA hostel* Glen Coe (6km E, warm and well-equipped, but may be little personal space, tel 01855 811219); *Inchree Bunkhouse*, Onich (5km N, basic with well-equipped kitchen, 2 bunkrooms and Alpine sleeping platform, new bunkhouse coming, and both right next to the pub!, tel 01855 821287);
Tourist offices Ballachulish (tel 01855 811296), Fort William (tel 01397 703781).

3 ► GLENLIVET
Cairngorms

Glenlivet is a Crown Estate in one of Highland glens east of Strathspey (location of Grantown and Aviemore). The estate is most ably run by an enthusiastic staff from the estate office to the south at Tomintoul (map ref NJ 172 182).

Where to ride
Dedicated routes
There are eight waymarked trails in the glen (some on tracks which don't appear on OS maps). These include the ride to the summit of *Carn Daimh* (561m, 181 250), the hairy rutted *downhill* (through 192 243) **to Westertown**, the spectacular remoteness of *Glen Livet* itself (at 260 233), followed, for the brave, by one of the straightest, roughest, fastest little downhills in Scotland.

Deer-stalking At certain times of year, this activity could shut parts of your trail. See the Aviemore entry

Mapping and literature
OS Landrangers 36 Grantown & Aviemore, 37 Strathdon (tiny section of Glenlivet). (The thin number tracks doesn't justify Explorers.)
See *Aviemore* for guidebooks.
Where to stay
SYHA hostel Tomintoul (open May-Aug, ring for confirmation, map ref NJ 165 190, tel 08701 553255).
Hotel Glen Avon Hotel, Tomintoul (map ref NJ 167 189, tel 01807 580218)
Tourist office
Tomintoul (Easter-Oct, tel 01807 580 285)

GLENTRESS - TWEED VALLEY
Scottish Borders
(see also Innerleithen)

standard-setting MTB venue, Glentress has superb built routes (featuring the Ewok Village with timber ramps and see-saws), a mountain biker's caff and a bikewash with a drain! The site revolves around the Hub (the home-baking cafe and bike shop), which is run by ex-champions Emma Guy (DH) and Tracy Brunger (XC). The pleasant base town is Peebles, and the area, which includes MTB venues Traquair Forest and Innerleithen, is known as the Tweed Valley. Go to website thehubintheforest.co.uk for full info on the site and activities, including a weather forecast.

Where to ride

Dedicated routes (all start from Red Squirrel car park)

Trail sponsored by Helly Hansen (black route)
...m, difficult, 3.5hrs, very exposed, caution at Ewok ...ge), start Red Squirrel car park, climb to highest point ...rest on the rocky Goat Track, descend the berms of ...hey Spears' to the Boundary Trail (rough singletrack ... jumps, berms and drop-offs), descend Deliverance ...climb Redemption back to Ewok Village, timber ...ps, see-saws and drop-offs, then berm back home.

...**route** - lots of fun (19km intermediate, 2hrs), start ...Squirrel car park, fast wooded singletrack, up to ...point over Tweed Valley, three more singletrack ...s, doubles at Spooky Wood, air on the Hairy Bear, ...uls in the Matrix and berms in Magic Mushroom.

...**ride red** - short and sweet (1.5km, beginner/inter-...iate), a short practice loop with jumps.

...**route** - you always remember your first time ...m, beginner/intermediate, 1.5-2hrs), a great intro-...ory route, that's less technical but still cracking on ...g singletrack, climbs and descents. Start at the Hub ...e Buzzard's Nest higher up the forest.

...**quest routes** - quest for the past. Pick up a leaflet ...ollow the checkpoints to learn about the forest's ...storic past, popular with families, on two routes, ...anet's Brae (2km) and **Green Hill** (7km). Both leave ...the higher Buzzard's Nest car park.

'Interpretation' route-skills loop (1.2km), great for novices and children, a smooth wide surface with obstacles that mimics the proper trails in miniature. A great confidence-builder, even has its own mini Ewok Village! Accessed by the Buzzards Nest car park.

Location Glentress and Red Squirrel car park lie on N side of A72 Peebles-Innerleithen, 2.5km E of Peebles.

Mapping OS Landranger 73, Explorer 337

Biking facilities The Hub-BIKE shop on site (demo bikes, repairs, guiding & tuition, open daily except Thursdays in winter, tel 01721 721736). Come here for hire, bike wash, trail advice and mapping, weather forecasts, bike hire, bike wash, parts and accessories

Where to eat The Hub Cafe, of course - serves real coffee with home baking! Run by Emma and Tracy at the centre of Glentress (on site, closed Thurs, tel 01721 721736, www.thehubintheforest.co.uk)

Where to stay See *Innerleithen* for MTB-friendly places. *Camping* Crossburn Caravan Park, Peebles (tel 01721 720501), Rosetta C&C Park, Peebles (tel 01721 720770); *Farm B&Bs* Lyne Farmhouse, Peebles (tel 01721 740255), Nether Stewarton, Peebles (tel 01721 730755); *B&Bs* Glentress Hotel (tel 01721 720100); Viewfield, Peebles (tel 01721 721232), Woodlands, Peebles (tel 01721 729882). **Tourist office** Peebles (visits in person only). If ringing, call Scotland central number tel 0870 6080404, or wwwvisitscotland.com.

Benurquhart and Cannich, see Great Glen

Slaves to the Slab: on the notorious
Hardrock Trail at Dalbeattie Forest (you
can miss it out).

14 ▶ GREAT GLEN
Highland

The Scottish continental faultline, with Fort William at the bottom and Inverness at the top, was made for cycling. Find stunning trails on both the classic, long-distance tougher-than-it-sounds Great Glen Cycle Route, and in the side glens where rides vary from tough expert grade to superb family routes. For local trail knowledge, ask at forest district offices en route (see below)

Great Glen Cycle Route

130km of signposted riding along the Caledonian Canal and Loch Ness. For MTBing, there's the 90km section from Corpach (just north of Fort William, map ref NN 099 766) to Drumnadrochit (21km south of Inverness, NH 508 300). Any doubts about the worth of this route, try to get an entry into the Fort to Fort (August to William) MTB race usually held in October!

The off-road route

Ride via Banavie (NN 113 770, an alternative start), Gairlochy (176 842), Clunes (220 899) then the harsh 96m climb at North Laggan (306 994), the reward being the loose wide downhill (which never seems to last long enough) into Mandally (NH 305 007). Singletrack presents itself at Invergarry (NH 306 011), where the weaving climb up through the rhododendron is quite a test. There is an 'intermission' of forest road at the top of the climb, but most of this leg to Bridge of Oich (335 035) is uneven singletrack. Relaxing canal towpath carries you NNE to Fort Augustus (378 092), then it is forest roads with big undulations to Invermoriston (420 168). The little hill out of Invermoriston used to be a loose road, but it is so steep it washed out every spring, so now it's tarmac. 'John's Link' (NH 428 168) is a precipitous snaking downhill to the lower forest road which continues through Creag Nan Eun to Alltsigh (at 456 191) (SYHA hostel on A82). Beyond Allt Sigh the route climbs severely on forest road topping out at 298m (the Thousand Foot Climb), but there is another good technical descent to the lower road in Ruskich Wood before the cut-off on to good singletrack at NH

494 236. The junction is signposted but the fast down approach makes it easy to miss. To all intents, the GG ends for mountain bikers at tarmac near Grotaig (at 4 238), but there is one final very steep downhill from 280 to the A82. Take care as vehicles also use this roa

Around and in the side glens;

Glen Loy is good for simple forest road trails and has path from the top round to the top of Kinloch Eil. It lie at the southern end of the Great Glen, 8km NE of Fo William off the B8004 at Strone.

Glen Garry (a western glen 30km NE of Fort Willian Invergarry at the mouth) has some of the best riding i the Great Glen, with good trails and circular routes o forest roads. The old public road from Tomdoun in C Garry to Skye is a hearty ride, but the loch in the mid can be hard to get over and you have to go round.

Auchterawe Forest, Fort Augustus (SW of FA) is scenic with unmarked routes, ask about them at the Caledonian Canal Heritage Centre in the village

Farigaig Forest, near Foyers, lies on the south bar halfway up Loch Ness. From the visitor centre at Inverfarigaig, enjoy narrow singletrack lanes. Cafe in Foyers village, and at hotels along the cycle routes

Glenurquhart and Cannich: West of Drumnadroc (W bank Loch Ness halfway up) is a selection of on-off-road riding. W of Cannich, further up the Glen, y can ride in the forest of Glen Affric (a remnant of the great Caledonian pine forests). E of Cannich are quie singletrack lanes on the east side of the River Glass.

Mapping and literature Cycling in the Great Gle leaflet from the forestry commission (Fort Augustus

ict tel 01320 366322, Lochaber district tel 01397
184); OS Landrangers 26 Inverness & Strathglass, 34
Augustus and Glen Albyn, 41 Ben Nevis, Fort
am and Glen Coe
e shops See Fort William
ere to eat/drink Lock Inn, Fort Augustus (good
, NH 378 091, tel 01320 366302)
ere to stay Camping most caravan sites allow
ping, but for some reason don't advertise the fact;
A Hostels Glen Nevis, Fort William (tel 01397
336), Loch Lochy (Mar-Oct, accessed from the
R by crossing the Caledonian Canal, map ref NN
972, tel 01809 501239), Loch Ness, Alltsigh (Feb-

Sept and winter weekends, NH 457 191, tel 01320
351274); **B&Bs** Braes Guest House, Spean Bridge (map
ref NN 233 821, tel 01397 712437), Sue Calcutt, Tigh
Na Mairi, Fort Augustus (map ref NH 373 091, tel
01320 366766), **Hotels** Invergarry Hotel, Invergarry
(NH 306 011, tel 01809 501206)
Visitor facilities At Fort William, Clunes, North
Laggan, Invergarry, Fort Augustus, Invermoriston,
Drumnadrochit and Abriachan
Tourist offices Drumnadrochit (open all year, tel
01456 459076), Fort Augustus (open Apr-Oct, NH 378
093, tel 01320 366367), Fort William (open year round,
tel 01397 703781). **Stations** Fort William, Inverness.

INERLEITHEN - TRAQUAIR FOREST
veed Valley, Scottish Borders
ee also Glentress)

ne to the renowned Red Bull downhill course, Innerleithen (actually Traquair Forest 1km south
own) is a full-on DH venue, with a weekend uplift service, club membership and tuition. The
ked black-grade cross-country course gets less publicity but is a worthy partner in grime.

me a member of the Innerleithen Riders to save
ey on the day pass and uplifts. Training days are
l for XC riders as well as DH wannabes.
ere to ride
Red Bull Downhill packed with high-life features;
uarry jump into dark woods, ski-lift jump into
ana, and the bombhole
k run cross-country (start/finish at the Red Bull
ar park), an expert course that climbs up to Minch
(576m) and beyond the Southern Upland Way.
inal descent teaches XCers how to DH!
ft Book in advance for the weekend van/trailer
e by ProGravity (go to info@innerleithenriders.
tel 07808 922478). £15/20 daily to members/
members, every weekend 9.30pm-4.30pm,
ing up to 10 runs a day (equall to 12,000ft climb).
ing (and race) days These could convert cross-
triers to DHing, go to Innerleithenriders.com

Innerleithen Riders MBC Membership of the home
club costs £20 per annum. It gives free use of the
course, and saves £5 per day on the uplift fee (tel 07808
922478, join online at www. innerleithenriders.com,
info@innerleithenriders.com)
Location From Innerleithen (on the Galashiels-Peebles
A72 road) head south on the B709 and go just over the
River Tweed, it's on your left (east).
Mapping OS Landranger 73, Explorer 337
Bike shop Probikesport, Innerleithen (bike and DH kit
hire, tel 01896 830880, www.probikesport.com)
Where to stay For more in Peebles see Glentress
entry. MTB Hostel ProBikeport Bothy, behind the
Probikesport shop, Peebles Rd, Innerleithen (self-
catering, same contacts as shop); Hotel Corner House
Hotel, Innerleithen (tel 01896 831181)
Tourist office Peebles (tel 0870 6080404).

2

THE ISLANDS
Colonsay, Oronsay, Raasay, Skye, North and South Uist, Berneray and Eriskay

Visiting these islands, where scallops are a basic food, is a whole new adventure and an educati
You must visit at least once, and by bike is the best way to do it. If the weather is good, you'll
return again and again. If it's not, you'll probably enjoy yourself just the same.

Where to ride

Apart from on Skye, long off-road rides are a rarity, but most of the local tarmac demands a mountain bike in any case! All the side roads are tiny. Even the main roads designated A865 and A867 are mainly singletrack with passing places, and in South Uist especially it is perfectly possible, and acceptable, to ride long stretches of beach which extend most of the island.

Field roads, which weave through the machair (sandy links pasture and 'hayfields'), often provide good link sections (eg, map ref NF 739 159 or 734 186, not shown on Landranger). Do not, of course, wander into the 'Danger Areas'. The list below is alphabetical, not preferential. All are excellent in their own peculiar way.

Colonsay The ferry only calls twice or thrice a week, but you can fill a couple of very good days by riding to the N end of Colonsay to Cnoc Corr (map ref NR 422 998), a stony test beginning with the 1:3 concrete at 406 983. With careful regard to the tides, **Oronsay** is a must, a damp technical ride across the Strand, then the reward of the best little monastery in Britain at NR 349 889 (but don't mention the skeleton in the wall!). Tide tables and crossing advice always to hand at the Colonsay Hotel.

Raasay Quite unique, you need first to get across to Skye, then ferry across the Narrows to Raasay before you start. Pier at NG 554 341. All the 'roads' are worthy of your attention, but of particular note are Callum's Road at the N end of the island (map ref NG 591 475) and the tracks around to Eilean Fladday (NG 591 495 and 595 493), some which are more than spectacular!

Skye Biggest and certainly one of the best. Locals will tell you the tracks aren't rough, but they are. The rewards however, are immense. For guided supported MTB holi-

days here contact Saddle Skedaddle (tel 0191 265 1 www.skedaddle.co.uk). Classics run through Glen Sligachan (from NG 486 298) to Camasunary (516 187), then SE over Am Mam to Kilmarie. In the same district the 'sharp' little mainly tarmac loop from Kilm is worth a hurl (NG 545 172); Elgol (518 135, 1:3 d to the harbour) - Glasnakille (NG 537 130) - Drinan Cadha nan Ingrean (at 552 162) - Kilmarie. Another classic, runs NNE from Torrin (NG 575 21 Strath Beg - An Slugan - Strollamus bridge (NG 593 265), and to both can be added the testing (!) track between Clach Oscar (NG 565 224) and Luib at 56 278, via Strath Mor, for a substantial loop.

Uists and Benbecula North Uist, Benbecula and South Uist make up the middle section of the Weste Isles, the Outer Hebrides or 'Long Isle', whichever y prefer. For some years now North Uist has been joi to Benbecula by a pair of mainly single-lane causewa what was the North Ford (NF 827 568) and likewis Benbecula to South Uist at what was the South Forc 801 472). Within the last three years, **Berneray**, between Harris and North Uist, has been linked to latter by a causeway (NF 911 759), and at the S end the chain a bridge now connects **Eriskay** and South (780 130) giving road links between all five islands.

Bike shops None, except a bike shack on South U Tobha Mor (NF 766 362) but it's a bit Hebridean!

Mapping and literature

Colonsay and Oronsay: OS Landranger 61 Jura, Colonsay, Explorer 354 Colonsay and Oronsay.

Raasay: Landranger 24 Raasay, Applecross and Loc Torridon, Explorer 409 Raasay, Rona and Scalpay. **S** Landranger 32 South Skye and the Cuillin Hills, Exp

Skye - Cuillin Hills. **North Uist & Berneray**: dranger 18 Sound of Harris & St Kilda, also part of dranger 22 Benbecula & South Uist, Explorer 454 th Uist & Berneray. **Benbecula & South Uist**: dranger 22, also part of Landranger 31 Barra and ounding islands, Explorer 453 Benbecula & South , **Eriskay**: Landranger 31, Explorer 453.

rist offices Colonsay (best info from Colonsay el, tel 01951 200 316); Lochboisdale, for South Uist, ay and Benbecula (Apr-Oct, tel 01878 700 286, Rd, South Uist); Lochmaddy, for North Uist and heray (Apr-Oct, tel 01876 500321, Pier Road, North ; Portree, for Skye and Raasay (all year, tel 01478 37, Bayfield Road, Portree, Skye); Raasay (best info Isle of Raasay Hotel, tel 01478 660222).

ries Caledonia MacBrayne (tel 01475 650100, v.calmac.co.uk) serves all the islands mentioned **ere to stay Colonsay** Camping only by prior gement. Colonsay Hotel (NR 389 941, tel 01951 16, has self-catering cottages and hosepipe - essen-you make the saltwater crossing to Oronsay).

Raasay: SYHA Hostel Creachan Cottage (NG 553 378, reopens 2005, mid-May-end Aug, tel 01478 660240); Isle of Raasay Hotel (map ref NG 550 364, tel 01478 660222), Raasay Outdoor Centre (Raasay House, map ref NG 547 365, tel 01478 660266). **Skye SYHA hostels** Broadford (NG 642 241, Mar-Oct, tel 01471 822442), Glen Brittle (NG 408 224, Easter-Sept, tel 01478 640278), Kyleakin (NG 752 264, open year round, tel 01599 534585); *Hotel* Sligachan Hotel (hotel, log cabins, camping, NG 485 298, tel 01478 650204); *Bunkhouse/Bothies* Croft Bunkhouse & Bothies, Portnalong (NG 351 349, tel 01478 640254).

South Uist Camping only by prior arrangement, *SYHA/Gatcliff Hebridean Hostels* (very basic, sleeping bag required) Howmore (NF 757 265, open year round, no tel), Berneray (NF 932 814, open year round, no tel); *Inn* Polochar Inn, Pollachar (map ref NF 747 144, tel 01878 700215), Mrs Morag McDonald, Lochside Cottage, Lochboisdale (map ref NF 783 202, tel 01878 700472).

NTYRE PENINSULA
gyll and Bute

ere to ride Catch one 22km-long linear route on t roads across the middle of the Kintyre peninsula: Ballochgair (east coast) through Glen Lussa lithic burial cairn signposted), alongside the W bank ssa Loch to Corputechan on the west coast.

There's parking at Ballochgair on the B842 Carradale road (north of Campbeltown). Come back the same way, or on road via the coast on the A83 and Campbeltown. **Tourist office** Campbeltown (tel 01586 552056).

33 ► KIRROUGHTREE FOREST
Dumfries and Galloway
(see also Galloway Forest Park)

Forestry Commi

Find first-class built singletrack and forest-road routes in Kirroughtree Forest, one of the dedicated 7 Stanes mountain bike sites. Watch the website www.7stanes.gov.uk for news of ne' trails. The forest lies in Galloway Forest Park (see entry) where Glen Trool to the north is the place to go for lochs and glens cross-country riding.

Where to ride
Singletrack At time of writing there is demanding singletrack around *Bruntis Loch* and *Larg Hill*, with technical riding on Larg Hill, spiced up with grippy rock. Singletrack will extend well up scenic *Bargaly Glen* in a stack loop trail that allows you to decide the trail length. Routes are open year round.
Dedicated routes
Start from the visitor centre, ride on forest roads.
Dallash (30km moderate), this is a longer ride out to the northeast
Larg Hill (11km moderate), twisting round Larg Hill and Bruntis Loch, via Curly Ride and Rally Corner.
Lochs and Glens NCN route 7 (Sustrans) runs 1km away (see Galloway Forest Park).
Location all routes start from Kirroughtree visitor centre; from Newton Stewart head SE on the A75, and

after 3km go left up into the forest
Kirroughtree visitor centre Open Apr-Oct, £1 and-display parking (tel 01671 402165, Galloway @forestry.gsi.gov.uk), cafe, information, shop and parking, Forestry Commission Scotland.
Mapping OS Landranger 83 Newton Stewart and Kirkcudbright, Explorer 319 Galloway Forest Park Sc good cycle route leaflet, £1, from the visitor centre
Bike shop Da Prato, 14 Victoria St, Newton Stewa (local route advice, sales and hire, tel 01671 402656
Where to eat Kirroughtree visitor centre, Central Cafe, Newton Stewart (baked potato-type dishes ar fish and chips), decent food at the Bruce Hotel
Location 3km northwest of Newton Stewart
Where to stay SYHA hostel Minnigaff (tel 0870 0(1142); also Scotland central reservations (tel 0870 1 3255), www.visitscotland.com.

15 ► LAGGAN - STRATH MASHIE FOREST
Highland
(see also Corrieyairack Pass)

An up-and-coming MTB venue with expert route, halfway between Fort William and Aviemor

Strath Mashie Forest, with its steep slopes and views, is due for a total of at least 14km of riding over three routes (including expert), with, possibly, bike facilities in the future. Find the trails in the *Auchduchil Woodland* in the forest SW of Laggan village on the A86 Fort William road. Laggan lies 11km southwest of Newtonmore in

Strath Spey, and is also the southern start point of th Corrieyairack Pass route. **Bike shops** Bothy Bikes, Aviemore (has more info on devts, hire, tel 01479 810111), Inverdruie MTBs (hire, tel 01479 810787 **Tourist offices** Aviemore (tel 01479 810363), Kingussie (tel 01540 661297).

OCH ALINE & SAVARY
ighland

ig on the Morvern peninsula opposite Mull, this 14.5km circuit climbs forest roads for
oramic views of the islands, and descends on 3km fast grassy singletrack.

ere to ride
d of Loch Aline & Savary trail (forest-road-red,
km, anticlockwise), starting from Lochaline (map ref
690 472, on A884, ferry to Mull), take the Strontian
for 3km, go left and follow red and blue
markers uphill 1.5km, at next gate go left on forest
, 4.5km climbing on Lag Mor road. Once over the
head of one feeder burn for the Savary river the
ent begins, watch out on left to take turn-off onto
drove road (grassy singletrack) down Savary Glen,
near to ruins of Savary village, go left at county road,
back to Lochaline.

ping and literature *Route leaflet* from Lorne

Forest District (tel 01680 300346); OS Landranger 49.
Bike shops David Graham, Oban (tel 01631 562069),
Oban Cycles (tel 01631 566996)
Where to stay *Camping* Fiunary Camping and Caravan
Park (lovely spot by the sea, and good for cycling from
4km W of Lochaline, tel 01967421225); *B&B* Fiunary
Cottage, Lochaline (tel 01967 421248); *Self-catering
cottages* on the Ardtornish Estate (views down loch and
over sound, tel 01967 421288, www.ardtornish.co.uk);
Lochaline Hotel (tel 01967 421657).
Tourist offices Strontian (tel 01967 402381), Fort
William (tel 01397 703781), Oban (tel 01631 563122).

MABIE FOREST
Dumfries and Galloway

34

Forestry Commis

With 4km of continuous handbuilt singletrack on the Phoenix Trail, and the black-grade Dark Si
loop, Mabie, one of Scotland's dedicated 7 Stanes MTB forests, comes with a top
recommendation. Sections include the Scorpion and Descender Bender! There's a bike shop w
hire on site, and base town is Dumfries. 7 Stanes neighbours include Dalbeattie 18km southwe
with Galloway Forest Park and Kirroughtree further west again.

Where to ride
Dedicated routes
Set off from the cyclists' car park, which is at the top of
the main car park.

Phoenix Trail (17km intermediate, difficult sections
coming, 2 hours, start at the top of the visitor car park
and follow the road in front of the ranger's office and
Mabie House Hotel), features 4km of unbroken classic
singletrack, fast descents, rock gardens and tight berms,
also the Twisty Bits killer climb and fitness-testing
Scorpion, plus a black-graded timber trail section.
Mini Jump Park and North Shore-style section
Mabie's Dark Side (4km, severe), steep rough, for
technical riders only

Forest Road loops
Woodhead Loop (11km easy/intermediate, 2 hours),
explore the forest on bash trails and gentle doubletrack.
Lochbank Loop (19km easy-intermediate, 3 hours), the
Woodhead Loop with an extension to the Lochaber
Loch forest nature reserve, using also lanes at Troston
Forest, good views over Loch Arthur.
Big Views Loop (5km easy, 1.5hours, start at cyclists' car
park at the top of the main car park), easy climbs leading
to views over the Solway Firth and Nith estuary.

Mapping and literature Landranger 84, Explorer
313; the *route leaflet* is available on-site, from the
Dumfries bike shop and from the rangers office (tel
01387 860247, Ae Forest District office,
feae@forestry.gsi.gov.uk), also www.7Stanes.gov.uk.

Bike facilities On-site bike shop (sales, spares and
repairs) at the start of the trails.

Mountain bike club Full Mental, the Mabie bikers
club, has built singletrack here since the start, organis
races and tutoring. They run the Sunday Muddy Sun
rides and, apparently, organize an excellent ceilidh.

Bike shops On-site, also Mikes Bikes and Boards,
Dumfries (tel 01387 255325)

Location Trails start at the car park near the Mabie
House Hotel, off the A710 (New Abbey Road) 7km
Dumfries (map ref NX 949 708). The entrance to th
forest is off a sharp left-hand bend. Parking is £1, wh
goes towards the upkeep of the trails

Where to stay
Camping Beeswing Caravan Park, Dalbeattie Rd (tel
01387 760242), Barlochan Holiday Park, Palnackie (
S of Dumfries, tel, 01557 870267)

Hostels Marthrown of Mabie (in forest, sleeps up to
tel 01387 247900); Barnsoul Farm, Shawhead, nor
the A75 10km west of Dumfries (four heated bothie
4/5 people, tel 01387 730249)

Self-catering Nunland (nr Dumfries, tel 01387 7302
Cairnyard Lodges, nr Dumfries (3* tel 01387 7302

Farm B&B Cowans Farm Guesthouse, Kirkgunzeon
A711 halfway between Dalbeattie and Dumfries (ar
£25 each, tel 01387 760284). **B&Bs** Locharthur Ho
nr Dumfries (tel 01387 760235), Abbey Arms Hote
New Abbey (10km S of Dumfries, 2* inn, tel 01387
850489), Rosemount, Kippford (7km S of Dalbeatti
tel01556 620214)

Tourist office Dumfries (tel 01387 253862)

EWCASTLETON
:ottish Borders
(e also Kielder)

35

w routes are due at this flatter venue on the border, the remotest of the 7 Stanes MTB projects.

nwhile, do the red route (and family routes), and do miss the *Cross Border Trail* (connecting with Kielder st in England). **Facilities** are eventually to include o bikes, hire and bike wash, and a cafe. The local ers on the project are from The Rush bike shop in urgh (www.therush.uk.com, see also 7stanes. uk). **Newcastleton** is the nearest town, in

Liddesdale. **Bike shops** The Rush at Jedburgh, 40km NE (tel 01835 869643), Hawick Cycle Centre (tel 01450 373352). **Location** Canonbie or Bonchester Bridge, B6357 to Newcastleton village, unclassified road at S end of village, follow signs for Dykecrofts. **Where to stay** *Holiday cottage* for hire just outside Jedburgh (sleeps 4, contact The Rush for details)

rth Uist, see Islands
onsay, see Islands

TFICHIE FOREST
erdeenshire

12

dedicated middling cross-country trails and a DH at Pitfichie west of Aberdeen. The forest is dily getting the MTB treatment, with the trail network due for completion around 2006. Ride e hills on singletrack and forest road, with steady-to-stiff climbs and equivalent descents.

re to ride
starts from the main Whitehills car park.
cated trails
total cross-country trails (waymarked oderate). Make up your own route over Green Cairn William and Pitfichie Hill on singletrack and road with a little walking. Excellent views from the ails. The informal Downhill track runs from the top chie Forest, and is being improved by volunteers.
route (waymarked blue/easy).

Mapping and literature See trails on the Ecurie Neep website (Pitfichie route information).
Location 25km W Aberdeen, 5km W Monymusk. From A944 Alford-Aberdeen, N on B993 (7km W Alford).
Mountain bike club Ecurie Neep, the active Aberdeenshire club (www.ecurieneepmtb.netfirms. com) rides every Sunday morning and Wednesday night. They also rides around Aboyne (including up to Mount Keen 939m), see website.
Tourist office Aberdeen (tel 01224 632727)

.say, see Islands

South Uist, see Islands
Skye, see Islands

24 ▶ THE TROSSACHS
Stirling

The Trossachs, the land of glens and lochs, are where bikers from Glasgow and Stirling go to pl
in Achray Forest, the Menteith Hills, and around Lochs Katrine, Ard and Venachar. Routes vary
from hand-crafted singletrack to waymarked family trails. The National Cycle Route 7 runs
through via Aberfoyle in the south via Callander and Balquhidder in the north.

Where to ride
Achray Forest Singletrack This forest, on the W side
of the A821 N out of Aberfoyle, features an 8km cross-
country singletrack loop hand-built by volunteers from
Glasgow MBC over the past four years and used for
cross-country racing each year. Variations have also been
used for the Loch Lomond Challenge. Plans are afoot for
a full waymarked black loop, and an easier red route.
Loch Katrine and Achray Forest route (58km hard),
starting from the car park at the end of Loch Katrine (for
full details see the source of the info www.mtbstuff.co.uk
and www.offroadroutes.co.uk)
Loch Ard route (red) A 12km forest-road loop with
views over Loch Ard, accessed from two Forestry
Commission car parks; Milton - B829 2km W of
Aberfoyle; and Kinlochard - B829 7km W of Aberfoyle.
Loch Ard orbital cycle route (yellow) Lying beneath
Ben Lomond, this 40km forest-road circuit provides
spectacular views over Loch Ard forest, the Menteith
Hills and the Carse of Stirling. Access from three
Forestry Commission car parks (shorten to suit all).
Glen Finglas a toughish 27km circular route with long
climbs/descents, and spectacular views. It starts in the
village of Brig O'Turk where there's a great tearoom and
pub. One alternative is to turn off and go to Balquhidder
or Strathyre, and return via a different route.
Glen Ample Hardish, good Land Rover/Quad track
route with great views, and sizeable burns to ford.
The Menteith Hills, east of the A821, provide another
very popular route, part track, part open moor. Great in
summer, but strictly for mud-lovers in the wet!
Sustrans Route 7 runs north-south through the heart
of Scotland, passing through Aberfoyle and Callander
Facilities The David Marshall Lodge, 800m north of

Aberfoyle off the A821, has a cafe, shop and toilets o
11 months of the year. A bike hire depot is planned f
the site, run by Wheels (see above).
Location Aberfoyle is 29km NW of Stirling, 35km N
Glasgow
Mapping OS Landranger 56, 57, Explorer 365
Bike shop Wheels Cycling Centre, Callander (repa
hire, guiding, trail advice and accommodation, on
Sustrans route 7, tel 01877 331100, www.scottish-
cycling.com)
Mountain Bike Club Glasgow MBC (Pete Siebelt
0141 563 3260, www.gmbc.org.uk); Stirling Bike C
has a site (www.stirlingbikeclub.org.uk) that's a mine
information about the routes above and others, incl
GPS downloads and route profiles. They are very ac
and usually have rides going on in and around the ar
They welcome to join them on rides.
Where to eat Aberfoyle has cafes and shops. Loca
pubs and hotels do food.
Where to stay *Camping* Cobleland C&C, Aberfoy
(on River Forth, open Easter-Sept, in-season tel 018
382392, out-of-season tel 0131 314 6505), Trossa
Holiday Park (tel 01877 382614); *Independent host*
Trossachs Backpackers, Callander (cyclist-friendly an
home of Wheels, tel 01877 331200); *B&Bs* Forth
House, Aberfoyle (tel 01877 382696), Barns of
Shannochill, Aberfoyle (tel 01877 382878), Altskeit
(pub and restaurant attached, 5km W Arberfoyle or
Loch Ard, tel 01877 387266). The hotels do good
and there are also pubs and cafes in which to eat.
Tourist offices Aberfoyle (open winter weekends
Easter-Oct tel 01877 382352), Callander (shut De
tel 01877 330342), Stirling (tel 01786 475019)

ing the Fort: on the international
hill course at Nevis Range

Into England

Home of the Dales, the Downs, the Lakes, the Peaks, the Wolds, the Moors and more.

Trail-building has boosted the riding in the Chilterns, Shropshire, Surrey, Cannock and Kielder. But can anything beat the craggy tracks of the Pennines, the South Downs or Dartmoor?

SOME CLASSICS...

- **The Calf and Bowderdale,** in the Howgills (p115) (a big exposed day on mountain & moor)

- **Mastiles Lane** in the Yorkshire Dales (high open riding) (p169)

- **Isle of Wight Off-road Randonnée** (80km round the hilly south coast island) (p117)

- **High Street in the Lake District (p123)**

- **Jacob's Ladder & Mam Tor** in the Peak District (p138)

- **The Cheviots** ridge and old roads (p87)

- **Coast to Coast** (the multi-day way over the Lakes and North Pennines) (p90)

- **South Downs Way** (1-3 days on superb coastal downland) (p156)

- **Mary Towneley Loop** (75km of the South Pennines at its best) (p157)

Rights of way
In Wales and England, the main legal tracks for mountain biking are bridleways, 'roads used as public paths' (RUPPS), byways and 'other roads with public access' (ORPAs).

Cotswolds
Buckinghamshire
Rowney Warren
Chilterns
Aston Hill, Chilterns
Ashton Court, Bristol
North Wessex Downs
Ridgeway Trail
Berkshire
Epping Forest
Eastway, London
Cardinham Woods
Dartmoor
Teignbridge
Exmoor
Combe Sydenham
Quantocks
Haldon Forest
Woodbury Common
Blackdown Hills
Mendips
Salisbury Plain
Cranbourne Chase
Blandford Forum
Freeride Park
Wessex Ridgeway
Dorset Coast
and Purbeck
Alice Holt Woodland Park
Bracknell Forest -
Swinley Forest
New Forest
Isle of Wight
Forest of Bere
Queen Elizabeth
Country Park
Surrey Hills West
North Downs
South Downs & SD Way
Surrey Hills East
North Downs Way
(Surrey & Kent)
Sevenoaks, Kent Downs
Deers Leap Park
Penshurst - PORC
Friston Forest
Bewl Water
Bedgebury Forest

ADDINGTON HILLS
(Shirley Hills), Croydon

Riding here is not goood for the place, and not encouraged. Please go south to the North Downs instead.

Things have changed in these Croydon hills since it was a competition site in the 1990s. The gorse heathland has very thin soil cover and its pebble beds were being dislodged and moving downhill. The hills are now a SMINC (Site of Metropolitan Importance for Nature Conservation) with a 'tread lightly' policy into which mountain biking doesn't fit comfortably.

ALICE HOLT WOODLAND PARK
Surrey-Hampshire

Here's a pretty family route nestling in the Surrey countryside at a forest centre with bike hire. Nice for days when you need a break from the sweat and grime of sporty offroad.

Where to ride
Family cycle circuit (5km), signposted, gently undulating with some loose gravel on descents and corners
Location Alice Holt Woodland Park is 5km south of Farnham on the A325 (map ref SU809416).
Stations Farnham, Bentley
Facilities Cycle hire (tel 07775 840807/01594 860065, open weekends May-Oct, Sun only rest of year, school and public hols). The Forest Visitor Cent is open year round (hot drinks and snacks, tel 01420 23666). Parking £2. Owned by the Forestry Commission
Bike shop Robin Cycles, Lindford (tel 01420 47661

ASHDOWN FOREST
East Sussex

There are only two bridleways through Ashdown Forest, a place where mountain biking is disli and discouraged.

If you ride at all, don't stray an inch off the rights of way! They'll be down on you like a ton of bricks.

SHRIDGE FOREST
edfordshire-Hertfordshire

u may ride just on the bridleways in the southern part of this National Trust estate in the north
ilterns, not freely around it.

ridge is a honeypot for family cycling only on the
n ground. The Ridgeway path here is footpath only

(no cycling). National Trust tel 01442 842488.

SHTON COURT
ristol

54

unexpectedly testing cross-country circuit starting from the top of the Ashton Court estate,
the Avon Gorge just 2km from the city centre. Lucky Bristolians.

ere to ride
dicated route
n *Timberland Trail* (11km, part of the Avon Forest),
k-steering level singletrack through parkland, with
:y sections in the Fifty Acre Wood; start from the
er gateway of Ashton Court estate (on Leigh Rd) and
d off anticlockwise beside the wall. 1km after
nging direction southwest, go right and cross the
d to ride the Fifty Acre Wood, returning on road then
odlands through the main estate. Rideable year
nd.

ation 2km west of the city centre. The upper
way of the estate is opposite the end of Bridge Road
ming from Clifton Suspension Bridge. Or ride up the
te road from Ashton Court house, accessed via
ver Ashton.

Mapping and literature OS Explorer 155; good
route leaflet from the Forest of Avon (tel 0117 963
9174, www.forestofavon.org.uk)
Visitor facilities Cafe in Ashton Court house, teahut.
The route is run by the Forestry Commission and Bristol
City Council
Station Bristol Temple Meads, 5km east
Major events Bristol Bike Fest
Bike shops Mud Dock Cycleworks, dockside near the
Arnolfini (tel 0117 929 2151); Dave Bater Cycles,
bottom of Park St (tel 0117 929 7368); Blackboy Cycles,
top end of Whitladies Rd near the downs (tel 0117 973
1420)
Where to stay *YHA hostel* Bristol, dockside beside the
Arnolfini (dorms and bedrooms, meals,
tel 0870 770 5726)

Guess whe
The Cotsw
south of B
Pipehouse L

STON HILL MTB AREA
Jear Wendover, Chilterns
ee also Chiltern Hills)

Thrilling dedicated MTB site on the steep slopes of the Chilterns scarp near Wendover. Aston
H is renowned for its adrenalin-filled downhills, 4Cross track and cross-country trails, hand-cut
00 acres of Forestry Commission woodland. To ride, you take out day or annual membership
the 800-strong Aston Hill Mountain Bikers club.

Here to ride
trails are open daily and maintained year round. All
signed according to the difficulty of the section (black,
and blue, hard to easy)
ck Downhill (hard, technical)
mate Pursuits Downhill (hard, technical)
3 (moderate/hard)
Downhill (moderate)
ss-country (9km), moderate with switchbacks and
holes, includes great descents
l/BSX (wear full face helmet and body armour)
n Hill Mountain Bikers
to www.astonhill.com (loads of info). You have to be
y/annual member of Aston Hill Mountain Bikers (day
mbership £5, full annual membership £45/30
or/junior). Day membership can be purchased in the
park at weekends. Membership provides 3rd party
ity insurance on Aston Hill, up to 10% discount in
cipating shops, social rides, discounted club clothing
secure parking.
club is run by Firecrest Mountain Biking (tel 01296
729, mob 07050 163421, info@firecrestmtb.com,
Box 12, Aylesbury HP21 7YJ). Teaching courses for
ilities from beginner to advanced, see website or
Firecrest
site is a partnership between Forest Enterprise and
rest MTB
lities Bike wash, spares and accessories on sale,
re car parking (the Chilterns has a problem with

break-ins to visitors' cars)
Events Aston Hill Downhill events, Southern Cross-
country, test days and product demos, see
www.astonhill.com
Opening days and times
These change, see the website, or telephone Firecrest
Location
Aston Hill (map ref SP 892 101) lies 3km northeast of
Wendover, 3km west of Tring, up off the B4009, about
800m from the A41.
Stations
Wendover (4km west) and Tring (7km northeast)
Mapping OS Landranger 165 Aylesbury; Explorer 181
Bike shops Mountain Mania, Tring (tel 01442 822458,
www.mountainmania.co.uk); Buckingham Bikes,
Aylesbury (tel 01296 482077 www.buckinghambikes.
co.uk)
Where to eat and drink Refreshments
Monday-Friday, on-site catering at weekends, pubs in
Wendover and Tring
Where to stay
(Try also www.visitbuckinghamshire.org)
B&Bs Mrs Drackford, Dunsmoor Edge (1km from
Wendover on Great Missenden Rd, tel 01296 623080);
Mrs McDonald, Lionel Ave, Wendover, (tel 01296
623426); Mrs Samuels, Icknield Close, Wendover (tel
01296 583285)
Tourist office
Wendover (tel 01296 696759, www.chilternweb.co.uk)

91 ► BEDGEBURY FOREST
Kent

A trail-building programme is planned at Bedgebury, meanwhile there is only family riding here.

Find the forest (office tel 01580 211044) northwest of Hawkhurst, accessed via Park Lane, the minor road that heads west off the A229.

BERE, see Forest of Bere

---

57 ► BERKSHIRE BRIDLEWAYS & BYWAYS
(see also Bracknell, North Wessex Downs)

Other than Bracknell and the North Wessex Downs, you can find a little Berkshire riding on farmland and woodland bridleways around Henley and Maidenhead.

Described rides Bowsey Hill (bridleways leading up to 140m height) and Maidenhead Thicket (permitted paths on National Trust land) both feature on the Knowl Hill Bridleway Circuit, an undulating 33km route using the best rights of way between Henley and Maidenhead. Free leaflet from the rights of way team at the Royal Borough of Windsor and Maidenhead (tel 01628 796407).

---

90 ► BEWL WATER, Kent

Find a flat but not dull circuit round this large lake.

The 19km flat circuit is rough in places as it runs around Bewl Water near Lamberhurst. The visitor centre has a cafe and the Bull pub lies halfway round at Three Legged Cross. The nearest station is Wadhurst.

LACKDOWN HILLS, DEVON
68

...de possibilities may be improved in the future, meanwhile, head south to Woodbury Common ...e entry) for better mountain biking than in these hills.

...u may ride here on the limited rights of way network ...idleways, RUPPS and BOATS), but the tracks tend to ...wet from the number of springs in the area and they are used heavily by horse riders. There are also sensitive areas, particularly the Iron Age hillforts, which are out of bounds.

LANDFORD FORUM FREERIDE PARK
72
...orset-Wessex
...ee also Wessex Downs)

...enowned southern venue for national events, the Freeride Park has a downhill course, dual ...om and cross-country trails, running over the steep contours of the West Wiltshire Downs ...ar Blandford Forum. The park is the creation of local bikers based around a mountain bike club ...Blandford, working with the Forestry Commission. Trails are being built along IMBA guidelines ...d are in development. Riders pay a day fee or annual subscription then ride as much as they ...e. The downs round here are rich in bridleways, see Wessex Downs

...ere to ride
...dicated routes In situ and on the plans are a ...mpetition downhill course, free-ride trails, a dual ...rse, Area 51 (access trails, trials, speed trials, jumps ...North Shore-like obstacles), a dedicated North ...re trail and jumps area.
...-navigating See Wessex Downs
...rmation Contact Justin Rowe, head of the park (tel ...58 458854, www.mtb-freeride.com).
...ation The Freeride Park is at Okeford Hill above ...ngstone, 8km NW of Blandford Forum. The car park ...n the yellow road S out of Okeford Fitzpaine at the ...of the down (at the Wessex Ridgeway). From there, ...entrance is E on the trackway to Shillingstone Woods.

Bike shop Offcamber, Blandford (38 Salisbury St, tel 01258 458677)
Mountain bike club The MTB-Freeride Club is based in Blandford (tel 01258 458854, www.mtb-freeride.com)
Where to stay *Camping* Inside Park Caravan & Camping, (4km SW of Blandford, Easter-Oct tel 01258 453719); *B&Bs* Gone Walkabout, 3 Alexandra St, Blandford (cyclists welcome, route info, tel 01258 455699, info@gonewalkabout.org.uk), Pennhills Farmhouse (Shillingstone, tel 01258 860491), Lower Bryanston Farm (working farm, Blandford, tel 01258 452009)
Tourist office Blandford Forum (tel 01258 454770)

BRACKNELL - SWINLEY FOREST
Berkshire

A diamond piece of riding in an otherwise innocent part of the south-east, Swinley Forest, bett known as 'Bracknell', has a fantastic free-ride MTB area, used by downhillers and cruisers, also testing forest roads, and a good visitor centre with a cafe, called the Lookout. Don't be deceive by its appearance on the OS map, with straight forest roads and plethora of pines, this is sharp hilly land absolutely full of twists and turns where it's a job not to get lost. Buy a £1 day permit every time you go (from the Lookout), and take your disbelieving friends. Great for beginner a experienced riders, honestly, and bikers with families, who can happily be left behind at the Lookout, or walking the forest roads.

At time of writing, Bracknell was a proposed 2012 Olympic MTB cross-country site.

Where to ride

MTB Area (free-riding off-track area) head south from the Lookout, to Surrey Reservoir. The MTB area is diamond-shaped to the south and pennant-shaped to the west. See the forest map. (Riding extends beyond these areas too). Routes include **Twisted Sister** and the **Full Nine Yards**.

Forest roads As long as you stay on the roads and observe the rare no-cycling tracks, you can ride for miles around the forest - note, the crowds tend to stick close to the Lookout.

Mapping OS Landranger 175 Windsor and Reading, Explorer 160 (better for true navigation on those forest roads); forest map 50p from the Lookout

Location Head for the Lookout visitor centre, off the B3430 Nine Mile Road, 4km south of Bracknell centre.

The Lookout visitor centre (tel 01344 354400).

Buy your £1 day permit here, cafe, adventure playground, hands-on children's science exhibition.

Bike shops In-Tention, near Crowthorne station, 2 west of Crowthorne village (tel 01344 773015), Mountain Trax, at the Wyevale Centre in Wokinghar (tel 0118 989 1333)

Mountain Bike Club Berks on Bikes MBC (Bob M www.bobmbc.com) is the club behind the MTB dev opment of the forest and the trail-building, and is ver active. They run rides most weekends in Swinley Fo and around the Crowthorne area; for the last 10 yea Gorrick MBC has been organising mountain bike cro country events in Berkshire, Hampshire and Surrey 1 riders of all abilities, including at Swinley Forest. Stations Bracknell, 4km to the north

Where to stay YHA hostel Windsor (meals, tel 08 770 6096) lies 13km northeast

BRINGEWOOD
hropshire
(ee Hopton Wood)

32

ropshire's classy national downhill and cross-country venue is available for open riding all year
und for free. Dave Pearce Cycles of nearby Ludlow runs a regular uplift service for downhillers
o. There is no way-marking, nor leaflets or facilities, but the trails are obvious in situ and Ludlow
very close, so no problem. Plans are afoot to develop Mortimer Woods on the opposite south
de of the lane a la Coed y Brenin.

here to ride
n up and follow your nose or a local.
ownhill The tracks are clear enough to find once on
e, and start from the trig point on top of the hill. For
d parking; from Ludlow, take the B4361 heading
uth out of town, but immediately after the town
dge, take the lane on the right (west) uphill. Watch for
 track signed Hazel Coppice on your right, and park
wn there in the quarry.
lift service Dave Pearce Cycles in Ludlow regularly
ves downhillers to the top of the downhill course
nerally alternating Sundays with Hopton Wood, see
ry). Book in advance (£10 per day, also private book-
s), cos it's popular. For dates, see the shop website or
 them (see below).
oss-country
n up and find the cross-country course, or ride
where in this open forestry site. For XC parking;
ow directions above from Ludlow, but continue past
 Hazel Coppice turning to the picnic area further on.
ation Bringewood Forest lies 3km southwest of

Ludlow, on the north side of the lane that heads west
away from town immediately south of the town bridge
– got that?
Bike shops
Dave Pearce Cycles, Fishmore Road, Ludlow (tel 01584
876016, www.pearcecycles.co.uk);
Climb On Bikes, 22 Bull Ring, Ludlow (tel 01584
872173)
Where to eat The Charlton Arms by the bridge is
good, with plenty of other cafes and pubs in town
Where to stay
Camping North Farm, Whitcliffe (on road from Ludlow
to Bringewood, tel 01584 872026); no YHA
Farm B&Bs Longlands, Richards Castle (tel 01584
831636), Hope Cottage, Orleton (tel 01584 831674)
Ludlow B&Bs Hen & Chickens Guest House, Old Street
(cycle-friendly, 01584 874318), The Mount, Gravel Hill
(01584 874084), Henwick, Gravel Hill (tel 01584
873338);
Tourist office Ludlow (tel 01584 875053)

II ▶ BROUGHTON MOOR - WALNA SCAR RD
Lake District

A single spectacular 20km-long high bridleway loop below the Old Man of Coniston west of Coniston, with a long off-road climb/descent with terrific views, in a peaceful area of open fells and a changing forest environment. There is a long road-section return.

Where to ride
Self-navigating route
From Coniston, yellow road SW (double arrow) to Walna Scar Road bridleway near disused quarry. Bridleway 4km, over Walna Scar, down to 90-degree LH bend, SW. Go down open fell beside river/beck to road near Stephenson Ground. Yellow road SE up to Broughton Moor forest, after 400m and a sharp RH bend, climb bridleway E round below Knott crag. Continue, via Appletree Worth Beck, to yellow road (disused quarry). Go left E Hummer Lane, to main A593, left NE via Torver back to Coniston.
Mapping OS Explorer OL6 (map ref 257 932)

Location From Coniston follow signs to Torver, then signs to Broughton. 1.5km after Torver go right, signed Broughton Mills, up Hummer Lane. Broughton Moor forest is on the right after 1.5km.
Bike shops and clubs see Grizedale
Where to eat Cafes in Broughton and Coniston
Where to stay
YHA hostels Coniston Holly How (not Coniston Coppermines YHA, meals, tel 0870 770 5770)
Tourist offices
Broughton-in-Furness (summer only, tel 01229 7161)
Coniston National Park Information Centre (tel 01539 41533).

UCKINGHAMSHIRE

50

side the arc of the Chiltern hills (see entry), the southeast has two country parks with a little sy-going off-road. Outside the hills and to the north is farmland with a series of low hills.

here to ride

ack Park and Langley Park Country Parks
ng just west of the M25 between Slough and bridge these neighbouring country parks feature a al of 7km pleasant easy off-road (link the pair, with e, crossing the A412), some of it beside the massive ge lots of Pinewood Studios (where they film *James d*). Black Park has a good cafe overlooking the lake m south of the main car park, walk the bike there). ch parks show the ride-legal tracks on signboards cks not shown on either the OS Landranger 176 or lorer 172). Pay & Display car parking. **Location**

from the motorways, exit at M40 J1, SW A412 5km, Langley Park south on white road, Black Park 300m later north on white road.
Dedicated route The Swan's Way (100km), a sign-posted bridleroute for horses and cyclists; from the north at Salcey Forest, Northamptonshire to the south at Goring. It crosses the Ouse Valley, passes through Milton Keynes, crosses the Vale of Aylesbury, climbs the hills of Waddesdon and Quainton, and continues to the Chilterns scarp to the Thames.
Get the route leaflet from the Engineers Dept, County Hall, Aylesbury, Bucks (tel 01296 382796).

URNHAM BEECHES, BUCKINGHAMSHIRE

ere's no mountain biking allowed here, no offroad at all, regretably.

nham's lovely beech woodland is a National Nature erve (managed by the Corporation of London), ere the trees' shallow roots get damaged by wheels hooves. Cycling is only allowed on the 5km of

tarmac roads. For off-road, go to the Chiltern bridle-ways, beginning 13km west (beyond Marlow), or the dedicated Aston Hill MTB area, near Wendover (22km northwest).

BURY DITCHES
Shropshire
(see also Hopton Wood, Shropshire Hills)

Bury Ditches features one short linear route, but is part of good riding throughout the Shropshire Hills, and boasts wonderful views to the Clun valley.

Where to ride
Bury Ditches (5km, linear), ride between the car parks at Bury Ditches and Colsley Woods, on undulating firetrack with loose corners and fairly steep fast sections. Stick to the way-marked route as Bury Ditches Hill Fort (a scheduled ancient monument) is not open to cyclists. The section is the off-road part of the Bury Ditches Dynamo, a 43km circular road route from the Secret Hills (Shropshire Hills Discovery Centre) in Craven Arms.

Location (map ref SO 435 825) 3km northeast of Clun. Bury Ditches car park is at map ref SO 332 839. Colstey Wood car park is at SO 304 842.

Mapping and literature Bury Ditches cycle route leaflet available from Secret Hills

Visitor information Secret Hills visitor centre (aka Shropshire Hills Discovery Centre), Craven Arms (tel 01588 676000, www.secrethills.com). Bury Ditches is Forestry Commission land

Bike shop Pearce Cycles, see Hopton Wood

Where to stay
Camping Green Camping Park, Wentnor (tel 01588 650605), Kempton Farm, Lydbury North (tel 01588 660250)

YHA hostel Clun Mill, Clun (self-catering only, tel 0870 770 5766)

B&Bs Llanhedric Farm, northwest of Clun towards Bicton (tel 01588 640203), Hurst Mill Farm, Clun (tel 01588 640224

Tourist office Ludlow (tel 01584 875053), Bishops Castle info point only (inside the Old Times shop, tel 01588 638467)

C2C, SEE COAST TO COAST ROUTE

CANNOCK CHASE
taffordshire

38

ıd an excellent choice of both specially-built and open riding in an Area of Outstanding Natural
auty (AONB) in the heart of a Midlands. Developed by Chase Trails, a very active group of
ıer-builders, backed by an on-site Swinnerton Cycles, there's a dedicated downhill area,
chnical long and short cross-country routes and easier trails for families. So enjoy the chase!

ıere to ride
dicated routes All these start from Birches Valley
or centre and are being built by 'Chase Trails' volun-
rs with the Forestry Commission and Swinnertons
les. See www.chasetrails.co.uk.
ow the Dog (10km technical singletrack)
ss-country race circuit (15km)
ıse around the Chase (40km-50km loop)
a Downhill area near Styll Cop, south of Rugeley
ls area
geback Family Trail
f-navigating Several bridleways run through the
ıse, but navigating them is difficult
ation Head for Birches Valley Forest Centre (2.5km
ıthwest of Rugeley, on the white road that forks right
th of before Sitting Mill (map ref 018171, tel 01889

586593, parking £1). (Cannock Chase visitor centre is
2km N of Hednesford but has less cycling connection).
Mountain Bike Club Chase Trails (www.chasetrails.
com) has a forum on its site where members can stay in
touch with each other. They also say "keep an eye out
for our trail crews and be prepared to pay the optional
'trail tax'. A few minutes of your time mid-ride to give us
a hand with a trail will really help."
Bike shop Swinnertons (hire, bikewash, repairs, open
daily, tel 01889 575170, swinnertoncycles.co.uk) at the
Birches Valley centre
Mapping OS Landranger 127/128, Explorer 244
Where to stay Camping Tackeroo (Forest Enterprise
Birches Valley, Lady Hill, Rugeley), *Silvertrees Caravan
Park* (Stafford Brook Rd, Penkridge Bank, Rugeley);
Hotel The White House, Marquis Dr, Cannock Chase

60 ▶ CARDINHAM WOODS
Bodmin, Cornwall

Cardinham Woods spread out over the beautiful Cardinham Water valley just southwest down o
Bodmin Moor. There are lots of routes to make up on the hilly network of forest roads and
tracks. Facilities include a cafe, toilets and a picnic area with barbeques.

Waymarked routes An easy cycle trail winds its way
along the valley bottom through scenic woodland.
Self-navigating On a network of forest roads and
tracks, including a climb to views across Bodmin Moor.
Mapping OS Landranger 200, Explorer 107. **Location**
E of Bodmin town, accessible from the A30 or A38.
Sustrans NCN3 Camel Trail 2km SW. **Station**
Bodmin Parkway, 3km SE. **Where to stay** Camping

Mena Farm C&C, Lanivet, Bodmin (tel 08456 44463!
Self-catering Deerpark Forest, 45 new Forestry cabins
(tel 01392 832262); **YHA hostel** Golant (14km S, mea
tel 0870 7705832); **B&Bs** The London Inn, St Neot
(10km, tel 01579 320263). **Where to eat and drin**
On site at Woodlands cafe (meals and snacks, daily
during school holidays, Thursdays & weekends the re
of the year). **Tourist office** Bodmin (tel 01208 7661

CHEVIOTS
Northumberland

e Cheviots form the eastern border between England and Scotland, and despite the high peat
ntent of the ground overlying ancient granite most of the tracks are eminently rideable - if you're
enough. This old glaciated ground tends to have steep sustained climbs out of the valleys, but the
ing tops provide superb elevated riding, where on a clear day you can see forever!

here to ride

ided and supported trips and MTB holidays in the
eviots (weekend or longer) contact Saddle Skedaddle
0191 265 1110, www.skedaddle.co.uk).

f-navigating

e ride (18km or 23km off-road, plus on-road return)
n Hexpethgate (map ref NT 871 160, literally a gate
Scotland on one of the old border crossings),
ghly SW to Coquet Head (at NT 772 082). Return
er via the valley road down Upper Coquetdale to
inton, or continue roughly S through the forestry
r Ogre Hill (from NT 776 073) via an additional 5km
vnhill on forest roads to the A68 at Byrness. Ideal if
have a friendly 'service crew'. The link into the
st, courtesy of the Border County Ride, a
serider's trail, is shown on the OS Outdoor Leisure
but not the Landranger, but is signposted.
pethgate can be accessed by following the ancient
nell Street NNW from the village of Alwinton (NT
063), the second half of the run being mainly down-
o Cocklawfoot on the Scottish side.

ther classic is a **traverse of the Street** from Upper
quetdale (NT 859 114), where there is a small car
at the road end, roughly NNW to the Border
e, then NW downhill to Hownam. With a little
gination, for a tough day out, the two can be joined
sing the farm track from Belford-on-Bowmont (at
814 206) to the hilltop junction at the gate in the
on Windy Law (at 792 190).

south-facing slopes of **Upper Coquetdale** have many
eways, it being possible to create short (but always
h) loops, often using a stretch of the dramatic
der Ridge as the connecting element. Riding the
et downhill from the Border Ridge is the best direc-

tion, the final 500m twin-track plummet to the River
Coquet being as steep as natural trackways come.

Mapping and literature

Guidebook: *Mountain Bike Guide - Northumberland*,
Derek Purdy, The Ernest Press, £7.50 (www.ernest-
press.co.uk, tel 0141 637 5492).

OS Landranger 80 Cheviot Hills & Kielder Forest (shows
the bulk of the Cheviots and the Border Forest Park),
74 Kelso & Coldstream (covers the extreme northeast
corner of the Cheviots providing links and finishes for
several cross-border routes).

OS Outdoor Leisure 16 The Cheviot Hills (vast double-
sided sheet covering all the Cheviots, but very little of
Kielder Forest. Waterproof editions provide enough
cover for two persons to stay dry - we've proved it!)

Location Alwinton (in Coquetdale, 15km W of
Rothbury) is a great place to start routes from.

Bike shops The Spar in Rothbury sells essentials (gear
cables, tubes, brake blocks and puncture kits).
For contacts, try the Rush (the Jedburgh bike shop and
enthusiasts, tel 01835 869643)

Where to eat Byrness has a cafe at the filling station,
much favoured by motor cyclists, and the Byrness Hotel
does the most excellent beef sandwiches.

Where to stay YHA hostel Byrness (lots of Pennine
Way striders, self-catering only, tel 0870 770 5740);
B&Bs Rose and Thistle (NT 921 063, tel 01669 650
226), Bonnie Barn (also upmarket self-catering, map ref
NT 934 047, behind the village hall, tel 01669 650 476;
Hotel Byrness Hotel (NT 771 024, tel 01830 520231)

Tourist offices Rothbury, for Upper Coquetdale
(seasonal, tel 01669 620887); Alnwick, for N
Northumberland (tel 01665 510665); Bellingham, for
Kielder and Byrness (all year, tel 01434 220616).

CHILTERN HILLS

(see also Aston Hill MTB Area, and Ridgeway)

Rich in byways and bridleways, the 50km-long Chiltern Hills run in an arc-shaped wedge betwee Reading (south) and Hitchin (north), and are known for their beechwoods, picturesque villages and country pubs. Make up your own routes climbing and descending the escarpment (100m height gain/loss), or go for the gentler inner valleys. Near Wendover, find the Aston Hill MTB Ar (see entry). The hills are an excellent destination for days out from London, served by trains fro Marylebone, Paddington and Euston. As you can't ride on footpaths, Ivinghoe Beacon and the northeastern end of the Ridgeway National Trail after Bledlow are out of bounds. The Chiltern Society cycle group identifies bridleways which get very muddy in the winter on their website www.chilternsociety.org.uk.

Where to ride
Guided and supported MTB holidays in the Chilterns (weekend or longer) contact Saddle Skedaddle (tel 0191 265 1110, www.skedaddle.co.uk).
Aston Hill MTB area (see entry).
Self-navigating Start points (tracks straight from town, secure pay & display parking, toilets, pubs and cafes) are Tring, Wendover, Princes Risborough, Marlow, Henley-on-Thames, Pangbourne and Goring & Streatley. Bridleway and byway routes are infinite. Include a descent/climb on the **escarpment**, linked perhaps by a bridleway section of the **Ridgeway National Trail** (13km flat and unbroken between Britwell Salome and Bledlow, but gets badly cut-up in wet weather). The riding 'in' from the escarpment is gentler.
Central The triangle between Chinnor, Bledlow Ridge and Stokenchurch is hilly and spectacular.
Southwest The area around Nuffield and Wallingford is more open and mellow. Also gentler are the bridleways around Ewelme (to Britwell Salome, Cuxham, Pyrton, Watlington, see described routes).
North The area around the Barton Hills between Luton and Hitchin is less ridden, with pubs below the hills at Sharpenhoe and Pegsdon, and good trails up from Lilley to the south.
The Icknield Way Riders Route is a long distance off-road route (mainly on bridleway) from Bledlow to Hitchin,

passing close to Princes Risborough, Wendover, Tring Berkhamsted and Dunstable, with plenty of climbs an descents. In effect it replaces the Ridgeway National Trail, which is in these areas is mainly only for walkers
Described routes
View and download routes by local organisations at www.chilternsaonb.org: *Bledlow Circular Ride* (16km *Ewelme circuit* (21km), *Judges Ride* (25km, shorter options: 6.4km, 16km, start at the Black Horse 800m north of Checkendon), *Sonning Common Health Ride No 4* (25km).
Where to eat and drink
Southwest Crown at Pishill, Bull & Butcher at Turville Stag & Huntsman at Hambleden, Fox & Hounds at Christmas Common, Chequers Inn at Fingest, Frog a Skirmett, Black Horse near Scot's Farm 2km west of Stoke Row, King William at Hailey.
Central The Lions at Bledlow, Red Lion at Whiteleaf, Plough at Cadsden, Rising Sun at Little Hampden, Greyhound at Wigginton, Full Moon at Cholesbury Common, Cock & Rabbit at The Lee, Valiant Troope Aldbury.
North The Old Hunters Lodge at Whipsnade, Red L at Studham, Lynmore at Sharpenhoe, Live & Let Live Pegsdon, Lilley Arms at Lilley.
Mapping OS Explorer 171 Chiltern Hills West, 172 Chiltern Hills East, 181 Chiltern Hills North, 182 St

ns and Hatfield, 193 Luton & Stevenage;
rangers 165 (north) and 175 (south)
te books *Local Bike Adventures* (Andrew Rickshaw
9, tel 01628 477020), *Great Cycle Routes - The
erns & The Ridgeway* (£7.99 Jeremy Evans) and
's Cycle Tours - Around London North*.
e shops Caversham, Pangbourne, Wallingford,
ow, Thame, Bourne End, High Wycombe, Princes
brough, Amersham, Chesham, Tring, Hemel
pstead, Dunstable, Luton and Hitchin.
e hire Rides on Air, Wallingford (tel 01491 836289);
ntain High, Pangbourne (tel 0118 984 1851);
le Safari, Marlow (tel 01628 477020); On 2
els, Bourne End (tel 01628 533003); Harpenden
es, Harpenden (tel 01582 461963)
ntain Bike Clubs Bucks MTB
ks_mtb@hotmail.com), Aston Hill Mountain Bikers
Aston Hill entry)

Sustrans routes NCN4 Thames Valley, regional
routes 57 and 30.
Where to stay
Camping Bridge Villa, Wallingford (tel 01491 836860)
YHA hostels Streatley, near Goring & Streatley station
(tel 0870 770 6054); Bradenham, Bucks, near
Saunderton station (tel 0870 770 5714), Ivinghoe, Bucks
(tel 0870 770 5884)
Farm B&Bs Old Callow Down Farm nr Bledlow (tel
01844 344416), Broadway Farm in Berkhamsted (tel
01442 866541)
B&Bs Little Gables in Wallingford (tel 01491 834426),
Lenwade in Henley-on-Thames (tel 01491 573468),
Manor Farm Cottage in Chinnor (tel 01844 353301),
Rising Sun in Little Hampden (tel 01494 488393)
Stations Listed towns are well-served by trains (from
London, Oxford, Milton Keynes and Bedford) and the
riding can start five minutes from the station.

LENT HILLS
orcestershire

37

very steep, compact set of hills on the southwest edge of Birmingham is covered with a web
ridleways and would be ideal for hill-pedallers if they weren't equally popular with the rest of
world and his dog.

utstanding local off-road site for Birmingham and
ley, 450-acre Clent Hills are nevertheless best
en during the week or out of season, when you
a chance to release the brakes for more than a
hent on numerous excellent downhills. If you don't
a hard sweat back to the top.
s extend to the Black Mountains in Wales on a good
and the choice of three hostelries lying at the end of
eways is very tempting.

Where to ride
Park on the north of the site at Nimmings Wood visitor
centre. Slow down for all other users.
Self-navigate Any number of bridleways on Adam's Hill
and Walton Hill (divided by a road), that run up to the
300m summit and the Four Stones, up and down the
slopes, or around the sides.
Where to eat and drink At the Hill Tavern (SW
slope), the Vine pub (SE slope on yellow road which
bisects the hills diagonally), and the Fountain pub.

4 ▶ COAST TO COAST, C2C
(see also Lake District, North Pennines)

As a big-country challenge, the 224km-long C2C (Coast to Coast) qualifies as a MTB classic due
its distance, the amount of climbing involved and the spectacular views. Running along paths, rail
trails and lanes, it connects the remote hills of northern England and demands not the quick
reactions of a singletracker but the resilience and strength of an explorer. Starting in Whitehaven
on the west coast of Cumbria the C2C crosses the Lake District, the North Pennines and the
Durham Dales before dropping to Consett and Sunderland on the east coast. It is best ridden
from west to east, for the sake of the prevailing wind, and for shorter climbs and longer descent
When you've finished you can get a souvenir stamped card from Sustrans to record your
achievement, also a 'been there, done that' C2C T-shirt (see www.rannerdale.co.uk)

Where to ride
You can complete in under 24 hours, but the average is
three to four days. Thousands of cyclists ride it annually.
The route (W-E): Whitehaven to Cleator Moor (8km),
Lorton (32km), Keswick (50km), Greystoke (77km),
Penrith (88km), Langwathby (95km), Hartside (112km),
Garrigill (123km), Nenthead (130km), Allenheads
(142km), Rookhope (152km)...(splits)...
...to Sunderland; Consett (178km), Stanley (190km),
Chester le Street (197km), Sunderland (212km), Roker
pier (216km).
...to Newcastle; Consett (178km), Rowlands Gill
(189km), Newcastle (203km), Jarrow (214km),
Tynemouth (224km).
Summits (approx distance/height); Whinlatter Pass
(40km, 300m), Old Coach Road (64km, 400m),
Hartside (120km, 570m), Black Hill (138km, 600m),
after Allenheads (147km, 500m), Rookhope Incline
(157km, 500m).
Off-road sections (there may be alternatives for easier
riding); Wythop Woods (singletrack descent), Whinlatter

Forest (forest track descent), the Old Coach Road
(elevated, isolated, rough and demanding), ascent of
Hartside (the hardest on the C2C, it is very steep in
places and can get sodden), Garrigill (very short, roug
hard climb), over Priorsdale and into Nenthead, the
Rookhope Incline (arguably the best section, with a lo
haul to the top and ruts and roughness on the descen
Sometimes closed in the shooting season, when an
alternative route is posted).
Mapping and literature The Sustrans C2C map
(Sustrans tel 0117 929 0888); website www.c2c-
guide.co.uk (all you need to know); guidebook *Ultim*
C2C Guide (by Richard Peace, £7.95, ISBN 1-90146·
17-2).
Where to stay etc The C2C is well documented on
the web (www.ctc-guide.co.uk) and in print (Ultimate
C2C Guide) so go there for accommodation, bike sh·
and hire, mapping and riding tips.
Souvenir T-shirt Contact Rannerdales (tel 01900 82·
462, www.rannerdale.co.uk)

COMBE SYDENHAM
rendon Hills, Somerset
ee also Exmoor and Quantocks)

hoop down this national downhill course in the Brendon Hills on the far-eastern edge of
moor National Park. Whoop back up in the occasional uplift service.

ere to ride

wnhill Course

n up and ride the current 250m-drop downhill
rse, open Feb-Oct, putting £5 in the honesty box.
enter a round of the national series when it's held
e. There's a second course in the park at Birds Hill,
two further courses under construction, the Colton
. More development is due for 2006.

ift days Local MTB club EMBC occasionally drives
rs to the top of the course for the day (£12
mbers, £15 non-members, ring Matthew Coxhead
1934 813689, www.sightdirect.co.uk/racing)

ation 14km east of Minehead; from the A39 turn
th 2km east of Washford, after 1.6km take the B3188
theast, Combe Sydenham country park (and hall) is
after Monksilver

untain Bike Club

BC: for cross-country and coaching contact Sally

Burnham (tel 01392 276122), for downhilling contact
Matthew Coxhead (tel 01934 813689)

Mapping and literature
OS Landranger 181 Minehead and Brendon Hills,
Explorer OL9; route leaflets (Holnicote Estate and
North Hill, Wimbleball, Dunster Woods) available from
the National Park centre (see below).

Where to stay See Exmoor entry for the majority.
Camping Quantock Orchard Caravan Park, Flaxpool (off
A358 SE of Crowcombe, tel 01984 618618, www.flax-
pool.freeserve.co.uk)
YHA hostel Minehead, Alcombe Combe (meals, tel
0870 770 5968)
Bike shop Pompys Cycles, Mart Rd, Minehead (tel
01643 704077)
Exmoor National Park Centres Dunster (tel 01643
821835), Dulverton (tel 01398 323841).

A great day out in the northern Lakes

49 COTSWOLD HILLS
Avon-NE Somerset-Glocs-Wilts-Oxfordshire

Long on loveliness, with clusters of excellent hilly rights of way, the Cotswolds are nevertheless often passed over by MTBers. They rise in a wedge from Oxford in the east, over a plateau riven with pretty valleys, to the western escarpment which runs from Wotton under Edge in the south to Cheltenhem and Winchcombe in the north. The hills also extend south to include Bath. The Cotswold lanes can be very quiet and scenic, so it's no grief using them as links.

The steepest riding is on the escarpment around Cleeve Hill (Cheltenham) and Winchcombe. The mellower rural bridleways and pretty villages are to the east.

Where to ride

Guided and supported Contact Saddle Skedaddle (tel 0191 265 1110, www.skedaddle.co.uk).

The Hell of the Cotswolds, springtime, 50km/100km, 1200m climb. Start Winchcombe (8km NE Cheltenham, route guide £2 at www.tracklogs. co.uk, organised by Winchcombe CC and Cheltenham & County CC.

Self-navigating

South, around Bath; Hilly circuits S, Hinton Charterhouse, Wellow (Pipehouse DH bdwy NW to Midford); also NW N (Cotswold Way to North Stoke, Langridge).

The edge around Wotton-under-Edge; Tor Hill (SE), Tyleys bottom (NE), Wotton Hill (NW) and around Ozleworth Bottom (SE).

Around Cam and Dursley; NE to Peaked Down, N-facing slopes Dursley to Bencombe, Nailsworth and Horsley.

The edge around Gloucester I; Upton St Leonards S bdwy to Painswick Hill; Cranham S to Cranham Common, S to Sheepscombe, NE to B4070, NE to Climperwell Farm and SE to Caudle Green.

The edge around Gloucester II; from Birdlip N on bdwys to Crickley Hill Ctry Pk, road link S side Leckhampton Hill (bdlwys N side of hill double-back on themselves).

The edge - Cheltenham to Winchcombe; Two ways up/down 160m:1km slope to ridgeline bdwy of Cleeve Hill (317m, no summit bridleway) NE of Cheltenham. Or climb Prestbury to top lane, N 1km to ridgeline bdwy N there. Meet B4632, continue to Nottingham Hill and Langley Hill (bdwys/access tracks to summit).

Northwest: Bredon Hill (294m), Alderton Hill (203m). **Central (mid plateau)**; circuits via Chedworth, Chedworth Woods, Compton Abdale, Notgrove, Cold Aston, Northleach and Hampnett (on bdwys of Monarch's Way, Diamond Way and MacMillan Way) N around Stow; Bourton, Lower and Upper Slaughter, also around Ilmington, also Upper Brailes.

Central west; the Dunstisbournes, Sapperton and Woodmancote (E NE Stroud), use 'other public access' (red dots on OS Landrangers), McMillan Way is bdwy 9km Sapperton NE to Woodmancote.

Cirencester N from Bowling Green (1km NW of centre) 5km to North Cerney.

Fairford NW via Quenington, Bibury, Ablington to Coln Rogers (to Cirencester via Chedworth, North Cerney), East Burford and Chipping Norton.

Mapping and literature OS Landrangers 163 (central, Cheltenham, Cirencester), 162 (W, Painswick and Stroud), 150 (NW, Broadway), 151 (N, to Stratford), 164 (E, to Oxford), 172, 173 (S, to Bath).

Mountain bike club Cheltenham and County CC (www.cc-cc.co.uk, MTB runs Tues, Sat, Sun); and Winchcombe CC (www.winchcombecc. org.uk).

Where to stay YHA hostels Slimbridge (7km to Cam, meals, tel 0870 770 6036), Stow-on-the-Wold (meals, central, tel 0870 770 6050).

Tourist offices Stow on the Wold (tel 01451 8310), Cheltenham (tel 01242 522878), Gloucester (tel 01 396572), Stroud (tel 01453 760960), Cirencester (tel 01285 654180).

OUNTY DURHAM
ee C2C, Hamsterley Forest, North Pennines)

ddition to the North Pennines, there's plenty more riding throughout County Durham. A
vy industrial heritage gives a variety of old railway and trolley lines forming a good network.

ere to ride
nsterley Forest is a valuable venue, see entry
skerley Way is easy riding but thrilling nonetheless
he views and isolation at the highest points. The
is part of the C2C route and runs from Sunderland
he way to the high Co Durham fells above Weardale.

Lots of moorland bridleways can be linked with the use
of a map and a sense of imagination. Just join the dots
(well, dashes).
Mapping OS Landrangers 87, 88, 92, 93:
Explorer/OL31, 307, 305

RANBORNE CHASE TO SALISBURY
iltshire-Dorset
ee Blandford Forum Freeride, Wessex Ridgeway)

71

road and little-visited area of fine downland with a choice of bridleway routes from a little hilly
ery hilly. Cranborne Chase extends 15km northeast from near Blandford Forum, with another
m of downland from there to Salisbury. The heights climb to over 250m and straddle the
nty border of Wiltshire and Dorset.

ere to ride
-navigating
e up loops on bridleways starting from Blandford
m/Stourpaine, Tollard Royal, Berwick St John,
sbourne Wake and Broad Chalke. A bridleway runs
the highest point at Win Green (277m, map ref ST
206), above Berwick St John.
eline routes (few contours on top, easy to navigate,
se as links) include the Ox Drove (20km), west-east,
Win Green on a mix of bridleway and rough

roadway to Coombe Bissett; also the northern ridgeline
(20km), west-east, from White Sheet Hill (above
Donhead St Andrew) to Salisbury.
Bike shop
Offcamber, Blandford (tel 01258 458677)
Where to stay
YHA hostel Salisbury (B&B only, tel 0870 770 6018)
Tourist offices
Blandford Forum (tel 01258 454770), Salisbury (tel
01722 334956)

18 ▶ DALBY FOREST
North York Moors
(see also North York Moors)

Conquer the stiff downhill course and signed cross-country trails at Dalby Forest, then take a shower, courtesy of the Forestry Commission! The largest recreational forest in Yorkshire is investing plenty of zloty to make its pines and trails attractive to MTBers, with everything in pla for 2005, all in a peaceful scenic landscape. As well as black and red waymarked routes (also blu and green), you have the open forest road network with links to the wider North York Moors National Park. Family cycling is also plentiful, for those seeking gentler days out.

Where to ride
Self-Navigating The network of forest roads covers the wooded valleys and plateaux of Dalby Forest's 8500 acres, with cycling both in the forest block and linking with other forests and moorland. There's parking and facilities on site, also at Thornton Dale nearby (North Yorkshire's prettiest village). Also, bridleway links to Saltersgate and the moorland beyond, and the new Moor-to-Sea route (130km of off-road linking Scarborough-Pickering-Whitby including forest, moor and coast, www.moortoseacycle.net)

Dedicated Routes
Extreme downhill (and push-up) purpose-built
Black route (10km) mostly singletrack with very steep climbs and descents
Red route (24km) challenging, some singletrack, needs good technical ability and fitness
Blue route (13km) moderate, mixed terrain and heights, can be combined with Green
Two green family routes 10km mostly flat, and 4km Ellers Way, from the visitor centre
Five *interlinking trails* due 2005 – the latest thinking!
Forest section of Moor-to-Sea route with planned extensions (www.moortoseacycle.net)
Location For Dalby Forest, follow brown signs from Thornton Dale (5km). Forest toll £5 per car (£2 evenings and out of season), walkers and cyclists free. The visitor centre is at map ref SE 856 874. The seasonal Moorsbus links with Bikebus for transporting people and bikes around the National Park (info tel

01439 770657, or Pickering tourist office, see below
Bike facilities Dalby Forest Bike Hire, bike wash, re and quick repairs (open daily Apr-Oct plus most wee ends, tel 01751 460400, mobile 07773 073262); cyclists cafe and showers in 2005.
Visitor centres Dalby Forest Visitor Centre (seaso tel 01751 460295), Forest Enterprise Pickering (tel 01751 472771. www.forestry.gov.uk/dalbyforest).
Bike Shops Dalby Forest Bike Hire (see Biking facili ties); Pickering Cycle Centre (tel 01751 472581), Richardson's Cycles, Scarborough (tel 01723 35268; The Bicycle Works, Scarborough (tel 01723 365594
Mapping and literature OS Explorer 27 North Y Moors East; Cycling in Dalby (waymarked routes); or guides for self-navigating available at the visitor centre and tourist offices, also www.moortoseacycle.net.
Tourist office Pickering (tel 01751 473791)
Station Malton (15km), via York
Sustrans Routes The Whitby-Scarborough rail tra shared by the Moor to Sea route
Where to stay See also North York Moors.
Camping High Rigg Farm (in Dalby Forest, tel 01751 460269), Spiers House Campsite, Cropton, Pickerir (open Easter-Sept, in season tel 01751 417591, out season tel 0131 314 6505); Horseshoe Inn, Levisha (camping behind the pub, 4km from forest by bike, t 01751 460240); *YHA hostel* Lockton (1.5km from forest, self-catering only, tel 01751 460376); *Self-catering* Easthill House, Thornton Dale (tel 01751 474561); see also www.moortoseacycle.net.

ARTMOOR
evon

, windy beautiful Dartmoor is a great place to go biking. Eroded stone-topped tors guard sweeping des, often boggy, often with magnificent open views. Old mineworkings dot the landscape iding silent water-filled quarries and rideable stone tramlines and rail trails. The valleys are in places tbreakingly pretty and leg-achingly steep. And it's all mapped on a Harvey walking/cycling map!

moor is graced with a dedicated waterproof MTB (from Harvey) which picks out and colour-grades ideable legal and permitted trails (many not shown S) according to difficulty and conditions. Compiled sustainable biking and 'Moor Care' in mind, in eration with the National Park, we say don't ride out it.

re to ride

ed and supported Saddle Skedaddle (ride the Country Way, tel 0191 265 1110, .skedaddle.co.uk).

navigating

moor is exposed and remote: carry foul-weather ng, snacks and repair and navigation kit. Many trails p are uncut and rough. Much of the northwest area sed military ranges where there is live firing - ve the signs - lying north-south between etown and Okehampton, and west-east between rd and Postbridge. You are asked to avoid open land in winter, to contain erosion (those tracks ed as dashed lines on the Harvey map).

igh Cleave/Manaton (east Dartmoor) Although ublicised as top-grade MTBing Lustleigh's steep re overused, popular with horse-riders and there rking problem in the village. The National Park lainly that you go elsewhere.

Tracey (east) Go W and S.

er/Postbridge (central) (access also Widecombe in oor) Go N to Fernworthy Forest, E to Pizwell, ons Down and through Chaw Gully round combe Down.

eet (central) 12km red/blue circuit from

Dartmeet, S to Saddle Bridge, NW Hexworthy, N Brownberry and Dunnabridge Pound, NE moor below Laughter Tor, via Stepping Stones to Babeny, S over and beside river to B3357.

Princetown (central) One of the classic Dartmoor routes runs out of wind-lashed Princetown S and W round to Sheepstor and Burrator reservoir. Return on trails N of the reservoir, then E, or on the gentle Princetown rail trail.

Ivybridge (south) Face a stiff 220m climb due north up to Butterdon Hill (364m) and return (12km) via Hanger Down to the west or (11km) Owley to the East.

Buckfastleigh (south) Red (difficult) trails W around Grippers Hill or NW around Michelcombe & Shuttaford.

Sticklepath/South Zeal (north) Go on a tough little route on red trails south round or up to Cosdon Beacon and to Little Hound Tor and back

Okehampton (north) Take the family on a classic piece of Sustrans rail trail (served summer weekends by the little Dartmoor Pony train line, tel 01837 55667 from Okehampton) to Meldon Viaduct. Easy trails south via Rowtor, East Mill Tor, Okement Hill and Scarey Tor.

Peter Tavy (west) A circuit E on Twyste Ln to Youlden Head, back via Bagga Tor. Also SE round Cox Tor to Merrivale. Link the two into a figure-of-eight.

Mapping and literature *Dartmoor for Off-Road Cyclists* map from Harvey (£7.50, tel 01786 841202, www.harveymaps.co.uk); OS Explorer OL28 Dartmoor (Landranger 191)

Location For south and central Dartmoor, from Exeter use the A38 Devon Expressway. For north Dartmoor, from Exeter take the A30. [CONT]

Stations Exeter, Newton Abbot, Plymouth
Events Newnham, north of Plympton outside
Plymouth is the venue for national .events and enduros.
Bike shops Tavistock Cycles, Tavistock (tel 01822
617630), for Exeter shops see Haldon Forest and
Woodbury Common entries
Where to stay *Princetown* - camping, bunkhouse and
B&B at the Plume of Feathers (1785 inn, tel 01822
890240, www.plumeoffeathers-dartmoor.co.uk);
Widecombe in the Moor - bunkhouse (and double/twin
rooms) at the Dartmoor Expedition Centre (tel 01364
621249); *Moretonhampstead* - Sparrowhawk
Backpackers (tel 01647 440318); *Manaton* - Great

Hound Tor camping barn (tel 0870 770 6113, camp
barns@yha.org.uk); *YHA hostels* Bellever (meals, tel
0870 770 5692), Okehampton (tel 0870 770 5978)
B&Bs Chipley Farm, Bickington, Newton Abbot (tel
01626 821947, louisa@chipleyfarmholidays.co.uk);
of Bells Inn, North Bovey (tel 01647 440375); *B&B
self-catering* Hele Farm, Gulworthy, Tavistock (tel 0
833084, helefarm.organics@talk21.com)
Tourist offices High Moorland Visitor Centre,
Princetown (tel 01822 890414, www.dartmoor-
map.gov.uk), Tavistock (tel 01822 612938), Ivybridge
(tel 01752 897035), Okehampton (tel 01837 5302C

---

87 ▶ # DEERS LEAP PARK
High Weald, West Sussex

Mostly aimed at families and groups, the park, which is part of a working farm, is a venue for
beginner and sport-level mountain bikers. It is also used for cyclo-cross and occasional mounta
bike racing, showing scope for harder riding. Covering 93ha of undulating West Sussex
countryside, there are sets of waymarked routes with sections from easy to moderate.

Where to ride
10km of purpose-built all-weather track winds through
the park, with 6km graded, colour-coded cycle path and
singletrack, through arable farmland, old clay pits and
woodland. Both sets of trails can be linked. There are
plenty of sharp uphills and a variety of terrain to test legs
and handling.
The venue is crossed by national cycle route 21, the
Forest Way and the Cuckoo Trail.
Mapping and literature OS Landranger 198 Brighton
& Lewes; Explorer 135 Ashdown Forest; Guide *Deers
Leap Park - Cycling for All* (tel 01342 325858)
Visitor facilities Park office (tel 01342 325858).
Refreshment hut, toilets, picnic and barbecue areas.
Open daily Mar-Oct; weekends and school holidays
from Nov-Feb, details on www.deersleappark.co.uk
Location Deers Leap Park lies 5km southwest of East
Grinstead (from the east, signposted from the B2110

from Saint Hill, and from the west from the A23).
Bike shops The on-site shop does repairs, mainte
nance and hire, and sells new and secondhand bikes
Future Cycles, Lower Square, Forest Row (spares a
accessories, tel 01342 822847)
Sustrans routes NCN 21 runs north of the park
between East Grinstead and Crawley.
Station East Grinstead (5km northeast)
Where to stay *Camping* Long Acre Farm, Newch
Road, Lingfield (tel 01342 833205); *B&B* Ardingly I
Street Lane, Ardingly (tel 01444 892214); *Hotels*
Brambletye Hotel, Forest Row (tel01342824144);
Chequers, the Square, Forest Row (tel 01342 8233
Tourist offices East Grinstead (tel 01342 410121
Crawley (tel 01293 545322)

ELAMERE FOREST PARK
heshire

Manley Hill cycle skills area in Delamere Forest Park is highly-rated, and whatever you want to make it. The forest also has two easy family trails, and you can ride on all forest roads. It lies in striking distance of south Manchester and Liverpool. Lottery funding has been used by the rs to put in the trails, which feature berms, drops and a dual course. Note: you have to ride ly and responsibly to ensure the continuation of freeriding at Delamere.

ere to ride

from Linmere Lodge, the main visitor centre, near mere station. There's parking nearer by on the on Road which runs east-west halfway up the park vest at Hatchmere). You can ride any of the forest s and all the junctions are numbered for navigation. ley Hill cycle skills area, the official site, is in the west corner of the park (around forest junctions 1, 42, 43, 44 and 45), with highly-rated tracks gh the tree compartments that include decent ents and rate highly with riders. The forester writes, skills area contains jumps and other features that riders may find difficult. Only those with a high e of cycling skill and bikes of a suitable standard d attempt to use it. The provision of the cycle skills s dependent upon the co-operation and respon- behaviour of bikers. The jumps and other features

are changed and rebuilt from time to time, and riders must check their route before riding."

Dedicated routes

There are two waymarked cycle trails: *Whitefield* (12km) and *Hunger Hill* (7km), both on a network of multi-use forest roads.

Facilities Cafe and shop (selling maps and emergency bike kit) at Linmere Lodge visitor centre (tel 01606 889792). Parking is £1 per car per day, season pass £10.

Location Delamere lies 13km E of Chester. From the A54 Chester-Northwich road, go N 3km east of Kelsall, 2km, visitor centre on left, near Delamere train station.

Mapping The forest guide shows the routes quite clearly, available at the visitor centre (tel 01606 889792); OS Landranger 117

Where to eat and drink Cafe at the visitor centre, Abbey Arms pub (south of the forest on the A556)

Winding up the Long Mynd

Delamere Forest Park wearing a mystical aura

ORSET COAST AND PURBECK

74

:e also Blandford Forum Freeride Park, Wessex Ridgeway)

ough not an MTB honeypot, the multitude of bridleways on the gorgeous coastal downland
leways of Dorset and Isle of Purbeck are fine enough for the area to deserve higher status in
off-road world. There are enough trails to challenge anyone to complete them, with easy-to-
combinations of favourite climbs and descents, ice cream vans and views.

, several times we share tracks with bridleway
ns of the long-distance paths (including the South
: Coast path), but don't forget, no riding on the
rity footpath sections (or stand-alone footpaths).

re to ride

led and supported Saddle Skedaddle (weekends,
91 265 1110, www.skedaddle.co.uk)
e three suggested circuits cover the highlights of the
central and east parts of the coastline between
ort and Studland. Being suggestions only, they can
be shortened and varied. If pressed, we would say
miss the Isle of Purbeck (the eastern part). Start
here en route.

: Dorchester and Abbotsbury circuit
, around 30km, hilly)
om Dorchester past Maiden Castle to the ridgeline
onkham Hill, Black Down (site of the Hardy
ment) and on to Abbotsbury near the coast. North
Abbotsbury to Little Bredy and Kingston Russel
nding and climbing the blind valley of the Bride
further bridleways or lanes back to Dorchester; NE
ck Down (site of the Hardy Monument)

ral: Between Osmington and West Lulworth;
ridleways close to the famous rollercoaster coast-
ut not on it).
Osmington or West Lulworth (visitor centre,
g, cafes and pubs). A circuit runs; Osmington, E on
yellow road to Upton, becoming bridleway above
Down Farm, E 6km to yellow road, E down to
Lulworth. Retrace to top of down, NW bridleway
aldon Herring, NE to before Winfrith Newburgh,
bridleway 5km (Five Marys, Moigns Down) back

to Osmington (option to continue NR from A353 before
Osmington to White Horse Hill.
East: Isle of Purbeck downland circuit (around
42km, hilly)
The complete circuit shows off the coastline and high-
points of Purbeck, and can easily be shortened. From
Corfe, E bridleway on Brenscombe Hill and Nine
Barrow Down, roads NE to Studland, bridleway climb
(push, and yield to walkers) SE E up round Old Harry
foreland, W bridleway on Ballard Down, SW down to
New Swanage. W out of Swanage on A351, to farm-
road bridleways S and W round Langton Matravers,
Priest's Way, to Worth Matravers (there-and-back S/N
bridleway to chapel at St Aldhelm's Head), NNE to
B3069, W to Kingston, SW to Swyre Head, NW to
Kimmeridge, W N to Steeple, NW road climb to top of
Purbeck Hills, E along ridge on public access road to
Corfe.
Purbeck: Also short circuits up and down
Brenscombe Hill and Nine Barrow Down.
Heathland riding (easy), on lowlying bridleways
through heath and woodland touching Poole Harbour at
Ower Bay (map ref SY 997 863), starting Corfe (W end)
or Studland (E end), on Rempstone Heath, Newton
Heath, Godlingston Heath and Studland Heath.
Mapping and literature OS Landrangers 194 195,
Explorer OL15 Purbeck & South Dorset
Location Reach Dorchester from the west via the
spectacular A35, from the east via the A35/A31
Southampton roads. Reach Purbeck from the east on
the A352 from Dorchester then B3071, from the west
from the A352 Poole/Wareham then B3070.   [CONT]

Where to stay *Camping* Bagwell Farm (west, 2km NW of Chickerell, tel 01305 782575), East Fleet Farm (west, 1.8km W of Chickerell, tel 785768); Durdle Door Holiday Park (central, 1.5km W of West Lulworth, atop the downs, tel 01929 400200), Norden Farm (east, 1.5km NW of Corfe, tel 01929 480348), Burnbake (east, towards Studland, 01929 480570); *YHA hostels* Litton Cheney (west, self-catering only, tel 0870 770 5923), Lulworth Cove (central, meals, open Ma Oct, tel 0870 770 5940), Swanage (east, meals, tel 0870 770 6058); *Independent hostel* Bournemouth Backpackers (east, Frances Road, Bournemouth, tel 01202 299491); *Hotel* Lulworth Beach Hotel (tel 01929 400404)

Tourist offices Dorchester (tel 01305 267992), Purbeck (in Wareham, tel 01929 552740)

---

59 ▶

EASTWAY CYCLE CIRCUIT
Lee Valley, east London

Find surprisingly challenging riding on a small piece of green space in a very urban area 1.5km from Stratford. Eastway is one of only two London off-road venues (the other being Hillingdor and is renowned for its high embankments and respectable bottom-to-top course height. It is home to the Beastway MTB series and cyclo-cross racing, as well as road-racing and time-trial on the high quality tarmac track.

However, at time of writing the Lower Lee Valley, which includes Eastway, is the proposed site of the 2012 London Olympics, bid permitting. This could change all details.

Where to ride

Ride freely around the course and embankments for a small fee. The race course is 3.2km and changes every event. There's also a 1,600m tarmac road-racing and time-trial circuit, and a small BMX track. Training days and schools days are organized (bikes provided).

Racing The Beastway series takes place on weekday evenings in the summertime (see www.londoncycle-sport.com for details) with categories for all abilities. Road racing and time-trialling are weekly activities: r the circuit manager for more details.

Facilities Free parking, changing rooms, a spacious club-room with refreshments on ride days. The circ manager is on tel 0208 534 6085. The site is run by Lee Valley Regional Park (all subject to change).

Location at the southern end of Hackney Marsh, 1.5km northwest of Stratford. It lies south of the ma A106 Eastway Ruckholt Road, Quarter Mile Lane (c sionally shared with travellers).

Development may change the access point.

PPING FOREST
ndon-Essex

ing Forest is a mountain biker's joy. You may ride off-track as well as on-track virtually
where over 5000 acres of glorious ancient woodland and grassland, on the border of the
ropolis, hardly ever repeating a ride. The forest is 19km long north to south and easy to get to
public transport. For insider wheeling hook up with Epping MBC, which excels in rides that
d horseriders and walkers. The forest was purchased by the Corporation of London to save it
n development and is run in the public interest. Watch out during the summer months for
-roaming English Longhorn cattle.

ere to ride

navigating Epping Forest MBC says get hold of the
ated OS Epping Forest map (1:20000) from the
it at High Beach (west side of the forest, half way
There's so much there.' You can loop the whole
t. You can head for the hills; Pole Hill, at south end
e forest has views of central London including the
on Eye and Canary Wharf. Yardley Hill nearby
s the same views if not better. When it comes to
hills, the forest undulates with short sharp hills and
s. See also Pole Hill and Claypit Hill and either side
ay Pit Hill road close to High Beech. Generally, the
hern half has more varied trails.

d the surfaced tracks though, which are horserides,
ugh other visitors may use them.

small number of places you may not ride are sign-
d; they include two Iron Age camps and Loughton
k, also listed Wanstead Park in the south.

ping OS Epping Forest 1:20,000, available from
formation centre and teahut at High Beach. OS
anger 167

tion

the forest at numerous points around the
eter. Accessible by train from the Central Line
ns Wanstead to Epping, and Chingford mainline.
you may not take bikes on the tunnel sections of
entral Line, only where it goes overground (due to
gulations).

shops Cyclone Cycles, Waltham Cross (5km west

of the northern end, tel 020 8399 0979), Heales Cycles,
Highams Park E4 (west of the southern urban forest
extension, 020 8527 1592)

Mountain bike club

Epping Forest MBC (www.epping-forest-mbc.co.uk).
Member Richard Castle says, 'After riding every week for
two years, I've done a different route every time. We
lose ourselves for three hours, and that's still following
the club policy of 'don't go on the horserides, and don't
ride the same track twice.'

Epping Forest Information Centre

High Beach (tel 020 7482 7073, on OS Epping Forest
map 1:20,000 map ref 412983)

Where to eat and drink

At High Beach tea hut and the nearby King's Oak pub
(lunches and hot meals). Here are also public toilets and
tap for rinsing the bike (it's a press tap so you need a
third hand).

In the south of the forest, near the Queen Elizabeth
Hunting Lodge, is the Butler's Retreat cafe (hot drinks
and food, just off Station Rd in Chingford)

At Whipps Cross, Snaresbrook, also at the south end, is
a tea hut (hot food and drinks, bacon butties, on the
south side of Hollow Pond)

Where to stay

YHA hostel Epping Forest (self-catering,
tel 0870 770 5822).

63 ▶ EXMOOR
Devon-Somerset
(see also Combe Sydenham)

Beautiful heather-clad Exmoor, on the north Devon and Somerset coast, is blessed with one of densest sets of bridleways in Britain, totalling 500km, with many other unsurfaced tracks being legal to ride as well. Follow them over what is largely high open moorland country dissected by deep combes. Exmoor also boasts a national downhill venue at Combe Sydenham country park (see entry).

Where to ride
Guided and supported Saddle Skedaddle (weekends and the West Country Way, tel 0191 265 1110, www.skedaddle.co.uk); Exmoor & Quantock MTB Holidays (Exmoor Challenge 130km overnight camping barn, tel 01984 632237, www.exqumtb.co.uk); Tom's Tours, Broadwood Farm, Dunster (tel 01643 821953)
Self-navigate the bridleways on coastal scarp and moorland, including the summit of Dunkery Beacon (519m). Steep ones near Porlock and open rolling ones on the top of the moor. Good start/finish places are Dunster, Withypool, Minehead, Winsford, Dulverton. Avoid routes that cross the boggy high moorland in the wet season.
Downhill course see Combe Sydenham country park
Dedicated routes
Dunster Woods: Explorer trail (15km, harder, brown), ascend to 381m Withycombe Common, great views; *Intermediate trail* (10km, orange) climb up to Croydon Hill. Start both from Nutcombe Bottom 21km SW of Dunster (*route map* from the tourist offices)
Wimbleball Reservoir, Brendon Hills: Explorer trail (19km, brown), climb to Haddon Hill, for views of the Brendons, long descent to Bury village, round lake. *Intermediate trail* (13km, orange), follow trails up and down round the lake. Start in Hartford SW of lake. Teashop at main car park (*route map* from tourist offices)
Holnicote Estate and North Hill: Explorer trail (21km, hard), start car park Selworthy Beacon (end of hilltop road via Bratton Ball up W out of Minehead) or Selworthy; ride anticlockwise, via Luccombe, Woootton

Courtney above Tivington, Selworthy and back. *Intermediate route* (12km, spectacular), coastal hill r along the approach road, with a drop to Selworthy (*route map* from the tourist offices)
Mountain bike club Exmoor MBC (cross-country coaching Sally Burnham, tel 01392 276122)
Bike shops Pompys , Minehead (tel 01643 70407 Lance Nicholson, Dulverton (tel 01398 323409)
Where to eat Horner Tea Garden in Horner, the Forrester's Arms in Dunster, Ship Inn in Porlock
Where to stay Websites www.exmoor-accommc tion.co.uk, www.exmoor-cottages.co.uk.
Camping Burrowhayes Farm, West Luccombe, Porl (tel 01643 862463), Porlock Caravan Park (camping 01643 862269), Wimbleball Lake (tel 01837 8715€ Westermill Farm Camping, Exford (tel 01643 8312: Doone Valley Campsite, Malmsmead (tel 01598 741267); *YHA hostels* Minehead, Alcombe Combe (meals, tel 0870 770 5968), Exford (meals, tel 087C 5828), Lynton (meals, tel 0870 770 5942); *Farm Be* Chapple Farm, Bury, Dulverton (tel 01398 331364* Warren Farm, Simonsbath (tel 01643 831283), Ker Farm, Winsford (tel 01643 851312); *B&B* Marsh Br Cottage, Dulverton (tel 01398 323197); *Self-caterr* Honeymead Cottage, Dulverton (2 bedrooms, tel 01398 323787), Liscombe Farm (cottages, tel 016∠ 851551), Ball Cottage, Winsford (tel 0207 622 675 Westwater Farm (cottage, tel 01643 831360)
Tourist Information
Exmoor National Park Centre, Dunster (tel 01643 821835); Dulverton TIC (tel 01398 323841).

OREST OF DEAN
/est Gloucestershire
ee also Wye Valley)

45

rt downhill pistes and the singletrack Fodca Trail make the atmospheric Forest of Dean a
ming place to ride. First-timers in this ancient hilly hunting forest should head for the
prehensively-equipped Pedalabikeaway cycle centre in the middle of the forest. The forest
has excellent family riding, so bring the brood. Base town is Coleford.

ere to ride
from Pedalabikeaway, see below
downhill tracks are short and sharp, but don't take
to climb back up.

ss-country The Fodca Trail cross-country (Forest of
Cycle Association - FODCA) is a singletrack trail
by rider-volunteers along the lines of Afan/Coedy
and growing). See fodca.co.uk for up-to-date info.

n riding On stoned forest tracks only, or anywhere
e 5km sq *Sallow Vallets free-riding area*. A favoured
is from *Pedalabikeaway to the Rising Sun* pub for
and return

ded riding Pedalabikeaway

ily cycling The dedicated family cycling trail is
ant and undemanding, and has direct access from
labikeaway. Miles of old mining railways now also
e excellent easy pedalling.

alabikeaway Cycle Centre What more could
want? A cafe, changing rooms with showers, toilets,
wash, shop and repairs, all under the amiable
dianship of Fred Carpenter (in Cannop Valley, tel
4 860065, www.pedalabikeaway.com (that's for
enue), www.pedalbikeaway.co.uk (that's for the
ess)).

ation For Pedalabikeaway (see map on www.pedal-
away.com), turn off the A48 at Lydney on the
4 to Parkend, follow signs to Lydbrook (don't go to
rook), then pick up the signs to cycle centre. From
40, follow the brown signs to the Forest of Dean,
e forest follow the signs to the cycle centre.

ntain Bike Club Bigfoot MBC. Ride hotline tel
6 262315. 'Centring on the Forest of Dean and

Cranham Woods near Gloucester, with the odd jaunt in
the Stroud or Cheltenham direction. We also feature a
once-a-month BIG Ride, which takes us further a field.'
Where to stay *Camping* The Forestry Commission has
three caravan/campsites in the Forest of Dean (open
Mar-Oct, in season tel 01594 833376, out of season tel
0131 314 6505). One is called Bracelands (Bracelands
Drive, Christchurch, Coleford); *YHA hostels* Welsh
Bicknor (northern forest, near Goodrich, Ross-on-Wye,
meals, tel 0870 770 6086), St Briavels Castle (southwest
of the forest, good for Wye Valley, St Briavels Lydney,
meals, tel 0870 770 6040); *Bunkhouse/B&B* Fountain
Inn (18thC inn with bunkhouse, Park End, tel 01594
562189, thefountaininn@aol.com); *B&Bs* Angel Inn in
Coleford (tel 01594 833113), Poolway House
(Coleford, tel 01594 833937); *Hotel* The Speech
House (Coleford, tel 01594 822607,
thespeechhouse.co.uk)
Mapping The *Forest of Dean Recreation Map* (see
advert p59) shows all the tracks open to cyclists, also
walker-only paths. Includes the family cycle trail, forest
rail-trail routes, four suggested circular routes and a
'round forest ride'. The reverse shows the free-riding
area and has loads of local tourist information.
OS Explorer 14 Wye Valley and Forest of Dean,
(Landranger 162)
Where to eat and drink The Fountain Inn at Park
End (see Where to stay), the Rising Sun in the middle of
the forest at Moseley Green (the cross-country riders'
haunt).
Tourist offices Coleford (tel 01594 812388),
Chepstow (tel 01291 623772).

FRISTON FOREST AND CUCKMERE
East Sussex

Friston Forest lies on the South Downs above the Cuckmere Valley 8km west of Eastbourne. There are cross-country trails inside the forest and bridleway connections to the South Downs Way which runs 2km north (see entry). Route advice and maps, meals and snacks are available the Seven Sisters Country Park visitor centre and tea shop, where you also find the Cuckmere Cycling Company (bike hire, repairs and route advice).

A summertime bike-bus serves the area, and accommodation is easy to find within striking distance.
The forest is owned by South East Water and managed by the Forestry Commission.

Where to ride

This is a good place for day-long cross-country riding, with one waymarked trail with technical sections, especially challenging in the wet. The trails are smooth mud paths, and better ridden in dry conditions.
Note: the off-route downhill sections are unofficial and due for removal because of erosion. Friston Forest is a water catchment area, or aquafer, and erosion risks causing sedimentation of the water supply. Also, being unofficial, the sections are not constructed to recognised standards or subject to safety inspections.

Self-navigating

Start points lead from the Bo Peep car park (north of the forest, off the A27 at Alfriston) or any of four Seven Sisters car parks. Explore myriad paths in the forest and towards Jevington (to the northeast). Bridleways lead to the South Downs Way.

Waymarked MTB trail (11km)

This starts from either the car park at Seven Sisters Country Park visitor centre or Butchershole car park, with steep slopes and winding singletrack in trees.

Mapping OS Landranger 199 Eastbourne & Hastings; Explorer 123 South Downs Way - Newhaven to Eastbourne
Location Friston Forest lies to N of the A259 between

Exceat and Friston. There are two car parks, one adjacent to the Seven Sisters Country Park visitor centre (map ref TV 518 995), the other, the 'Butchershole' park, is off the Friston to Jevington Road (TV 555994) Nominal parking fees contribute towards the maintenance of the car parks and the MTB trail.
The summertime **Hiker Biker Bus** carries bikes free a trailer one-way anticlockwise round the eastern South Downs (every two hours, Sun & Public Hols, July-September adult/child £2/£1), from Lewes via Newhaven, Exceat Eastbourne, Folkington and back to Lewes.

Bike Shops

Cuckmere Cycle Company, Seven Sisters Country Park visitor centre, Exceat (hire, parts, repairs, route advice maps, tel 01323 870310, www.cuckmere-cycle.co.uk

Stations

Seaford (4km west), Eastbourne (13km east), Berwick (8km north).

Where to eat

Country park visitor centre tea shop, Golden Galleon pub, Exceat (tel 01323 892247); Sussex Ox, Milton Street (real ale, by South Downs Way 1.5km NE of Alfriston, tel 01323 870840)

Where to stay

Camping/Bunk barn Foxhole Campsite and Camping Barn, Seven Sisters Country Park, Exceat (tel 01323 870280).
YHA hostel Alfriston (meals, tel 0870 7705666).
B&B Exceat Farmhouse (tel 01323 870218)
Tourist office Seaford (tel 01323 987426)

ЭREST OF BERE
̄ampshire

̄e a small amount of easy-going off-road in an ancient hunting forest 10km NW of Portsmouth.

:h a short mountain bike route and a family loop just ɔm the south coast in the lovely Meon Valley in ٦pshire. You can connect north with the South ٮns Way (the Meon drains the downs). in Wickham (in the Meon Valley, on the A32 coming ٦ out of Fareham) and follow the old railway line to

the forest, or drive up Hundred Acres Road. Parking also in West Walk car park (£1, toilets). Fareham is the nearest station. There's a free map guide in the car park, while the OS map is Landranger 196. For post-ride refreshments go to cafes in Wickham There's an ice cream van there in summer

---

̄rest of Bowland, see Trough of Bowland

̄ISBURN FOREST
ɔrest of Bowland, Lancashire
̄ee also Trough of Bowland)

13

٦er forestry riding in Gisburn can be combined with open-country riding in the Forest of Bowland. ̄ect beautiful rolling land on the doorstep of the Yorkshire Dales, near Settle and Clitheroe.

̄ere to ride Starting from Cocklet Hill car park (map ̄D 745 551), on colour-coded trails on forest roads ٥ingletrack, wind through mixed woodland, views ٥s the Hodder Valley to the surrounding fells. The ٦ark map details the three routes, all best cycled anti- ٤wise.

٥marked routes Purple (9km), forest road and ٤track, short steep descent and ascent. Green ̄6km), similar, combine with red route. Red (16km) ٤ challenging with steep climbs, descents, mainly ٤track, passes Martin's Laithe shelter, a barn with ٤ tables.

٦ping OS Landranger 103 Blackburn & Burnley; ɔrer OL41 Forest of Bowland and Ribblesdale ̄ation Gisburn lies on the east side of the forest, off

the B6478 between Tosside and Slaidburn. Settle is 13km northeast, Clitheroe is 17km south
Bike Shops Pedal Power, Clitheroe (hire, tel 01200 442066)
Stations Settle (8km NE), Long Preston (8km E)
Where to eat In Slaidburn - Hark to Bounty Inn (meals and real ale) and village shop; Settle - Naked Man Bakery & Cafe and Settle Down Cafe; Tosside - village shop
Where to stay Camping Langcliffe Caravan & Camping Park, Langcliffe, Settle (N edge Settle, tel 01729822387); **YHA hostel** Slaidburn (5km from forest, tel 0870 7706034); **B&Bs** Hark to Bounty Inn, Slaidburn (tel 01200 443246); Brooklands, 9 Pendle Road, Clitheroe (tel 01200 422797);
Tourist Office Clitheroe (tel 01200 425566)

10 GRIZEDALE FOREST PARK
Lake District National Park

A premiere Lakeland MTB destination, this beautiful working forest (between Windermere and Coniston Water) has a wealth of quality cycling including excellent singletrack, signed routes and bridleways. You get spectacular views, climbs and descents, and the chance to admire and puzzle over sculptures on the way. Bike facilities include a spares and repairs shop, hire and bike-wash.

Where to ride

Guided and supported Saddle Skedaddle (tel 0191 265 1110, www.skedaddle.co.uk).

Signposted forest road routes (moderate-demanding, map £1 from visitor centre)

Singletrack route coming!

Goosey Foot Tarn (3.5km, 30 mins, moderate, red sign one-way clockwise), starts from Moor Top car park, the shortest in the forest but still has hills.

Grizedale Tarn (10km, 1.5hrs, moderate, black signs), starts at Bogle Crag car park, on the slow ascent look out for sculptures, heads for the only natural tarn in the forest.

Moor Top (11.5km, 1.5hrs, moderate, purple signs), starting from Grizedale visitor centre or Moor Top car park, ride up to the top of the moor and down.

Hawkshead Moor (17km, 2.5hrs, demanding, green signs), starts from Grizedale visitor centre, Moor Top car or High Cross car park, covers a large part of the western forest with wonderful views of the Old Man of Coniston, the Langdales and Helvellyn.

Silurian Way (23.5km, 3.5hrs, demanding), starts from Grizedale visitor centre, Moor Top car park or Force Mills car park, passes many sculptures on both sides of the Grizedale Valley, get ready for hills and panoramic views

Self-navigating

(all anticlockwise, using combinations of tracks)
Use Explorer OL7, to extend these outside Grizedale Forest

Parkamoor ridgeway (30km, start/finish at Grizedale visitor centre for tea and cakes, spectacular high thrills in

day's ride), start visitor centre, either go N brown road to Hawkshead Moor for SW bridleway through Grizedale Moor, or bridleway via Broad Piece/Park Plantation. At crosstracks (near 253m) SW bridleway, Parka Moor (stunning views, high ridgeway). To Low Parkamoor, pick up S green-dotted cycleway, good descent near Grass Holme, round E, via Three Foot Oak to High Ickenthwaite. Pick up Corker Ln NE, via Force Forge Farm to past Force Mill, for NW bridleway to Satterthwaite. Then NE bridleway via Breasty Haw (good climb to ridgeway, good descent off) to yellow road, Low Scar Wood. NW on waggly bridleway (nice singletrack) to 203m. Return to visitor centre on green dots.

Singletrack Descents Loop (16km, start/finish Grizedale visitor centre, fast and tech descents, rideable climbs stunning views, short forest road sections). Visitor centre, NE on green dots to 189m mark, loop round forestry track via Ormandy Intakes to brown road, and briefly N for bridleway SW through Grizedale Moor, Park, to Low Parkamoor. E bridleway for fantastic descent to the main road (muddy but rideable, good views) and lane to Satterthwaite. NE bridleway via Breasty Haw (good climb and descent for ridgeway with steep finish to main road. NW waggly bridleway (nice singletrack) to 203m mark, return to visitor centre.

All Day Ride via Hawkshead (30km, singletrack, climbs/descents and stunning views, tea & cakes Grizedale, Hawkshead). Start/finish in Hawkshead; S climbing on permissive bridleway to the forest (green dots, white road, mapped as footpath, forest track) to road below Hawkshead Moor. SW on bridleway

ugh Grizedale Moor, the Park, to Low Parkamoor, E
leway (fantastic descent to main road and views) and
to Satterthwaite. NW bridleway past Breasty Haw
d climb and descent on and off ridgeway), steep
n at main road. Pick up NE bridleway over to brown
below Long Slack, N to Ees Hows, to Near
rey, bridleway N (past disused quarry) into Claife
st (good climb, stunning views to Ambleside Fells,
tarns). Bridleway to crosstracks beside Holling Band
tation, NW to crosstracks near Long Height, W via
gh Hows and down a good descent to Colthouse
tation back near Hawkshead.

ping and literature OS Explorer OL7 (map ref
944), *forest cycle routes map* (£1) from centre
ation Follow signs to Hawkshead then Grizedale
st Visitor Centre and car parking Grizedale visitor
re (tel 01229 860010, www.forestry.gov.uk/north-
england), car parking at centre £2 half-day, £3 all
free at outlying car parks High Cross, Moor Top,
e Mills, Blind Lane
shop/hire Grizedale Mountain Bikes (on-site, hire
sales, open daily mid-Feb-Oct, weekends in winter,
1229 860369, www.grizedalemountainbikes.co.uk);
Croft (Hawkshead, hire, tel 015394 36374); Bike

Treks Ambleside (sales and hire, tel 015394 31245),
Ghyllside Cycles (sales and hire, tel 015394 33592)
Mountain Bike Clubs Bog Trotters (Lancaster-based
call Simon 01524 843474 or Paul 01524 416388), Bike
Treks in Ambleside organises rides on Tuesday nights
Where to eat Grizedale visitor centre cafe; in
Hawkshead; the Eagles pub in Satterthwaite; the Tower
Bank Arms in Near Sawrey
Where to stay *Camping* The Croft, Hawkshead, also
bike hire, self-catering flats and caravans for rent (tel
015394 36374, enquiries@hawkshead-croft.com);
Independent hostel Rookhow Centre, Rusland,
Grizedale, 3km south of Satterthwaite south of the forest
(tel 01229 860231, rookhow@tesco.net); *YHA hostels*
Hawkshead 5km (meals, tel 0870 770 5856), Coniston
Holly How (meals, tel 0870 770 5770), Windermere,
15km via ferry (tel 0870 770 6094, meals); *B&Bs*
Walker Ground (bike-friendly, Hawkshead, tel 015394
36219)
Events GNBC and Ace races, festivals
Tourist offices Hawkshead (tel 015394 36525),
Ambleside (tel 015394 32582), National Park visitor
centre Brockhole (015344 46601)
Station Windermere (20km).

---

uildford, see North Downs and Surrey Hills

ALDON FOREST
xeter, south Devon
e also Dartmoor, Teignbridge)

66

letrack is growing steadily at hilly Haldon Forest, 8km SW of Exeter on the Haldon Ridge,
re you can also freely ride on the forest roads. Take your own snacks, there are no facilities.

re to ride
navigating On challenging, hilly cut singletrack and
forest tracks in a 'take us as you find us' condition.
ping OS Landranger 192 Exeter & Sidmouth;
rer 110 Torquay & Dawlish, Explorer 114 Exeter &
xe Valley
ation Park at Buller's Hill; from the A38 at Exeter
course follow signs to Dunchideok, go 1.5km and
ar park is on the lefthand side.
Shops Partridge Cycles, Kennford (tel 01392
'03), Freewheel, Fore Street, Exeter (tel 01392
91); Mud Dock, Commercial Road, Exeter (tel
2 279999); hire bikes at Saddles and Paddles on
Quay, Exeter (tel 01392 424241)

Mountain Bike Clubs Exeter Mountain Bike Club
(very active, www.embc.uk.net). For the trail-building
see www.yucca.co.uk/trail.
Station Exeter (9km from Buller's Hill)
Where to eat Nearest cafes and shops - Exeter 8km
Where to stay *Camping* Haldon Lodge Camping &
Caravan Park, Clapham (tel 01392 832312); *YHA
hostels* Exeter (meals, tel 0870 775826); Steps Bridge,
nr Dunsford, Exeter (self-catering only, tel 0870
7706048); *B&B* Gissons Arms, Kennford, Exeter (tel
01392 832444)
Tourist Office Exeter (tel 01392 365700)

5 ▶ HAMSTERLEY FOREST
County Durham

Foresters and mountain bikers in the eastern Pennines have built a highly-respected downhill course, cross-country singletrack and jumps area at Hamsterley, making it an MTB name. There are family trails too, on well-surfaced roads. The forest spreads across three valleys, with tracks leading from the valley floor to the moor tops at around 450m.

It costs £2 to enter the forest (ticket machine at the main entrance).

Where to ride
Guided and supported Saddle Skedaddle (tel 0191 265 1110, www.skedaddle.co.uk), Grit Mountain Biking (tel 0798 559 2163, www.gritmtb.co.uk)

Self-navigating
From the visitor centre car park, access the wider countryside using local bridleways and OS maps.

Waymarked routes
Trails are colour-graded for difficulty, varying from 5km to 16km. They can be also be linked via forest tracks and bridleways. Route leaflets are available in the visitor centre, and are pinned to the noticeboard when the centre is closed.

Downhill area
This is in the central forest, south of Grove House. Park in the Grove car park, then do a 10-minute ride over the bridge and along a waymarked cycle route to the top of the course.

Hamsterley Forest Visitor centre
see Location for directions (open Apr-Oct, tel 01388 488312), snacks available
Mapping OS Landranger 92 Barnard Castle, Explorer OL31 Teesdale & Weardale. Waymarked trail maps are available at the visitor centre in season, and the rangers office the rest of the year.
Location From the A1, the A68 north to Darlington leads to West Auckland and Toft Hill. 800m from Toft Hill turn left into Hamsterley village. The forest is signposted from this junction (map ref NZ 092 313)
Station Bishop Auckland (branch line from Darlington).

Bus to Hamsterley village.
Bike shops Avanti Cycles, Auckland (tel 01388 608397); Hamsterley Forest Cycles, Barnard Castle 01833 690194); Iron Horse Cyclery, Darlington (tel 01325 284500, www.ironhorsecyclery.com); Hamsterley Forest Cycle Hire (tel 01388 488188)
Mountain Bike Clubs
Grit Mountain Biking is an informal club for the forest and its surrounds, which runs guided rides (www.grit mtb.co.uk); Hamsterley Trailblazers do cross-country trail-building in the forest (www.hamsterley trailblazers.co.uk); Club Descend is the Hamsterly downhill club (www.descendhamsterley. co.uk)
Sustrans
NCN7, the Coast-to-Coast route and NCN14, the National Byway, run within 16km of the forest
Where to eat
Get snacks at the visitor centre and shop, also snack in the car park (daily in summer, weekends in winter) Hamsterley tearoom in village (open Apr-Oct).
Where to stay
Camping High Shipley Farm (Mrs CJ Atkinson, tel 01 764620)
YHA hostel Langdon Beck, Forest-in-Teesdale, Barnard Castle (meals, tel 0870 7705910, langdonbeck@yha.org.uk)
B&Bs Grove House (Mrs H Close, tel 01388 4882C Dryderdale Hall (tel 01388 488494)
Tourist offices
Barnard Castle (tel 01833 630272)
Bishop Auckland (tel 01388 604922).

OPTON WOOD
ropshire
e also Shropshire Hills)

31

of Shropshire's two venues that specialize in downhill with a chauffeur uplift service. The
d also features 32km of forest roads, track and singletrack for cross-country. It lies in the
ly Shropshire Hills between Shrewsbury and Ludlow. There's parking and a picnic area, and
tacular views from the top of the hills. Lift your eyes from the trail and you might also see
, buzzards and goshawks. Or, actually, better stay looking where you are!

re to ride
wood's forest roads, tracks and singletrack feature
ur-graded (easy blue to difficult black), with
ered posts at every junction, which you follow
onsite signage and the cycle guide.

icated trails
route, Hopton's downhill runs – for seasoned
s only – with berms, jumps & turns
r route, challenging
oute, adventurous

t service
Pearce Cycles in Ludlow drives downhillers to the
of the black runs on regular Downhill Days. You
to book (£10 per day, also private bookings), cos
popular service with up to 80 riders a time. For
, see the shop website or ring Pearce Cycles (see
w).

ping OS Landranger 137; waterproof leaflet
ntain Biking in the Forest - Hopton Wood is avail-
from the Forestry Commission (tel 01889 586593)
arce Cycles (tel 01584 876016)

tion Find the wood 13km west of Craven Arms,
e B4385 to Clun, adjacent to the village of Hopton

Castle (map ref SO 347 777)
Bike shops Dave Pearce Cycles, Fishmore Road,
Ludlow (tel 01584 876016, www.pearcecycles.co.uk).
Dave and Lindsay Pearce have contributed greatly to the
development of mountain biking around here.
For visitors Nearest visitor centre is Secret Hills (the
Shropshire Hills Discovery Centre) at Craven Arms (tel
01588 676000, secret hills@shropshire-cc.gov.uk,
www.secrethills.com), see also the Forestry Commission
website www.forestry.gov.uk
Mountain Bike Club
No local MTB club (Ludlow CC likes road riding), so for
biking buddies, best contact Pearce Cycles.
Stations
Hopton Heath 3km east, Bucknell 4km south
Where to stay
YHA hostel Clun Mill, Clun (self-catering only,
tel 0870 770 5766)
Major events Pearce Cycles organises downhill racing,
see website.
Tourist offices
Ludlow (tel 01584 875053)
Knighton (tel 01547 528753)

A packhorse trail in the South Pennines

Summer (above) and winter (below)
in the fabulous Quantocks

19 ▶ HOWARDIAN HILLS
North Yorkshire
(see also North York Moors)

Lying just south of the North York Moors, the Howardian Hills are a low ridge of wooded lumps peaking at 172m, with a small number of bridleways. The best trails lie at the southern end, in the Castle Howard area, where you can find a couple of descents. Otherwise, they tend to be discontinuous, and get muddy in winter.

Mapping and information
OS Landranger 100, see ww.howardianhills.gov.uk

Where to eat and drink
Most villages have pubs. You find cafes in Hovingham and Terrington, also attached to Yorkshire Lavender near Terrington and at Castle Howard. Find village shops in Ampleforth, Brandsby, Hovingham, Huttons Ambo, Slingsby, Terrington and Welburn.

Where to stay
Camping Lakeside Holiday Park, in Castle Howard grounds (30 tent pitches, Castle Howard estate office, tel 01653 648316)

YHA hostel Helmsley (meals, tel 0870 770 5860)

B&Bs Grange Farm, Castle Howard, Bulmer (dairy farm on Castle Howard estate, tel 01653 618376, www.grangefarmbulmer.co.uk); Gate Farm, Ganthorpe Terrington (on the Castle Howard estate, tel 01653 648269, www.ganthorpegatefarm.com)

Tourist office Malton (tel 01653 600048)

HOWGILLS
Cumbria
(see also Yorkshire Dales)

14

Located on the hills on the western edge of the Yorkshire Dales, the Calf (676m) and Bowderdale make up a classic route, with Sedburgh the base town.

Where to ride
Self-navigate The Calf/Bowderdale/Ravenstonedale
Common route (42km, 1285m climbing, 6-7hrs dry/wet)
This is a big ride, so allow time for delays and go prefer-ably when it's dry and there's enough daylight.
Start/finish Sedbergh, pub at Ravenstone.
*[Ride anticlockwise: Sedbergh, A683 E, 800m left unclas-sed road/bridleway, past view of Cautley Spout to Narthwaite Farm, right downhill only as far as a 90 degree right-turn ('Handley's Bridge' means you've gone too far), stop and go thru gate across field (vague) to another gate at a streamside (Wandale Beck) and enter woodland, bridleway thru trees to Murthwaite Farm, next bridleway is re-routed slightly so follow blue arrow markers N to road north of Adamthwaite Farm. Road N to Ravenstonedale. Road W to Calbeck, bridleway W to Cockstones, farmroad W to Weasdale, farmroad NW to close to main road, farmroad W to Bowderdale Farm, farmroad S becomes bridleway after 400m, bridleway S inside Bowderdale Beck to Great Force Gill Rigg, bridleway SW to the Calf.
Note: dismount and walk the 400m section from the Calf to Bram Rigg Top (a big dip). As a black dashed line its status is sensitive. Walking is worth it, because the alternative 100% bridleway route to the Calf has much less off-road.
To give you the option, it runs; from the Calf down to Howgill, via White Fell and Castley Knotts.]
bridleway S to Rowantree Grains, bridleway SW as*

bridleway forks before Winder take the lefthand S option towards Lockbank Farm, road into Sedbergh.
Location Sedburgh is 8km east from M6 J37, on the A684 Wensleydale road.
Mapping and literature OS Landrangers 91, 97, 98; Guidebooks *Mountain Bike Guide: The Lake District, the Howgills and the Yorkshire Dales* and *More routes in The Lakes, Howgills and Yorkshire Dales* (both by Jeremy Ashcroft, £7.95/8.50, The Ernest Press)
Where to stay
Camping Pinfold Caravan Site, Sedbergh (just outside village on A684 to Hawes, tel 015396 20576)
YHA hostel Kirkby Stephen (meals, tel 0870 770 5904)
Farm B&Bs Ash Hining Farm, 1.5km from Sedbergh (direct up on to Howgills, tel 015396 20957), High Greenside, Ravenstonedale (northeast of Howgills, 3-day deals, tel 015396 23671)
B&B Brownber Hall Country House, Newbiggin on Lune (north side of Howgills, around £27, tel 015396 23208, www.brownberhall.co.uk)
Where to eat
Sedbergh - Red Lion and Dalesman pubs in Sedbergh, Post Horn tearooms do evening meals in season on request
Ravenstonedale - Fat Lamb (northeast of Howgills, A683 turning into Ravenstonedale, tel 015396 23285)
Tourist offices
Sedbergh (tel 015396 20125)
Kirkby Stephen (tel 017683 71199)

48 ▶

IRONSTONE HILLS
Oxfordshire-Warwickshire

Enjoy bridleways, picturesque villages and wonderful country pubs in the gentle, little-explored Ironstone Hills on the northeastern tip of the Cotswolds. One highpoint is Shenlow Hill at 227m, another, the wonderful range of excellent local country pubs, described below!

Where to ride
Self-navigating
Plenty of good permutations up and down the hills, and
Two suggested routes;
South Newington-Great Tew estate (17km, good tracks and great estate scenery)
From South Newington south on bridleway to Great Tew and the Falkland Arms, east on bridleway next to pub, minor road to Ledwell, through village, east on bridleway skirting Worton Wood. North on minor road through Over Worton, west to Nether Worton. West on minor road/bridleway, north on bridleway over Raven Hill and steep hill climb back.

Swalcliffe-Epwell (15km)
From Swalcliffe village hall, northwest on green lane past Swalcliffe Mill, west on bridleway (Roman road) to Epwell, northwest on yellow road, S yellow/orange road, south on bridleway to Traitor's Ford, south on yellow road to Sharpe's Hill, east on yellow road/bridleway to Swalcliffe Common, north on bridleway, yellow road into Swalcliffe and pub.
Mapping OS Explorer 191 Banbury, Bicester &
Chipping Norton, Landranger 151 Stratford upon Avo
Warwick & Banbury

Where to eat & drink
Real ale and nice (but pricey) food at the Stags Head, Swalcliffe (tel 01295 379378, closed Mon) and Wykha Arms, Sibford Ferris (tel 01295 352377).
At Hook Norton, 100m from the Hooky Brewery, fantastic range of ales at the Pear Tree Inn (tel 01608 350331).
Handy for the hills is the refurbished Lord Saye & Sele Broughton (more lovely beer and food), not forgetting the Blinking Owl at North Newington (tel 01295 419398).
Also the Falkland Arms at Great Tew (tel 01608 68365 'an absolutely lush pub, good cheap lunches and fab re ale, right en route too'.
Bike shops Banbury Cycles (56 Broad St, tel 01295 259349), BGM Banbury (2 Bridge St, by the station, te 01295 272757 www.bgmuk.com).
Where to stay www.visit-northoxfordshire.co.uk,, a info from Cherwell District Council

SLE OF WIGHT

sunny little piece of off-road paradise, the Isle of Wight is not a major MTB destination but
ould be, considering its contours and coastline, shown off on an 80km round-island classic ride.
n extension of the South Downs, the south of the island is dominated by wonderful chalk
ownland, which you can traverse barely touching tarmac. Bikers get demanding climbs and
allenging descents, as well as relaxed riding through wooded valleys and quiet country lanes.
ne council is proud of its well-maintained and protected trail network, which amounts to over
0km of bridleway, cycleway and byway across the 35km-long island. Take a short ferry ride
ross the Solent, and it's like travelling abroad without having to find your passport.

here to ride

ided and supported

cle Wight offers guided riding with back-up service
d bike hire (also self-catering accommodation, Steve
arce, tel 01983 761193, www.cyclewight.com).
ghtOffRoad (groups up to 30, day rides or longer with
commodation, bike hire, www.wightoffroad.com).
f-navigating With so much bridleway and byway,
d all marked on a single OS map for the whole island,
ute-planning is easy. The four **MTB maps** and **12-route**
le guide (see Mapping) are also worthwhile aids. Use
es to connect bridleways, and you can cover a lot of
und.
ghstone Forest is good for singletrack and forest trails.
panoramic views do the **ridge ride** along the
nyson trail or on **Stenbury Down**. For route details,
the Extremists MBC website
ww.extremists.co.uk).
ssic ride: Tackle the 80km Isle of Wight Off-road
ndonnée, a one- or two-day (depending on your
ty) round-island route, proudly designed by the
remists (see Mountain Bike Clubs for website).
ymarked The 100-km Round the Island Route road
te (RTI) takes eight hours, and is fully waymarked in
h directions. Use this in its own right on roads and
ntry lanes, or to link bridleways and byways criss-
ssing the island.
pping and literature All available in tourist offices;

OS Landranger 196 The Solent and Isle of Wight,
Explorer OL 29 Isle of Wight.
Four maps detail the island's bikeable byways and bridle-
ways (**NE, SE, W and South Central**) to be used with the
OS maps.
Guidebooklet: A Guide to Cycling Trails on the Isle of
Wight (12 circular cycle routes and map of the RTI, the
Isle of Wight Council with Cycle Wight)
Guidebook: Philip's Cycle Tours - Hampshire and the
Isle of Wight (£8.99, two mapped IoW routes)
Ferry Terminals are at Portsmouth, Southampton and
Lymington.
Ferry operators are Red Funnel Ferries (tel 0870
4448889, www.redfunnel.co.uk), Wightlink Isle of Wight
Ferries (tel 0870 5827744, www.wightlink.co.uk),
Hovertravel (tel 01983 811000,
www.hovertravel.co.uk). Cycles free on all services.
However, the Portsmouth-Ryde fast ferry and Southsea-
Ryde hovercraft have limited space so avoid busy times
and check availability.
Bike Shops
Sales, spares and repairs:
Offshore Sports, Cowes (tel 01983 290514) and
Shanklin (01983 866269); First Gear Cycles, Newport
(tel 01983 521417); Wight Mountain, Newport (tel
01983 533445); The Bike Shed, Perreton Farm,
Merstone (tel 01983 868786); Extreme Cycles, Ventnor
(tel 01983 852232). [CONT]

ISLE OF WIGHT
(Continued)

Repairs and hire: Autovogue, Ryde (tel 01983 812989); Battersbys, Ryde (tel 01983 562039).

Hire only: Funation Cycle & Mountain Bike Hire, East Cowes (tel 01983 200300, 07703 20299); Isle Cycle Hire, Wavells B&B, The Square, Yarmouth (tel 07801 623652); High Adventure, Freshwater Bay (tel 01983 752322); Bike Mech, Freshwater (tel 01983 756787); *Mobile hire* (free delivery and collection): Island Cycle Hire (tel 07712 363134).

Mountain Bike Clubs
Extremists IOW MTB Club (ride info, newsletter from Dave Stratford, tel 07880 690093, www.extremists. co.uk). Vectis Cycling Club may help with ride buddies, but is more for road racing (Martin Hall, tel 01983 612476). Offshore Sports also gives route information and perhaps ride buddies.

Stations Trains run twice hourly from Ryde to Shanklin. Information available from Southern Vectis (tel 01983 827005)

Where to stay Lots of accommodation for all tastes and budgets. Try the central number for tourist information (tel 01983 813818), accommodation booking line (tel 01983 813813).

In west Wight:
Camping Heathfield Farm Camping, Freshwater (west, tel 01983 756756, www.heathfieldcamping.co.uk), Stoats Farm Caravan & Camping, Totland (southwest, tel 01983 755258, www.stoats-farm.co.uk), Chine Farm Camping Site, Atherfield (southwest, tel 01983 740228)

YHA hostels Sandown (east, meals, tel 0870 770 6020 Totland Bay (west, meals, tel 0870 770 6070)

Self-catering Cycle Wight, Newclose Farmhouse, Thorley (tel 01983 761193, email Madmudderbiker@ cyclewight.com), Rose Cottage, Thorncross Farm, Brighstone (southwest, tel 01983 740291, www.thorn cross-holiday-cottages.co.uk), Cheverton Farm Cottag Shorwell (southwest, tel 01983 741017)

B&B Chilton Farm B&B and cottages, Brighstone (sou west, tel 01983 740338, www.chiltonfarm.co.uk)

Where to eat/drink
The island is packed with pubs, cafes and tearooms. B check those contours before merrily riding off in searc of sustenance.

Events Wight Diamond Festival, annually, May Bank holiday. Two-day orienteering event for both serious racers and families (there's even a cream tea category King of the Hills competition (be the quickest to bag th five highest points on the island). Entry includes marqu with food, drink and entertainment, plus bike games a competitions. Contact Trailbreaks (tel 0118) 976 249 www.trailbreak.co.uk

Tourist offices
There is a central phone number for all offices (tel 01983 813818).
In person at Cowes (Fountain Quay), Newport (High Street), Ryde (Union Street), Sandown (the Esplanade Shanklin (High Street), Ventnor (High Street), Yarmou (the Quay).

Find superb riding in the expanse
of the Forest of Bowland

34 ▶ JACK MYTTON WAY
Shropshire
(see also Long Mynd)

A long, hilly linear route that shows off the best of the Shropshire hillscapes, including Wenlock Edge and the Long Mynd, on rural byways, bridleways and quiet country lanes. Starting at Ray's Farm 8km south of Bridgnorth, and finishing 112km later at the Welsh border near Llanfair Waterdine, it is named after the notorious but affectionate Shropshire character 'Mad Jack', wh performed foolhardy stunts, usually with horses, such as trying to leap crossing gates with the horse still in the trap!

Towns and villages en route allow plenty of opportunities for food and overnight stops.

Where to ride
Two-thirds of the route is off-road on varied surfaces, with challenging climbs, notably on to the Long Mynd (rewarded with a short, rocky descent into Eyton). You have to follow the OS map as the way-marking needs clarification. For route details see Mapping.

The route (112km): starting at Ray's Farm, Billingsley, go along a wooded valley, climb up and along Wenlock Edge, then woodland trails to Jacobs Ladder descent, the Long Mynd plateau (views of the Berwyns and Wrekin), through Clun and towards the Welsh border at Llanfair Waterdine (additional loop: from the start at Billingsley, down to Cleobury Mortimer, to Rushbury, and rejoin)

Literature and mapping Get the *Official Route Guide to the Jack Mytton Way* (laminated cards) from Shropshire Books, Shropshire County Council (tel 01743 255043). Maps: OS Landranger 137 Ludlow & Church Stretton, 138 Kidderminster & Wyre Forest; Explorer 201 Knighton & Presteigne; 217 The Long Mynd & Wenlock Edge; 218 Kidderminster & Wyre Forest.

Location For the start at Ray's Bridge, take the B43 Bridgnorth-Bewdley road. Ray's Farm is signposted v 'Ray's Farm Country Matters' (map ref SO 713832)

Bike shops Terry's Cycles, Church Stretton (hire, p repairs, tel 01694 723302); Pearce Cycles, Fishmore Road, Ludlow (full-on MTB shop, tel 01584 876016 Stations Church Stretton (halfway round), Knighton (6.5km from end at Llanfair Waterdine), Highley (Sev Valley Railway, 4.5km from start).

Where to eat In towns and villages en route

Where to stay For more see Shropshire CC list at tourist offices. *YHA hostels* Clun Mill, Clun (self-cater only, tel 0870 770 5766); Bridges Long Mynd, Ratlinghope (meals, tel 01588 650656); *B&Bs* Billing Hall Farm, Covert Lane, Billingsley (tel 01746 86187 Gaskell Arms, Much Wenlock (tel 01952 727212), C Farm House, Clun (three pubs/restaurants with 150r the farmhouse, tel 01588 640432)

Tourist offices Church Stretton (tel 01694 723133 Ludlow (tel 01584 875053); Bridgnorth (tel 01746 763257); Much Wenlock (tel 01952 727679)

IELDER FOREST PARK
lorthumberland and Borders
ee also Newcastleton, Scotland)

2

gland's largest forest lies on the Scottish/English border and offers a lot of cycling, some of ich, as long as you are selective, makes good mountain biking. Much is on forest roads through onotonous conifer plantations, which makes the experience of leaving the close thickets more citing, as fantastic views open out unexpectedly. The Cross Border Trail is highly recommended.

ere to ride
re are a small number of good off-road sections,
plans to develop permanent technical trail.
ations and junctions can be confusing, and some of
fast descents need care. Many roads have deep
ows of loose stone which can throw a wheel off
rse easily.
ss Border Trail (Lewisburn-Dykecroft 18km one-
; Lewisburn-Kershopefoot 27km one-way, 35%
oad/65% forest road, both demanding, blue signs).
is the real gem of the area. Take the southern fork
Villowbog, into Scotland and follow the thrilling
cent alongside Corby Linn and Kershope Burn. Loop
clockwise, back over the border at Bloody Bush
Pillar, fast descent rejoining where you left. Just
ond here stop and look at the ancient packhorse
ge on the righthand side at Akenshaw Burn, a true
ak moment. This route is planned to slot into the
ned dedicated trails at Newcastleton Forest (see
tland, 7 Stanes), which will make it really special.
Swinburne Selection A combination of trails west
e water, with different start points; Leaplish, Kielder
tle and Lewishburn Picnic Place.
A (13km, 7% off-road, demanding, includes the
ling Greenside descent and fearsome Serpent Brae);
B (9.5km, 5% off-road, moderate, undulating);
C (16km, 20% off-road, demanding, climb for
ctacular views of the forest, and the Skyspace sky
pture)
vood (27km, 15% off-road, demanding, heart of the
st with a thrilling descent beside Belling Burn,)
pping A hard-to-decipher cycle routes map is avail-

able from visitor centres; OS Landranger 79, 80, 86, and Explorer OL42
Location On the English side of the border with Scotland, reach the water from the southeast from Bellingham, or from the northwest from Hawick via Saughtree
Bike facilities Kielder Bikes hire, spares, repairs and bike wash at Kielder Castle (tel 01434 250392); bike wash at Leaplish Waterside Park
Bike shops Hexham (30km south), The Rush at Jedburgh, 16km N of forest (tel 01835 869643)
Visitor information www.kielder.org; Kielder Castle centre (N end of water, tel 01434 250209), Leaplish Waterside Park (W bank, halfway up, tel 0870 240 3549) and Tower Knowe (SE bank, tel 0870 240 3549)
Where to eat At the three visitor centres
Where to stay *YHA hostel* Kielder in Kielder Village (meals, tel 0870 770 5898), Byrness, 20km northeast of Kielder Castle in Redesdale Forest on the A68 (self-catering only, tel 0870 770 5740); *Log cabins* Leaplish Waterside Park (brochure and bookings tel 01434 250294); *Hostel/self-catering* Reiver's Rest, Leaplish Waterside Park (shared bunk area, double and family rooms, tel 01434 250294); *B&Bs* Lyndale Guest House, Bellingham (tel 01434 220361), Snabdough Farm, Bellingham (tel 01434 240239), Pheasant Inn, Falstone (tel 01434 240382, www.thepheasantinn.com), Woodside, Falstone (tel 01434 240443)
Event Annual Kielder Reiver Trailquest (What's On guide, tel 01434 220242)
Tourist offices Bellingham (tel 01434 220616) Kielder Partnership (tel 01434 220643)

KINVER EDGE
Worcestershire

A popular outcrop and beauty spot, Kinver Edge is mostly no-go footpaths, but here's a fine towpath/bridleway circuit that uses the superb permissive bridleway on the western flank. This area around the Stour and Severn valleys is worth devoting a long weekend or week to.

Where to ride
Self-navigating circuit (2-3hours, 21km, anticlockwise, download towpath permit from britishwaterways.co.uk. The lane off the Edge to Blakeshall gets busy, ride with care). Start/finish Wolverley (map ref 839 793), N towpath (Staffs & Worc Canal) 8km, to where towpath meets lane E of Million forestry. W lane, W bdwy through The Million. Cross Enville Common road, A458 (straight ahead, W), into Enville, left S estate road to hall, S road/bdwy 2km (finish on good climb White Hill Farm), right S lane to crossroads below Kinver Edge, permissive bdwy (opposite) S parallel to lane 1.4km, left (E) bridleway (tough techy climb) to top Kinver Edge; strictly legal route: straight ahead down to lane, right to Blakeshall (not strictly legal route but well used: from top of Edge, right on clear track, downhill with care (Kingsford Country Park), join white road to Blakeshall). Left (E)

out of Blakeshall to rejoin towpath north of Cookley, back to Wolverley.

Location Kinver Edge lies above Kinver town, 7km west of Stourbridge, 8km north of Kidderminster (M5 J3).

Mapping OS Landranger 138 Kidderminster & Wyre Forest

Bike shop Smith Cycles, Kidderminster (3 New Road, tel 01562 823721). It's worth going the extra kilometres south to MTB shop Stourport Specialist Cycles (tel 01299 826470, manager is Tim)

Where to eat and drink Kinver is the place to go cafes and a chippy. Pubs in Wolverley, Cookley, Enville

Where to stay Camping Wolverley Camping & Caravanning Club, Westhead Park, Wolverley (open Mar-Oct, tel 01562 850909)

Tourist office Bewdley (tel 01299 404740)

AKE DISTRICT
Cumbria
;ee Broughton Moor, Grizedale and Whinlatter Forest Parks)

8

ne Lakes is one of the best areas in the country, where a wide variety of year-round riding and
)pious opportunities for pub and cafe stops are set against a fabulous and often dramatic
ickdrop. You can divide the region quite simply into North and South, Keswick being the centre
the North, and Ambleside the hub in the middle of the South. From the highest point in
igland to which you can legally ride a bike – Helvelleyn – to gentle lakeside cruises, the Lake
strict has it all! As a general rule the further south you come the more rideable riding there is.

is is a summary of the area, there are separate entries
Broughton Moor-Walna Scar Road, Grizedale Forest
d Whinlatter Forest. The Lake District fills to the gills at
iday times, so book accommodation in advance.

here to ride

ided and supported Saddle Skedaddle (tel 0191
5 1110, www.skedaddle.co.uk), Adventure Cycling
iding, contact Steve, Penrith-based tel 01768
2589, www.adventurecycling.co.uk).

lf-navigating
:eland riding is split between lower-level, predomi-
itly rideable trails, and big mountain adventures,
ich involve some pushing and carrying.

** issic rides**
ere are two classic high-level routes, 'High Street',
owing the course of an old Roman road, and
lvellyn. Both are big-mountain proper days out.

h Street is best approached south to north, which
es a short, sharp climb up and a lovely long downhill.
t from Ambleside or Troutbeck, ride the full ridge to
oley Bridge, and return via the lakeshore path around
iswater, or over Boredale Hause, finally riding over
:stone Pass to return to your start point. Allow 4-6
irs, and carry your own food and water. Its not that
innical, but you'll know you've been in the mountains
a day. Plan an easy ride next day!

lvellyn Although there are bridleways up almost all
ects of the mountain, it is best tackled from
nridding on the east side. This is the most ride-able
, but still involves a hefty push/carry, although the

views from the summit make it all worthwhile. Follow
the bridleway from the car park in Glenridding, up past
Greenside Mines and climbing Keppel Cove to make the
summit ridge. To make a decent ride, from the summit
backtrack north and head past Raise (where there is a
permanent ski tow!) before passing over Sticks Pass en
route to the great rounded humps of the Dodds. Finally
dropping down to the Old Coach Road, where a right
turn will take you back, all downhill, to Dockray, for a
well-earned pint at the Pub, or on to the cafe at Aira
Force (waterfall) before returning to Glenridding.
Low level: The area between Windermere and Coniston
lakes has some wonderful mountain biking. Highlights
are Parka Moor (see Grizedale) on the east side of
Coniston lake, Loughrigg Terrace near Ambleside,
Grizedale Forest (see entry), Tarn Hows Area. Look for
the bridleways on the OS map, there are lots of options
to join them all up!
The Undiscovered Gem is the area around Broughton In
Furness, on the southern boundary of the National Park.
When the central Lakes are at bursting point in mid-
summer, here you find deserted singletracks. Take a
peek at the map.
Mapping and literature OS Explorers four sheets –
OL4 North-west, OL5 North-east, OL6 South-west,
OL7 South-east; Guidebook *Mountain Bike Guide – the
Lake District, the Howgills and the Yorkshire Dales* and
More Rides in Lake District etc (22 mapped routes,
Jeremy Ashcroft, Ernest Press, £7.95, tel 0141 637
5492www.ernest-press.co.uk), *Philip's Cycle Tours –*

Cumbria and the Lakes (nine mapped routes, Nick Cotton, £8.99)

Bike shops Biketreks, Ambleside (tel 015394 31245), Keswick MTBs (hire, repairs tel 017687 75202), Lakeland Pedlar shop and cafe, Keswick (tel 017687 75752)

Where to stay See also Grizedale.

YHA hostels Ambleside (meals, tel 0870 770 5672), Black Sail (meals, tel 07711 108450), Borrowdale (meals, tel 0870 770 5706), Buttermere (meals, tel 0870 770 5736), Coniston Holly How (meals, tel 0870 770 5770), Coniston Coppermines (meals, tel 0870 770 5772), Derwentwater (meals, tel 0870 770 5792), Elterwater (meals, tel 0870 770 5816), Ennerdale (meals, tel 0870 770 5820), Grasmere (2 hostels, meals, tel 0870 770 5836), Hawkshead (meals, tel 0870 770 5856), Helvellyn (meals, tel 0870 770 6110), Keswick (meals, tel 0870 770 5894), Patterdale (meals, tel 0870 770 5986), Wastwater (meals, tel 0870 770 6082), Windermere (meals, tel 0870 770 6094).

Self-catering Portland House Cottage, Keswick (tel 017687 74230).

Independent hostels Grasmere Independent Hostel (tel 015394 35055, www.grasmerehostel.co.uk), Walkers Hostel, Ulverston (tel 01229 585588).

B&Bs Croyden House, Ambleside (tel 015394 32209), Broadview Guesthouse, Ambleside (tel 015394 3243 Paddock Guest House, Keswick (tel 01768 772510), Gilpin House, Keswick (tel 017687 75186), Shepherd Arm's Hotel, Ennerdale Bridge (tel 01946 861249), Trevene, Buttermere (tel 017687 70210)

Tourist offices
Windermere (tel 015394 46499) Ambleside (tel 0153 32582), Keswick (tel 017687 72645)

---

39 ▶ LEICESTERSHIRE
see also Rutland

East and southeast of Leicester, you can enjoy 3-4 hours pedaling if you link bridleways and lane

Where to ride
You can divide runs into *north* (round Tilton-on-the-Hill) and *south of the A47* (Leicester-Peterborough road). You can also trek along the *Via Devana*, the Roman Road that heads SE from Leicester as far as Glooston (where there's a nice pub), on all manner of surfaces. Branch off on various bridleways and lanes for good circuits. There are also enjoyable bridleways to the south of Leicester around Wistow, where there's a nice cafe at parking.

Mapping OS Landranger 140, 141, Explorer 233

LINCOLNSHIRE WOLDS

...e mellow Lincolnshire Wolds rise to 150m in a long low ridge that parallels the east coast, ...signated an Area of Outstanding Natural Beauty. They feature a small number of bridleways, ...veral of which appear in published off-road routes in the north Wolds.
...e on/off-road Southern Wolds cycle route, which starts from Snipe Dales Country Park, has fine ...ws, and there's an excellent cafe at nearby Hagworthingham for tea and cakes.

...here to ride

...f-navigate Use the OS maps, perhaps getting ideas ...m the following rides;

...utes (by the British Horse Society and Lincolnshire ...unty Council)

...thern Wolds cycle route (17km, from Snipe Dales, ...unty council) mixture of quiet lanes, stone tracks and ...en lanes exploring the southern wolds. From Snipe ...es country park (no cycling in the park) go to Lusby, ...n Hagworthingham, white road, track to Bag ...derby, track on Ancient Green lane then N NE NW ...SW round to Somersby, lane to Ashby Puerorum, ...e S Stone Road to A158, cross, via Winceby back to ...antry park.

...inton-le-Vale route (23km, northeast of Market ...en, BHS), mixture of bridlepaths and links from ...nton to Rothwell, via Hills Brough Fm to Normanby ...Vold, Walesby, Risby, Stainton.

...brook, also Stainton (29km, northeast of Market ...en, BHS), from Binbrook to Swinhope, W then N to ...organby, Croxby, Thoresway, Stainton, Kirmond le ...e, Thorpe then S E N back to Binbrook

...esby (12km, northeast of Market Rasen), from ...esby SE to halfway to Teaslby, then SW, W and ...ough the end of Willingham Forest and Walesby ...odlands, N to Claxby, SE (view) to the Viking Way ...r Mill Farm, and back. Link also to Normanby le ...d, over to the Rothwell Bridle Trail.

Where to eat There's a cafe at Hagworthingham, and a tearoom in Walesby. Also, buy local Lincolnshire food (an idea promoted by the AONB to boost the local economy and please your taste buds).

Where to stay

Camping Walesby Woodlands Caravan Park (Walesby Road, Market Rasen, tel 01673 843285), West Ashby (4-star camping and caravanning, tel 01507 527966, ashbyparklakes@aol.com, www.willerby.com)

YHA hostel Woody's Top, Ruckland, 8km south of Louth (self-catering only, tel 0870 770 6098); Hostel Viking Centre Hostel in Claxby (near Normanby le Wold)

Location

For **Snipe Dales Country Park**, between Horncastle and Spilsby, signposted off the A158, entrance off yellow road NW of Lusby (map ref TF 331 682).

For **BHS trails**, head for your chosen start village (Stainton, Binbrook, Walesby or any en route)

Facilities at Snipe Dales; car park (50p) and toilets

Mapping and literature

OS Landranger 113, Explorer 273, 282. Routes published in the cycle trail pack from Lincolnshire County Council (£5, tel 01522 553127, www.lincswolds.org.uk).

Station Market Rasen

Tourist offices

Horncastle (tel 01507 526636)
Louth (tel 01507 609289)

33 ▶ LONG MYND AND WENLOCK EDGE
Shropshire Hills

The Long Mynd and Wenlock Edge are among Shropshire's finest hills for riding, full of bridleway that lead numerous ways up and down the humps and summits, continuing west to Stiperstones and east to Brown Clee Hill. The Mynd is a great broad, bare steep-sided mound with wonderfu views and plentiful open tracks. Wenlock Edge is an 18km ridge of open slopes and woodland, with traverses between Ape Dale to the north and Corve Dale to the south. You can link routes using the Jack Mytton Way (see entry) a long-distance bridleway. Church Stretton is the base town, overlooked by the Mynd to the west and Hope Bowdler Hill to the east. Please keep to t bridleways, says local owner the National Trust, and watch out for walkers and equestrians.

Where to ride- *Self-navigating*
Long Mynd. National Trust recommended summit circuit: (21km, mostly undulating, some steep climbs). From Carding Mill Valley to Church Stretton, to Little Stretton. Right past the Green Dragon, left and right heading for Minton on lane. Through Minton, after 1km right onto 2nd bdwy on right. Climb to junction with the Shropshire Way (map ref SO403 906), right N following Shropshire Way, past Gliding Club to Pole Bank (SO 415 944). Continue on well-defined track, crossing Ratlinghope road, heading NE. At next road right, after 250 metres right NE (following the National Trust boundary) fast downhill (take care). After 1.5 km right at Bullocks Moor, road down to All Stretton, right back to Church Stretton, right to Cardingmill Valley
Hope Bowdler Hill Directly above Church Stretton, this is crossed by one steep bridleway (no riding on neighbouringCaer Caradoc Hill and hillfort).
Wenlock Edge. *Start points* Church Stretton and Craven Arms (at the SW tip, has facilities). The southern end has good offroad traverses but there's no ridge route (from SW to NE; Callow Hill/Seifton Batch, Westhope to Corfton Bache/Bache Mill, Eaton to Bache Mill). The Jack Mytton Way runs along the N side, traversing at Eaton.

Location *Church Stretton;* is off the A49 Ludlow-Shrewsbury. Cardingmill valley; take the white road V off the town road just N of town. *Craven Arms* lies or the A49 12km south. **Station** Church Stretton
Facilities Church Stretton has all facilities. For Long Mynd; parking, cafe, toilets and shop at the NT Visito Centre in Cardingmill Valley (map ref SO 445 945).
Mapping and literature OS Explorer 217 (Landranger 137)
Where to stay Camping Little Stretton, Marshbroo Prolley Moor and Wentnor; **YHA hostels** Bridges Lor Mynd (NW side of Long Mynd, meals, tel 01588 650656), Clun Mill (self-catering, tel 0870 770 5766) Wilderhope Manor, Longville-in-the-Dale (on Wenlo Edge, meals, tel 0870 770 6090)
Bike shops and hire Onny MTB Hire (Flowers Coffee Shop, Craven Arms, tel 01588 672710), Wh Wonderful Cycling, Petchfield Farm, Elton, Ludlow (h centre and cycling holidays, tel 01568 770755), Pear Cycles, Fishmore Rd, Ludlow (tel 01584 876016, Hopton Wood uplift service), Climb On Bikes, 22 Bu Ring, Ludlow (tel 01584 872173), Terry's Cycles, 6 Castle Hill, All Stretton (tel 01694 723302)
Tourist offices Church Stretton (seasonal, tel 0169 723133), Ludlow (tel 01584 875053)

1ALVERN HILLS
Herefordshire-Worcestershire

e great hump of the Malvern Hills is covered by a useful network of bikeable bridleways and lker-only footpaths. But please stay off the main ridge and fall-line trails, as erosion is a major ncern. Instead, enjoy sustainable well-mapped routes in the area that surrounds the hills.

ls are best explored on quieter weekdays, with neone with local trail knowledge.

pping Use the dedicated *Malvern Hills East* and *vern Hills West* (14 routes for a range of abilities). ites 12 and 13 will challenge experienced bikers. 0 and 13b are for families (£2.99, from local bike ps and tourist offices);

Landranger 150, Explorer 190, 204

ere to stay *Camping* Robin Hood Campsite

(Castle Morton, tel 01684 835212), Berrow House Campsite, Hollybush, nr Ledbury (tel 01531 635845) *B&Bs* Orchid House, Upper Welland (east of hills, tel 01684 568716); Bank Cottage, Hollybush, nr Ledbury (tel 01531 650683)

YHA hostel Malvern Hills (meals, tel 0870 770 5948)

Tourist offices Malvern (tel 01684 892289, www.malvernhills.gov.uk/ tourism) Ledbury (tel 01531 636147)

The Malverns Offroad Cycling Maps

Map 1 - East
Six circular routes on bridleways and quiet lanes to the east of the Malvern Hills

The Countryside Agency

Published by Offroad Cycling

FOREST OF DEAN RECREATION MAP
Central Area
A GUIDE TO THE
TRAILS AND FORESTRY TRACKS
OF THE CENTRAL DEAN AREA
FOR CYCLISTS AND WALKERS

Scale 1:30.000 2 Inches = 1 Mile
3.3cm = 1 Kilometre

Showing approved cycling trails plus suggested recreational bike routes

Published by Offroad Cycling
With acknowledgements to Forest Enterprise
Third Edition

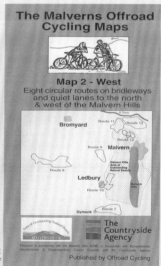

The Malverns Offroad Cycling Maps

Map 2 - West
Eight circular routes on bridleways and quiet lanes to the north & west of the Malvern Hills

The Countryside Agency

Published by Offroad Cycling

The Offroad Cycling Maps of the Malverns and the Forest of Dean. £2.99 per map from local TIC's & bike shops.
Mail order (+31p p/p) from Offroad Cycling, Coddington, Ledbury. Herefordshire. HR8 1JH. Tel: 01531 633500

69 ▶ MENDIPS
Somerset
(see also Quantocks)

One of the best MTB destinations in the southwest, the limestone Mendip plateau has steep sid
and an exposed moorland top, peaking at Beacon Batch 325m on Black Down. The hills feel
satisfyingly high and remote (more than they are), while the climbing and conditions take streng
rather than technique and suit intermediate and expert riders. The main area is Black Down and
Rowberrow Forest, a large area of heathland and forest at the northern end above Cheddar, wi
something like 26km of trail. A limited number of disconnected bridleways exists above Wells.

The hills have two bonuses for MTBing; one, an excellent free mini trail-guide with colour-graded bridleways,
and two, a MTB-friendly holiday park, Broadway House,
run by an MTB enthusiast where you can get trail advice
and full facilities. Broadway House also hosts an annual
institution, the Cheddar Challenge cross-country race,
which uses the escarpment.

The Mendips are a place for local bikers to explore again
and again, and for visitors to stay for a weekend.
Attractive Cheddar and Wells are on the doorstep, with
other good places to stay and eat.

Where to ride
Warning: Black Down is exposed; wear suitable clothing
according to the weather.

Self-navigating
Start from Cheddar on the south side, and climb the
gorge road or the parallel bridleway to the top of the
plateau, then pick bridleways into Rowberrow Warren
(along the West Mendip Way), or to Beacon Batch on
the top, and include a flying descent down Black Down -
the Mendip highlight.

Start from Burrington Combe car park (map ref ST
476587) on the north side, up Black Down; it has three
black-grade ascents and one red - yikes!

Recommended trail guide
Even experienced map-readers should get the free
Black Down and Rowberrow Forest MTB trail-guide,
from the Mendip Hills AONB service (Area of
Outstanding Natural Beauty, tel 01761 462338,
mendiphills@somerset.gov.uk). This laminated mini-

map colour-grades the numerous bridleways, showir
the wide choice of trails and helping you to design rid
from moderate to hard.

Other mapping and literature
OS Landranger 182, Explorer 141, 153, 154;
Guidebooks: Haynes' *Bristol and Bath Cycle Rides* ha
mapped Cheddar/Black Down ride; *Philip's Cycle Tou
- Dorset and Somerset* (ISBN 0 540 08200 7) and -
Around Bristol and Bath (ISBN 0 540 08196 5) have
mapped Cheddar-based and Wells-based routes.

Location 16km southwest of Bristol, the Mendips
AONB stretches from Weston-super-Mare on the
Bristol Channel, to Wells 20m inland. It includes Che
Valley Lake and Blagdon Lake (low-lying to the north)
and is crossed by the A38 and the M5. Approach
Cheddar from the A38, or M5 J22 (then NW on the
A38, via Axbridge).

Station Yatton (10km northwest)

Where to stay
Camping Broadway House Caravan and Camping Pa
(NW of Cheddar on A371, tel 01934 742610,
www.broadwayhouse.uk.com)
YHA hostel Cheddar (meals, tel 0870 770 5760)
B&B Bay Rose House, Cheddar (tel 01934 741377)

Where to drink
The Burrington Inn (north side on the B3134, map r
ST 476589),
The Swan Inn, Rowberrow (northwest side, map re
451583)

Tourist office Cheddar (tel 01934 744071)

NEW FOREST
Hampshire

77

Open and singletrack mountain biking has been resisted in the New Forest, but you can ride on approved trails on public gravelled forest roads. There may be no hard slopes but the moorland and woodland area is large, atmospheric in places and explorable, and the tracks remain rideable all year round. Brockenhurst and Lyndhurst are nice towns and villages, and half-a-dozen civilised campsites are dotted about the place. Stop and greet those short, shaggy, riderless ponies when you meet them.

Where to ride
Get the cycling pack from the tourist offices.
You can ride anywhere on 160km of forest roads, also on quiet lanes between the villages. All the tracks are signposted and only the vulnerable forest areas and places where work is going on are barred.
The trails are well maintained and all-weather-proof. Most of the roads have a 40mph speed limit; 'Be a sport, ride with thought - stay under 40mph' (This apparently greatly reduces the number of accidents involving ponies, cattle and deer, let alone cyclists).

Mapping
The *New Forest cycling map pack* (£3.50) and the *New Forest official map* (£1.50) are both available from Lymington tourist office (see below). All routes are also marked on the OS Explorer OL22.

Bike hire
New Forest CyclExperience (Brockenhurst, tel 01590 204, www.cyclex.co.uk)

Bike shops HE Figgures Cycles, Lymington High Street (tel 01590 672002)

Where to stay *Camping* For all Forestry Commission caravan and camping sites tel 0131 314 6505, they are; Ashurst (open Easter-Sept); Denny Wood, Lyndhurst (open Easter-Sept); Matley Wood, Lyndhurst (open Easter-Sept); Hollands Wood, Brockenhurst (open Easter-Sept); Roundhill, Brockenhurst (open Easter-Sept, tel 0131 314 6505); Ocknell & Longbeech, Fritham (open Easter-Sept, Longbeech has no toilets, tel 0131 314 6505); Setthorns, Wooton, New Milton (open year round)

YHA hostel Burley (meals, tel 0870 770 5734); Lyndhurst, Brockenhurst

Stations Brockenhurst, Ashhurst

Tourist office
Lymington & New Forest (central office for the New Forest, tel 01590 689000), Forestry office (tel 02380 283141)

16 ▶ # NIDDERDALE
North Yorkshire

One of the least known of the dales, Nidderdale is considerably more desolate and less-visited than better-known sisters Wharfedale and Swaledale. Riding here is fantastic, with a real feeling exploration of the natural and industrial heritage of the area. Expect long, loose rocky climbs an tooth-jarringly fast descents on a variety of moorland access trails. Facilities are limited, for bett or for worse, without the plethora of tearooms and tourist shops found elsewhere in Yorkshire.

Where to ride

Self-navigating *The Nidderdale Classic*, this starts at Lofthouse, rides the steep tarmac climb to Middlesmoor, goes up over the old road to Scar House reservoir, crosses the dam and turns right, then follows the ridge-line all around the eastern side of the valley on bridleway and ORPAs, and descends back into Ramsgill.

Other quality routes include **Lofthouse/Ramsgill over to Kirkby Malzeard** via the moors, *Scar House dam to West Burton via Coverdale*, and *Scar House dam to Gollingslith Foot or Jervaulx*.

Dedicated riding Volunteer-built technical freeride trail at Hunters Stones (NY 210 499), constructed by Singletraction, Yorkshire's MTB trail-building group.

Mapping and literature Harvey Maps' *Dales - East* (waterproof, 1:40000, one of four MTB trail maps covering the Dales); OS Landranger 98 and 99, Explorer 298; *Philip's Cycle Tours - Yorkshire Dales* (£8.99) has a mapped route between the two reservoirs. Website www.mtbroutes. com has a downloadable route.

Location A59 Harrogate-Skipton road, to Pateley Bridge, then north to Lofthouse. **Station** Harrogate

Bike shops Moonglu in Ripon (tel 01765 601106), Boneshakers in Harrogate (tel 01423 709453), Psychlosport, Harrogate (tel 01423 545413), and Otley

Where to stay *Camping* Studfold Farm Park, Lofthouse (views, open April-Oct, tel 01423 755210, www.stud foldfarmactivitycentre.co.uk); *Self-catering cottages* Abbey Holiday Cottages, Middlesmoor (above Lofthouse, tel 01423 712062, www.abbeyholiday-cottages.co.uk); *B&B/Bunkhouse* The New Inn,

Appletreewick (classic MTB hostelry, 15km SW Patele Bridge, tel 01756 720252); *Independent hostels* Wes End Outdoor Centre, Whitmoor Farm, West End (ov looks Thruscross reservoir 10km S Pateley Bridge, te 01943 880207), Skirfare Bridge Dales Barn, Kilnsey, Wharfedale (tel 01756 752465); *YHA hostels* No shortage! Ellingstring (connected by road to Lofthous 15km SW, self-catering only, tel 0870 770 5812); Kettlewell (in Wharfedale next W from Nidderdale, meals, tel 0870 770 5896), Linton (SW of Nidderdale near Grassington in Wharfedale, meals, tel 0870 770 5920); *Farm B&Bs* Bewerley Hall Farm, Bewerley, nr Pateley Br (tel 01423 711636, www.bewerleyhallfarr co.uk), Nidderdale Lodge Farm, Ripon Rd, Fellbeck, Pateley Br (tel 01423 711677); *B&B* Dale View, Old Church Ln, Pateley Br (tel 01423 711131)

Where to eat Crown Hotel, Lofthouse (Black Shee beer on draught, tel 01423 755206), New Inn at Appletreewick (at time of writing the 'MTB Arms', w proper beer, best place to ask for route advice, could revert to an ordinary moorland pub), The Sportsmar Arms Hotel, Wath-in-Nidderdale, nr Pateley Br (natic winner of Honest Food Competition for using local fc and drink, tel 01423 711306).

Mountain bike clubs Trailblazers MBC (year roun Weds/Suns rides, call Pete (at Psychlosport, Harrogat tel 01423 545413); North Leeds MTB club (informa group on the Forum of www.singletrackworld.com).

Tourist offices

Pateley Bridge (open Easter-Oct tel 01423 711147) Harrogate (tel 01423 537300)

ORTH DOWNS
urrey
ee also North Downs Way, Surrey Hills east)

82

e North Downs ridgeline in Surrey bursts with good tracks and testing slopes. The scarp rises
t of Guildford and runs via Ranmore Common to the steeps of Box Hill and Mickleham Downs
th of Dorking. Together with the easterly Surrey Hills (south across the valley, including Leith
and the Redlands built trails), this is where Londoners come to play bikes.

ere to ride

ded and supported Lets Offroad (tel 020 8402
2, www.letsoffroaduk.com) and Saddle Skedaddle
0191 265 1110, www.skedaddle.co.uk).

-navigating
from Guildford, Gomshall, Dorking, Westhumble &
ill (station) and Mickleham.
the rich bridleway/byway network along the top of
carp, and up and down the south face.
North Downs Way provides a bridleway mainline
ranch off. Create loops that head south towards
lake and Leith Hill. Or, north of Ranmore Common,
National Trust estate Polesden Lacey and back-
ds Tanners Hatch YHA hostel.

ping OS Explorer , Landranger 186 Guildford, 187
ing Reigate. See www.redlandstrails.org. Trail
ts coming out, on sale from Nirvana (see below)

and other bike shops.

Location Defined as the land between Guildford and
Dorking north of the A25. **Stations** Guildford,
Westhumble & Box Hill, Dorking, Gomshall

Bike shops Nirvana at Westcott (guiding and hire, tel
01306 740300), Beyond Mountain Bikes at Cranleigh
(guiding tel 01483 267676)

Where to eat & drink Boxhill servery and the caravan
at Headley, big barn tearoom at Bockets Farm (on A246
south of Leatherhead, just west of junction with A24).
Dorking has major shops and supermarkets.

Where to stay (see guided, supported riding); *YHA
hostel/Camping* Tanners Hatch (tel 0870 770 6060,
tanners@yha.org.uk, self-catering only, no access for
cars, camping)

Tourist offices Guildford (tel 01483 444333)
Dorking/Mole Valley visitor centre (tel 01306 879327)

ORTH DOWNS WAY
ee North Downs, Surrey Hills)

85

-bridleway, this high-ground route gives passage through the Surrey Hills and Kent Downs

North Downs Way national trail runs through
heast England for 246km on a chalk downland cres-
from Farnham in Surrey via Dorking, Westerham in
, Trosley and Detling to Boughton Lees where it
into two routes, one direct to Dover, the other via
erbury. 50km (20%) is ride-legal bridleway or

byway, so you can't ride the full trail but you can make
loops at points along. The best sections are around
Guildford in the Surrey hills, and between Maidstone
and Canterbury in the Kent Downs. The route is
waymarked throughout, with blue arrows on the bridleways. See www.nationaltrails.gov.uk/northdowns.

Alpine scenes on Afan Argoed's awesome singletrack (south Wales).

► NORTH PENNINES
Durham Dales
(see Coast to Coast/C2C, County Durham, Hamsterley)

Famously called 'England's last wilderness', in all seriousness the moors and valleys of Teesdale a Weardale are wild. En route for High Cup Nick and Cross Fell expect mountain weather and mountain conditions, and consider safety a priority. The area is littered with old mine-workings where navigational skills are a vital component of your toolkit. Climbs are long and flowing, descents are the same, and the views are phenomenal. Trails vary from old drove roads to narrow moorland singletrack and impenetrable seas of heather. Expect wet feet in winter!

Where to ride
Self-navigating
High Cup Nick is unmissable; park at Cow Green reservoir (a National Nature reserve with rare alpine plants such as Gentian Violet: the most fabulous blue colour). Follow the tarmac south, past the waterfall, then continue over the moors to the head of the nick. Also accessible from Dufton; see www.mtbroutes.com for a full route details

Numerous ancient trails lasting from the days of lead-mining allow good access to the area;
Cross Fell (893m, the highest point in the Pennines) is worth exploring, with long and isolated moorland bridleway routes
Mid Fell claims the highest tarmac road in England with bridleway access to near the top - a thrilling 7km 600m descent (or climb if you're that way inclined) reminiscent of 'Le Tour' with an off-road option too.

Dedicated routes see Hamsterley Forest

Mapping and literature
OS Landranger 87 91 92, Explorer OL31. See also www.mtbroutes.com
Location
The North Pennines lie between the Lake District and Durham city. To the west is the M6 and the east the A1(M). Scenic roads lead in from the surrounding towns.

Base towns
Alston, Middleton in Teesdale, Stanhope
Bike shops
In Penrith: Harper Cycles (tel 01768 864475) and Arragons Cycle Centre (tel 01768 890344)
Stations Hexham, Haltwhistle and Penrith
Where to stay
Camping Sayerhill Farm (Teesdale, tel 01833 622203) Westgate Caravan & Camping site (Weardale, 10 ten pitches, tel 01388 517309)
Independent hostel Mill Cottage Bunkhouse, Nenthe (Weardale, tel 01434 382037, email administration.office@virgin.net)
YHA hostels Alston, 13km north of Cross Fell (meals 0870 770 5668, alston @yha.org.uk), Langdon Beck (Teesdale, meals, tel 0870 770 5910), Dufton, on so west edge of NPs, 8km from Cross Fell (meals, tel 08 770 5800, dufton@yha.org.uk)
B&Bs Outdale, Forest (-in-Teesdale) (Teesdale, tel 01 622303), High Brandon, near Rookhope (off Wearda tel 01388 517673), Bonny Moor Hen, Stanhope (Weardale, tel 01388 528214), Bee Cottage Farm, Castleside (C2C, northeast edge of NPs, tel 01207 508224)
Tourist offices
Stanhope (tel 01388 527650), Alston (tel 01434 382244), Middleton in Teesdale (tel 01833 641001) Hexham (tel 01434 652220)

NORTH WESSEX DOWNS
Viltshire
(see also Ridgeway)

55

NATIONAL TRAIL

his large area of mid-south downland has the Ridgeway arcing round its northern edge, but
fers far, far more than that. Running from Devizes in the west to Basingstoke and Reading in the
st, named downs include Pewsey, Marlborough, Lambourn and Watership, and the hills
ackpen, Haydown, Inkpen and Walbury.

here to ride

lf-navigate

e rights of way on the OS Landranger maps. The
owing scratches the surface;

ansdyke Path (runs W-E from SE of Calne to
arlborough)

und Marlborough (west) Go NW to Hackpen Hill on
e Marlborough Downs

und Pewsey (start Pewsey for facilities, start Oare to
e north for proximity) Go N and NW for Tan Hill
ay/Wansdyke Path, go S for Pewsey Down

rth Tidworth/Ludgershall Take your pick of bridle-
ys/byways N and W

ayfarer's Walk (22km, slightly discontinuous and you
ist observe the no-go footpath sections); Inkpen Hill
Walbury Hill to Watership Down, to North and East
kley near Basingstoke (continues to Portsmouth).

ydown Hill Start at Vernham Dean (ride W around
e hill)

Around Lambourn Broad choice of routes, including an
orbital, W, N, E and S

Mapping OS Landranger 173 Swindon and Devizes,
174 Newbury, Wantage. Guidebook *Philip's Cycle Tours
- Hampshire and the Isle of Wight* (£8.99, mapped
routes of Inkpen/Walbury Hills and Kingsclere/Overton)

Bike shop Boltons Bikes & Tandems, Ludgershall
(10km northwest of Andover, tel 01264 791818)

Where to stay *Camping* Postern Hill Caravan &
Camping Site, Savernake Forest (open Easter-Oct, in
season tel 01672 515195, out of season tel 0131 314
6505)

Tourist offices Devizes (tel 01380 729408),
Marlborough (west, tel 01672 513989), Swindon
(northwest, tel 01793 530328), Andover (southeast, tel
01264 324320), Newbury (east, tel 01635 30267)

17 ▶ **NORTH YORK MOORS**
North Yorkshire
(see also Dalby Forest)

The North York Moors are a vast plateau incised by steep-sided dales, fringed on the west by a huge escarpment and criss-crossed by trackways, many of considerable length. There are no distinct summits as such, but the sense of elevation and space is quite special. Be prepared for long rides in an exposed district, unique in the United Kingdom.
The main thoroughfares are well defined, often paved by sandstone and frequently used, but sor of the lesser bridleways, the real gems, need a navigator's skill, a deal of strength and a trials rider's technique in places, and reward with some great riding.

Where to ride (see also Dalby Forest)
Memorable downhills
These run off Urra Moor (through map refs NZ 578 032, 580 024 and 570 007), down into Baysdale (through 629 060), down towards Sleights from Black Brow at (NZ 866 060) and even desperate tarmac descents into Rosedale Abbey (through SE 732 967 and 722 950). Several of these cannot be ridden uphill!
Spilling off Rudland Rigg are a variety of downhills, the bridleway through NZ 625 011 being little more than a sheep trod, very peaty and loose, the old road at SE 656 971 is very slabby but loose, and the Rigg road itself from SE 653 950 can shake your head off when riding SSE.
Atop the escarpment the rocky run down the side of Black Hambleton (SE 478 945), and subsequent scoot to the car park (at 480 958) is a fitting end to any ride, but if it's pure technicality you seek, make your way further S to the super-steep bridleways (through SE 503 867, 504 838 or 510 816) near Sutton Bank.

Cross-country classics
The choice is enormous. The best approach is to ride the classics first, then, when you are attuned to the place, add your preferred loops;
The East The *Whitby-Scarborough rail trail* (32km) runs along the extreme eastern fringe of the Moors and makes excellent family riding, or a good alternative when the weather on the moors is too rough. From the north, the path starts at Larpool (S of Whitby town at NZ 896

094), runs 8.2km to Robin Hood's Bay (NZ 950 054) then a further 8km to Ravenscar (map ref NZ 980 01 then the final 16km to Scarborough town.
Note: a hairy diversion between Middlewood Lane, Fylingthorpe (map ref NZ 947 042) and Stoupe Brow Bridge (NZ 960 024), which removes the 'family' grading and elevates this section to the 'determined' category, has been in place for some time, but should completed by the time you read this. If not, be prepar for a sustained muddy carry up both sides of Mill Beck
Also in the East are good waymarked **forest rides in** **Langdale**, starting at SE 927 925 and *Dalby* (SE 877 900), and some serious loops across **Fylingdales Moo** the track over **Cock Lake Side** (map ref NZ 900 008) being a favourite.
The Central Moors Between the classic Rudland Rig in the west and the A169 Pickering-Whitby road in the east is really excellent riding; **Rudland Rigg Classic** This the old, and at one time most important, road across Rudland Rigg: from map ref SE 659 926 near Bog Ho (where it is irresistibly signposted 'Stokesley 16, Unsuitable for Motors') go NNW for a stony 9.8km t Bloworth Crossing (NZ 616 014). Bridleways join at West Gill Head (SE 644 969) near Three Howes (63 986) and the Crossing itself, and another old road crosses at Ouse Gill Head (SE 640 974), making seve loops possible - but all involving steep climbs and/or descents.
In the Danby district, four contrasting surfaces can

)ven into a demanding loop, all thoroughbred twin cks. The **Clitherbeck bridleways;** from NZ 726 087 ughly NW to 712 102; from 712 100 S to Danby age; the **Park Nook bridleway** E from NZ 684 086 to 7 085 near Park End then NNE to the tiny wood at Z 703 094. The **old road from Robin Hood's Butts** Z 712 115) **WSW to White Cross** is virtually moor- d 'motorway', until you hit the water-filled ruts! And ally, for a great day out, there are two little slab-paved ns that steal through the heather from **Sand Hill** at Z 670 105 to 667 104, then again from **Rosedale** ake at 707 095 to the moor road at 710 098.

e South

ouple of splendid long bridleways run through the st side of **Cropton Forest**. Very popular with serious ers is the mixed surface route through SE 764 924 l 757 977 over **Owlet Moor**.

e West

dland Rigg could claim to be a western route, but the doubted classic along the lip of the huge escarpment is mbleton Street or Road (depending which bit of the o you look at), which runs SSE from a bleak car park ap ref SE 479 959) above Osmotherley, to the top of ck Yate Bank (at 509 877). Loops can be made to the sing the bridleways down into, and up out of **Hawnby** ap ref SE 542 897), or down the west side of the p into the hamlets of **Kirby Knowle** (at 479 873), wick (470 909) or **Boltby** (491 866). There are also marked routes in **Boltby Forest** from high Paradise n (SE 503 888) and the route can be further ended S to Whitestone Cliff near Sutton Bank (at 503), using bdwys which double as the **Cleveland Way**.

pping and literature

ps The combination of the two OS Outdoor Leisure s gives best coverage and value; 26 North York ors Western area, 27 North York Moors Eastern area OS Landrangers 93 Middlesbrough & Darlington , 94 Whitby & Esk Dale, 100 Malton Pickering & ounds, 101 Scarborough & Bridlington).

debooks **Mountain Bike Guide - North York Moors** ah & Gary McLeod, The Ernest Press, £6.95); ntain Biking in North Yorkshire, and **Mountain**

Biking around Ryedale, Wydale and the North York Moors (both booklets, by J Brian Beadle, Trailblazer Publishing (Scarborough), £2)

Bike shops In Whitby - Dr Cranks, 15 Skinner St (tel 01947 606661); Great Ayton - Biketraks, 39 High St (tel 01642 724444); Northallerton - Cowley Cycles, 12 Zetland St (tel 01609 776656); Thirsk - Millgate Cycles, 13 Millgate (tel 01845 527666)

Where to eat Cafe at the Moors Centre, Danby (weekends only in winter)

Where to stay

Independent hostel Harbour Grange Backpackers, Whitby waterfront (dorms/family rooms, tel 01947 600817); **YHA hostels** Osmotherley (meals, tel 0870 770 5982), Lockton (self-catering only, tel 0870 770 5938), Helmsley (meals, tel 0870 770 5860), Whitby (meals, tel 0870 770 6088)

MTB-friendly inns and B&Bs

East: For eateries and accommodation go to Robin Hood's Bay, Scarborough and Whitby; **Inn** Fylingdales Inn, Fylingthorpe (NZ 944 050, tel 01947 880433); **B&B** Mrs Cook, Burgate Farm, Harwood Dale (run by Catriona Cook of the British Horse Society, see Introduction pages, trail advice, map ref SE 970 950, tel 01723 870333).

Central: Inns Fox & Hounds, Ainthorpe, Danby (NZ 704 076, tel 01287 660218); The Lion, Blakey Ridge, Kirkbymoorside (SE 679 997, tel 01751 417320); Barn Hotel & Tearoom, Hutton-le-Hole (SE 706 898, tel 01751 417311); **B&B** Roy & Kath Atherton, High Blakey House, Blakey Ridge (opp. The Lion, map ref 679 997, tel 01751 417 186).

West: Three Tuns Restaurant & Motel, Osmotherley (NZ 457 971, tel 01609 883301); **B&Bs** Mrs Jean Jeffray, Cote Faw, Sutton Bank (SE 522 830, tel 01845 597363); Allan Abbott, Vane House, Osmotherley (457 971, tel 01609 883301).

Tourist offices Danby (Moors Centre, Danby, open year round, tel 01287 660654), Helmsley (seasonal opening, tel 01439 770173), Scarborough (open year round, Valley Bridge Rd, tel 01723 373333), Whitby (open year round, Langbourne Rd, tel 01947 602674).

26 ▶ PEAK DISTRICT - THE DARK PEAK
Derbyshire

The northern part of the Peak District is big country; a rugged peat-covered moorland plateau incised with edges and steep-sided valleys between Manchester and Sheffield. Millstone grit or gritstone, is the underlying rock, famed for its grip. It wears smooth beneath feet and tyres, but you do encounter freshly broken rock you will be surprised at the traction.

The climbs vary between long hard slogs and steep long hard slogs (only kidding, no I'm not!), and not all the downhills are high-speed scoots, many are quite technical. Reminders of an industrial past are ever-present, mainly from quarrying and mining when most of the product was won by hand. The myriad of tracks at all levels are the legacy of these industries, and if you take your bait in the lee of a high-level dry stone wall take time to ponder the effort by man and horse to work this exceptionally hilly country.

Edale, the start of the Pennine Way walking route, is a good base, with parking, two campsites, a pub & station.

Where to ride
Guided and supported Lets Offroad (tel 020 8402 6652, www.letsoffroaduk.com, 4 skill levels), and Saddle Skedaddle (tel 0191 265 1110, www.skedaddle.co.uk).
Classic self-navigating rides
Edale (map ref SK 124 853) is the start point for biking loops that embrace three classics; *Jacob's Ladder* (SK 085 862) on the bdwy between Upper Booth (SK 102 853) and Coldwell Clough near Hayfield (SK 056 858); the *Roych Road* (SK 083 837); and the *Lord's Seat/ Mam Tor* complex (110 834/ 125 835).

Jacob's Ladder is the shortest, doubling early with the Pennine Way, and so steep that Gritstone blocks have been cemented together to limit and repair erosion. The spectacular downhill is usually thick with pedestrians. In contrast, the second half of the crossing, from Edale's Cross (546m) at the top of the Ladder down to Coldwell Clough, is an eternal fast, stony descent.

Roych Road runs between Mount Famine (SK 052 84° and the A625 (091 825) via Roych Clough, where the fords are interesting but usually rideable. A rough sect also occurs at South Head (063 845), even the lumpy downhill is uncomfortable! Try hard to ride from the M Famine direction towards Roych Clough.

West of the A624, just opposite Mt Famine, is a great little network of bridleways, mainly old trackways and roads, but now reduced to stony singletrack, often doubling as streams, on the high ground of *Chinley*, Chinley Churn (451m, map ref SK 035 836) being th highest point, with most riding above 300m. The dea straight, broken-surfaced downhill through 027 865 is recommended.

The *Sett Valley rail trail* between Hayfield (big car pa at 035 869) and New Mills (003 858) can be a useful link/return route avoiding the main road.

West of the A624, in the triangle bordered by the A6 B6102/A6105 and A624, is the most intricate netwo of bridleways and old roads (with great names: Knarr Nook, Butchers Piece Farm, Dirtylane, Podnor, Bottom's Hall and Gird Lane).

Mam Tor area: Parallel with the A625, the old track fr Mam Tor (SK 124 833) roughly W over Lord's Seat (542m), actually down to the A625 (at 093 825), sta with a tough climb to the ridge where a 'footpath' ru along the N side of the fence and a 'bridleway' runs along the south side, eventually combining at a gap i wall about 600m W of the summit. The 'good' sectio only if you are riding WSW, starts at 099 829, with continuous drop-offs for 500m down to the main ro

ld Mam Tor Road: The old main road on the eastern
de of Mam Tor, circumventing Winnat's Pass (from SK
31 833, just beyond the entrance to the Blue John
avern, to 133 837) is subject to continuous landslips
d has slid several metres down the hillside, leaving
eat fractured sections of carriageway that still bear
hite lines, the first drop being the biggest! You can
eave through the difficulties, then swing right onto big
rmac corrugations on the lower slopes, which lead into
ong long downhill into Castleton. One of the wackiest
ishes to any ride.

dybower Reservoir: Find good tracks on the eastern
le, notably behind Ladybower House (SK 204 865) on
e heights of Derwent Edge (198 882) and a long ride
rough the trees on the east side of the Derwent and
owden Reservoirs (through 173 906 and 169 935).
ne bridleways over Bridge-end Pasture (SK 176 878),
tween the two arms of Ladybower, and the Roman
ad (at 168 863) between the western arm and the
lway are also worth riding.

per Derwent Valley/Cut Gate (SK 170 953): At the
rthern end begins the wild moorland track over Cut
te. A less-frequented long tough 8km route that
ans committing. Riding south-north the initial stages
ough Cranberry Clough involve carrying, and on
aining Margery Hill (529m, 186 960) you have
nbed at least 250m, or more. The reward is
tracted singletrack descents either to North America
nest! SK 202 997) or the more northerly fork to the
stern end of Langsett Reservoir (197 008) or there-
outs. It's debatable whether the north-south descent
ough Cranberry Clough is any easier.

gdendale/Woodhead Pass rail trail: This exposed part
the Trans Pennine Bridleway, and classic in its own
nt, runs across the northern edge of the High Peak
m Hadfield (SK 024 960) just north of Glossop, ENE
ove the reservoirs of Valehouse, Rhodeswood,
side and Woodhead, over the Woodhead Pass and
wn to Penistone (SE 251 032), over the M1 between
and J37, around the south side of Barnsley (at SE

351 035) and all the way into East Yorkshire. From the
hamlet of Woodhead (SE 096 000) to Gallows Moss
(416m at SE 141 005) the route is not railway, it uses
the stony original pass road which is a tremendous
downhill E-W, but a toil W-E.
The railway sections make excellent family rides in
dramatic countryside; Hadfield - Woodhead Reservoir
(9km), Woodhead - Dunford Bridge (9km), Dunford
Bridge SE 157 023 - Worsbrough Museum (24km),
Worsbrough SE 351 035 - Wombwell 390 043 (5km).

Bike shops
Allens Cycles, Wombwell (tel 01226 756281), High
Peak Cycles, Glossop (tel 01457 861535), Lex's Cycles,
Penistone (tel 01226 763763)

Stations
Bamford (5km on the A6013 to Ladybower), Barnsley
(3km to Trans Pennine Bridleway), Chinley (for Chinley
Churn and Mount Famine), Edale (for Edale Loops and
Jacob's Ladder), Hadfield (start of Longdendale/TPB),
Hope (for Castleton, Mam Tor and SW Ladybower),
Penistone (on TPB)

Where to stay (see also 'Guided and supported' riding
Bunkhouse Thorpe Farm Bunkhouses, Hathersage (tel
01433 650659)
Independent hostel/B&B/self-catering
Pindale Farm Outdoor Centre, Hope
(tel 01433 620111)
YHA hostels Crowden (meals, tel 0870 770 5784),
Edale (meals, tel 0870 770 5808), Langsett
(self-catering only, tel 0870 770 5912)
B&Bs Wayside Cottage, Padfield (tel 01457 866495),
Potting Shed, Chapel-en-le-Frith (tel 01298 812656)

Mapping and literature
OS Outdoor Leisure 1 The Peak District, Dark Peak;
Landranger 110
Guidebook *Mountain Bike Guide - Derbyshire & the
Peak District* (by Tom Windsor, Tim Banton and Andy
Spender, The Ernest Press, www.ernest-press.co.uk,
tel 0141 637 5492, £7.50)

Tourist offices (all open year round)
Barnsley (tel 01226 206757), Glossop (tel 01457
855920), Sheffield (tel 0114 273 4671)

27 ▶ PEAK DISTRICT - THE WHITE PEAK
Derbyshire

There's classic riding in the White Peak, the southern area of the Peak District, defined as south of a line between Macclesfield through Castleton to Sheffield, and down to Ashbourne, northwest of Derby. The famous Tissington, High Peak and Manifold rail trails provide fascinating links to other tracks along old industrial roads and bridleways, which have both swooping and steep slopes through agricultural upland. This is limestone country, hence the name, and less rugged and more lush than its northern Dark Peak sister.

Due to the way limestone breaks and weathers, no matter how well defined, the surfaces can demand great strength to ride. There are places where the stony centre of the well-worn tracks is best avoided, and you find yourself riding off-camber singletrack right at the edge! Four river valleys, roughly parallel north to south, cut through here, so, like the name of one of those rivers, the climbs are manifold, with brilliant downhills too. Unless you stick to the rail trails, you cannot devise a route without a stiff climb, and matching descent. The main start towns Castleton, Eyam, Hathersage, Buxton, Ashbourne.

Where to ride
Guided and supported Lets Offroad (tel 020 8402 6652, www.letsoffroaduk.com, 4 skill levels) and Saddle Skedaddle (tel 0191 265 1110, www.skedaddle.co.uk).
Self-navigating Through the southern half of the area, rail trails provide excellent rides in their own right and useful links.
Tissington Trail (22km) start point Ashbourne (map ref SK 175 470) runs N through Tissington (178 521) to Parsley Hay (147 633) on gently graded rail trail. At Parsley Hay, the Tissington Trail meets the **High Peak Trail** (doubling as part of the Midshires Way) which provides another 4km NW to Sparklow (SK 127 660) in the Buxton direction, or ESE all the way to Bolehill (SK 289 555) just S of Matlock 21km away.
Ordance Survey now indicates 'white' roads that are

rights of way (red dots on Landranger, green dots on Explorer Outdoor Leisure) under the 'other route with public access' category (ORPA). Landranger 119 for th area is one of the best in the country for this.

In the **Chatsworth** area is a rattling good downhill to Edensor (through SK 240 697), good old roads near Rowsley (244 664) and Beeley Hilltop (270 684) and a wacky descent into Two Dales (through 284 633) whe the last 300m to the B5057 resemble a boulder field. I comparison, the elevated grind between Darley Bridge and Upper Town (via 250 618) verges on civilized.

Monsal Trail This much shorter rail trail, accessible between Coombs Road (SK 230 680) and Thornbridg Hall (197 711) keeps you out of the traffic in the Wye valley and puts you in reach of a good little network of 'other routes' between the A6 and A623 E of Buxton.

Eyam Have a look at the intricacies around Eyam (SK 215 765) S of the A623 on the heights of Longstone Moor (204 743), and a tiny track through Silly Dale (1 767) just to say you were there.

Castleton Climbs out of Castleton are hard and sustained but gain height quickly. Winnats Pass, the tarmac road, gets you up to the Mam Tor zone in no time, and another road S out of the village puts you straight into 'Limestone Way' country, with plenty of

dleways, often on stony roads. The Rebellion Knoll
p around Shatton Moor (SK 191 810 and 182 806) is
d to beat. Do it clockwise, then a lot of the
sperate) climbing is on good tarmac.

rthern Arc Don't miss the limit of White Peak lime-
ne, on high ground immediately S of Castleton (SK
0 830), Brough (184 825) and Hathersage (230 815)

ke shops BeSpoked, Bakewell (tel 01629 815076),
rn Stanley, Matlock (tel 01629 582089)

pping and literature
Landrangers 119 Buxton and Matlock, 110 Sheffield
Huddersfield (very important 2% for Castleton area);
lorer OS2 Peak District-White Peak, OL1 The Peak
trict-Dark Peak (2% for the area S of Castleton).
bsite: mapped routes on MTBroutes.com.
idebook: *Mountain Bike Guide - Derbyshire and the
k District* (Tom Windsor, Tim Banton and Andy
encer, £7.50, the Ernest Press, tel 0141 637 5492)
ations Bamford (for Northern Arc), Buxton (western
as), Cromford (for High Peak Trail), Darley Dale,

Dove Holes (western approaches), Hathersage
(Northern Arc), Hope (Northern Arc), Matlock Bath,
Matlock Riverside
Where to stay
Camping Pindale Farm, Hope (tel 01433 620111)
Bunkhouses Reckoning House, Mandale Farm, Haddon
Grove (5km SW of Bakewell, tel 01629 812416),
Thorpe Farm, Hathersage (tel 01433 650659)
Self-catering Pindale Farm, Hope (tel 01433 620111)
YHA hostels Bakewell, Bretton, Buxton, Castleton,
Elton, Eyam, Hartington, Hathersage, Ilam Hall, Matlock,
Ravenstor and Youlgreave!
B&Bs The Hollow, Little Longstone (map ref SK 190
717, tel 01629 640746); The Old Orchard, Stoney
Lane, Thorpe (map ref 158 503, tel 01335 350410);
Mandale Farm, Haddon Grove (5km SW of
Bakewell, tel 01629 812416), Pindale Farm, Hope
(tel 01433 620111)
Tourist offices
Ashbourne (tel 01335 343666), Bakewell (tel 01629
813227), Buxton (tel 01298 25106, five figs only)

EDDARS WAY
Norfolk
ee also Thetford)

NATIONAL TRAIL  42

ost of the inland half of this flat East Anglian long-distance trail is MTB-legal. The full trail starts
Knettishall Heath and runs NNW on a Roman road through the Brecks and open farmland to
olme-next-the-sea (continuing out-of-bounds on the Norfolk Coast Path footpath). Ride-legal
ctions are, from south to north; the A11 via Stonebridge to Little Cressingham and South
kenham (18km). (Short road stretch to) North Pickenham to Castle Acre (8km), and all the
y to Fring (29km). To reach the coast from Fring follow road sections. You can combine the
uthern section with riding in Thetford Forest, which lies 5km to the west.

Landrangers 144, 132; *Peddars Way National Trail
de* (Bruce Robinson, Aurum Press); info and
dleway mapping on www.nationaltrail.co.uk/
ddarsway; guide with accommodation by the Norfolk

Ramblers (tel 01953 861094). Castle Acre, halfway
along, is a little medieval walled town with an independent hostel, the Red Lion (a former pub, tel 01760
755557). See also *Thetford* for accommodation.

22 ► PENNINE BRIDLEWAY

NATIONAL TRAIL

This National Trail-in-development runs up through northern England and is specifically designed for mountain bikers and horse-riders (and walkers).

In 2008, once the Pennine Bridleway is finished and open, it will run from the High Peak Trail in Derbyshire to Byrness in Northumberland, a distance of 560km. The trail is signposted and has no stiles or steps, just easy-to-use gates and special road crossing points. As the official line goes, 'let nature be the only challenge!' For *mapping and literature* contact the Pennine Bridleway team (tel 0161 237 1061, www.thepennine-bridleway. co.uk). For the Mary Towneley Loop, see the entry for the South Pennines .

For where to stay, the British Horse Society produces a nationwide guide *Bed and Breakfast for Horses* with some Pennine Bridleway places (BHS bookshop tel 08701 201918, if out of stock, see also B&Bs on www.bhs.org.uk).

88 ► PENSHURST (PORC)
Kent

Doubles, table-top, jumps and lines. Get it all at PORC (Penshurst OffRoad Club), a small, steep and perfectly-formed piece of woodland on the High Weald near Tonbridge, in an area otherwise surprisingly devoid of good riding. It's excellent for high-jumpers and BMXers, cross-country too, and has been the host of national competitions.
The faster you reach the bottom, the faster you're back at the top.

Where to ride
4km downhill short-course and cross-country single-track, dual slalom course and jump quarry. Good for all skill levels, from beginners to pros - a great place to learn the jumpy end of the sport, as well as straight pedalling.
Mountain Bike Club The home club is PORC (manager Rob tel 01892 870136, mob 07736 429417, www.porc-online.co.uk).
Location From the A26 halfway between Tonbridge and Tunbridge Wells, turn off west on the B2176

(towards Bidborough). Continue past Penshurst Place stately home and through Penshurst, then outside the village, take the first right just over the stream. Climb 800m, and the entrance is on the left, heading uphill.
Facilities and charge Camping, food and drink on site. £4/2.50 adults/children per day. Instructors available.
Bike shop Wild Side Cycles, 77 Camden Rd, central Tunbridge Wells (tel 01892 527069)
Tourist office Tunbridge Wells (tel 01892 515675)

65 ▶ QUANTOCK HILLS
Somerset
(see also Combe Sydenham)

A national MTB treasure, the red sandstone Quantocks are a bridleway-rich treat for body and mind. The 16km ridgeline has a choice of over 15 big climbs/descents up steep combes and hillsides, rewarded by lovely floaty tracks on the top plateau, with views over the Bristol Chann
The climbs are around sea-level to 300m, a height difference you can easily plan in twice (or more!) per ride.
In the autumn the hills burn with the colour of turning bracken and the picturesque villages bel
shelter fine country pubs. Holford is a popular start, heading straight up Hodder's Combe.

Where to ride
Guided and supported Lets Offroad (tel 020 8402 6652, www.letsoffroaduk.com) and Saddle Skedaddle (tel 0191 265 1110, www.skedaddle.co.uk); Exmoor & Quantock MTB Holidays (holiday caravans, tel 01984 632237, www.exqumtb.co.uk)

Self-navigating
The north half of the hills have the striking riding.
Start from the car park in Holford (NE, start of Hodder's Combe). Other start villages include Nether Stowey, Crowcombe and Bicknoller
For a start-height advantage there are car parks on the traversing lane (central, Crowcombe-Nether Stowey) and off that on the north side of Great Wood.
Combes/slopes include: (from Holford clockwise) Hodder's Combe, Holford Combe, above Nether Stowey, forest climbs in Great Wood above Adscombe and Aley, up Bagborough Hill, above Triscombe, just east of Crowcombe, above Halsway, Thorncombe to Thorncombe Barrow, Bicknoller Combe, above Weacombe, the north end, Smith's Combe and Pardlestone Hill.
Maps of a tough route and the top downhills, credited to 'WA', can be found on www.chocolatefoot.co.uk/routes.
The ridgeline is bridleway/rupp for 6km from the northern tip at Beacon Hill (310m) to Great Hill (337m) and the Triscombe Stone in the centre. If you avoid the footpaths, you can also continue south.
Mapping and literature OS Landrangers 181 (the less

interesting southeast area is on 182, and southernmo area on 183), Explorer 140
Location M5 J23, to Bridgwater, A39 (Minehead ro to Nether Stowey and Holford, or via Over Stowey over the hills (1:4 down) to Crowcombe and Bicknc
Stations Bridgwater (17km E of Holford), Taunton
Bike shops Bicycle Chain, Bridgwater (tel 01278 423640); Bicycle Chain, Taunton (tel 01823 252499 Bike Zone, Taunton (tel 01823 252499); Newmans Cycles, Taunton (tel 01823 332762); Ralph Colman Cycles, Taunton (tel 01823 275822); St John Street Cycles, Bridgwater (tel 01278 441500); Roger Josep Cycles, Bridgwater (tel 01278 663545)
Where to stay See also 'Guided and supported'
Camping Quantock Orchard Caravan Park, Flaxpool (west side, off A358 SE of Crowcombe, tel 01984 618618, www.flaxpool.freeserve.co.uk)
YHA hostels Quantock Hills (NE end, 2km W of Holford, self-catering only, tel 0870 770 6006); Crowcombe Heathfield (W side, 1.5km SW of Crowcombe, meals, tel 0870 770 5782)
B&B The Manse - 10% discount mentioning this bo Lime St, Nether Stowey (keen cycling owner and tr advice, tel 01278 732917).
Where to drink and eat
At pubs in Holford, Nether Stowey, West Bagborou Triscombe and Crowcombe and Bicknoller.
Tourist offices Bridgwater (tel 01278 427652), Taunton (tel 01823 336344)

QUEEN ELIZABETH COUNTRY PARK
Hampshire
(see also South Downs, South Downs Way)

80

Hampshire's best-known country park boasts the highest point on the South Downs (Butser Hill 270m) and is the starting point of miles of excellent cross-country biking.

Where to ride

Off-navigating The South Downs Way runs directly through the park, leading to routes across East Hampshire and West Sussex. See www.hants.gov.uk/cycling

Dedicated routes

Orange trail (5km, experienced, off-camber singletrack, early climbs and descents)

Purple trail (5km, novice, gravel roads, forest tracks and short piece of singletrack)

Country Park Visitor Centre With cafe (tel 023 9259 5040), www. hants.gov.uk/countryside/QECP). Parking £1 Mon-Sat, £1.50 Sun and bank hols. The country park is run by the Forestry Commission and

Hampshire County Council

Mapping OS Landranger 197, OS Explorer 120, park trail guide 75p, Hants County Council offroad routes (two packs of 12 routes £2.99 each)

Location The park lies 7km south of Petersfield on the A3 Portsmouth road.

Station Petersfield (5km north)

Bike shops Sensible Bike Co, Petersfield (tel 01730 266554), Owens Cycles, Petersfield (tel 01730 260446)

Mountain Bike Club
None officially, but try the friendly crew at Sensible Bikes in Petersfield

Tourist offices Petersfield (tel 01730 268829), Havant (023 9248 0024)

56

RIDGEWAY TRAIL
(see also Chilterns, North Wessex Downs)

NATIONAL TRAIL

A classic progress across southern England, the 72km western upland half of the Ridgeway National Trail is long and relatively easy to cover as it runs along the top edge of the North Wessex Downs. It is marked by big skies and ancient sites, particularly the Uffington White Hors

As well as suiting experienced bikers, in dry weather the route is good for families. After a prolonged rainy spell expect delay due to mud and ruts.

The lowlying eastern half of the trail runs along the flat base of the Chiltern escarpment and is discontinuous bridleway (see the *Chilterns*).

Where to ride
Western half (North Wessex Downs)
This is all MTB-legal upland track (RUPP), starting in the west at Overton Hill near Avebury, finishing in the east at Streatley in Berkshire.

Streatley/Goring make a good start/finish point at the eastern end for out-and-back riding.

For loops that partly use the Ridgeway (see North Wessex Downs) start from Marlborough, Wantage, Lambourn, West and East Ilsley and Compton

Mapping and literature - western half
Ridgeway Circular Riding Routes Pack (£2.35 + £1p+p, from the National Trails Office, tel 01865 810224); Guidebook *Philip's Cycle Tours - Around Oxford* (£8.99, mapped routes around Lambourn, Uffington, above Wantage, Chilterns east of Goring, Stoke Row, west from Henley/Nettlebed).

Eastern half (Chilterns)
This section is more broken and wooded, but with a 13km stretch of bridleway/byway between Britwell Salome and Bledlow in Buckinghamshire.

(The Ridgeway National Trail continues mostly on footpath to Ivinghoe Beacon, no cycling).

Stations Swindon (7km north), Didcot (7km north-

east), Goring (en trail)

Historic highlights (western half)
Avebury World Heritage Site (village in a stone circle); Iron Age Forts at Uffington, Barbury and Liddington; The White Horse of Uffington (which some consider more canine than equine).

Where to eat and drink
In the western half, there are no facilities up top, bar t occasional watertap, so carry food and water. The on pub en route is the Shepherds Rest at Fox Hill.

Nearest towns
From west to east: Marlborough, 6.5km east of start; Wantage, 3km north of trail; Streatley and Goring en on the Thames; Wallingford, 1.5 km north of trail, Princes Risborough and Wendover en trail; Tring, 2km west.

Mapping and literature - general
OS Landranger 173, 174, 175, 165
Guidebook: *Ridgeway National Trail Guide* (Neil Curt Aurum Press)
Website: www.nationaltrail.co.uk

Where to stay
Camping Forestry Commission Postern Hill Campsite Marlborough (tel 01672 515195); field at Westfields Farm, Ogbourne St George (no toilets, tel 01672 841373)

YHA hostel Ridgeway (above Wantage, meals, tel 087 770 6064, Court Hill, Wantage)

Tourist offices
Avebury (tel 01672 539425)
Marlborough (tel 01672 513989)
Swindon (tel 01793 530328)

RIVINGTON
Lancashire

21

The main local mountain biking north of Manchester is no easy option: the climb to Rivington Pike worthy of any remote upland. There's another bonus in that the low-level start point is the Lever Park estate, where the Great House Barn has a cafe and visitor centre. You'll anticipate that finishing cuppa during the ascent to Winter Hill at 456m (with its huge mast).

Where to ride
Self-navigating Start from the Great House Barn car park in Lever Park. Climb on steep Sheep House Lane to the top, contour round past Rivington Pike on a ridged moorland bridleways, eventually to the conifer plantation, Wilderswood, descend steep narrow Old Rake lane then first right to a concessionary bridleway. You can continue all the way down to the reservoir. Lever Park has friendly family cycling and routes on Lancashire Country Rides

Location For Lever Park estate: M61 J6, N A6027 past the striking Reebok Stadium (home to Bolton Wanderers), left A673 NW to Horwich. After a big roundabout in Horwich enter the park on the right.

Mapping and literature
OS Landranger 109
Two routes here are mapped in the routes book *Manchester Cycle Rides* (Neil Simpson, Haynes, £10.99, www.haynes.co.uk)

3 ▶ ROTHBURY AND COQUETDALE
Northumberland
(see also Cheviots)

For long high rides in remote upland moors and forests, head for pretty Coquetdale, to the southeast below the Cheviot Hills (see entry) near the border of England and Scotland. Here is a limitless set of memorable self-navigating rides on tracks you will probably have all to yourself. Make Rothbury or Alwinton your base.

Where to ride
Self-navigating
Follow rights of way for a bundle of big-country trails around Simonside, Rothbury Forest, Thrunton and Kidland.
See the locally-produced www.coquetdale.com/mtb for insider descriptions of riding around the area.
The website features seven mapped described MTB routes (*Roond Simonside, Roond Rothbury, Roond Elsdon, From and Alniwick Moor (say annick), Ewartly Shank, Usway* and *Kidland*)

Mapping and literature
Guidebook: *Mountain Bike Guide – Northumberland* (mapped routes for Carriage Drive/Rothbury and Harwood Forest, Derek Purdy, £7.50 The Ernest Press, www.ernest-press.co.uk, tel 0141 637 5492).
OS Landrangers 80, 81, Explorers OL16, OL42 (and 332 for Thrunton).
Website: lots of ride info on www.coquetdale.com.
Location A1, NNW A697, left at Weldon on B6344 8km to Rothbury town. For Alwinton continue 6km on B6431, at Flotterton go right on minor road, continue 9km to Alwinton)

Where to stay
Camping Coquetdale Caravan Park, Whitton (1km S Rothbury, open Apr-Oct, (tel 01669 620549)
Farm B&Bs Lee Farm, The Lee (3km SW Rothbury, te 01665 570257), Tosson Tower Farm, Great Tosson (3.5km W Rothbury, tel 01669 620228)
B&Bs The Byre Vegetarian B&B, Harbottle (for Uppe Coquetdale and Kidland Forest, 12km W from Rothb tel 01669 650476), Cross Keys Inn, Thropton (one room in good pub, 4km W of Rothbury tel 01669 620362), Rose & Thistle Inn, Alwinton (for Upper Coquetdale and Kidland, 14km W of Rothbury, tel 01669 650226).
Self-catering cottages List on www.visit-rothbury. co.
Bike shops
The Spar in Rothbury sells spares for repairs. For contacts try the Rush (the Jedburgh bike shop and en siasts, tel 01835 869643)
Where to eat and drink
Cross Keys pub at Thropton (4km W of Rothbury, or room B&B, tel 01669 620362)
Tourist office Rothbury - National Park Tourist Information Centre (tel 01669 620887)

ROWNEY WARREN WOOD - CHICKSANDS
Ampthill Forest, Bedfordshire

`◀ 51`

Here's the fun home ground of Beds Fat Trax MBC, whose members have created a cool MTB course of testing woodland singletrack with jumps and twists, in cooperation with the Forestry Commission and the Southill Estate. All tracks are shared, so keep your eyes peeled.

Where to ride
Mix up types and grades of riding on singletrack and forest roads, with links to open-country bridleways. All riding in the Warren takes place on the northwest side of the lane. The car park is on the southeast side of the lane, where a mapboard shows the routes.

Dedicated riding *Challenging hilly red route* (5km) and *easy blue route* (3km). The air-filled *Freeride* area and *dual slalom course* are at the north end of the Warren, reached from the cross-country routes.

Self-navigating A long bridleway section of the John Bunyan Trail runs from the southern edge of the wood all the way into Bedford. At the northwest corner is a bridleway section of the Greensand Ridge Walk (continuing southwest to Clophill and northeast towards Sandy - avoid footpath sections)

Location 12km southeast of Bedford. Go to the main car park in Sandy Lane, which is the lane to Chicksands 2km northwest of Shefford off the A600

Mountain bike club Beds Fat Trax (membership tel 01234 720955, www.bedsfattrax.supanet.com)

Where to eat and drink At the pubs in Shefford 2km to the southeast

RUTLAND WATER

`◀ 51`

Stretch your legs on the signposted 27km circuit round this large reservoir.

The navigating is easy, and, on a sunny Sunday, there's lots to watch that's happening en route. Good for families too. There's a visitor centre at Empingham (tel 01572 653026), and pay and display car parks at Normanton, Barnsdale, Whitwell and Empingham. For refreshments go to the Waterside cafe near Normanton, or to pubs at Edith Weston, Empingham, Whitwell, Hambleton and Manton. You can hire bikes at Whitwell (tel 01780 460705 on the north shore), and Normanton (tel 01780 720888). The nearest station is Oakham, 2km west.

SALISBURY PLAIN
Wiltshire

There's a healthy buzz of mountain bikers around Salisbury Plain, despite the whizz-bang of missiles from the firing ranges. As long as you observe the Danger Area notices, there is typical hearty downland riding to be had on long open tracks, which can feel exposed and remote. The local club, SPAM Biking (see below) is very active, and supplements its club runs with organizing major events such as the annual Salisbury Plain Challenge and the Lavington Blast.

Military areas

Generally speaking, out-of-bounds military areas are very well marked. Signs on the boundary of exercise and live-firing areas are placed every 50m or so and the main entry points to the plain (byways) are manned by civilian wardens when anything potentially dangerous is happening. As a rough guide, the area of the plain to the east of the A360 from West Lavington to Shrewton is open at weekends but there are exceptions. Common sense prevails here so if you're not sure, don't go there.

Where to ride
Self-navigating

Riding is mainly on fire-track so the going is good any time of year.

Neither of the following routes is technically challenging but both are great hacks. There are very few snack stops en route, so stock up before you go.

There's good parking at the Lavington Vedette (map ref 024 553, Explorer 130 north sheet) and from here there are loads of options;

Route A: Do the loop S towards Tilshead swinging E towards Netheravon and then N towards Urchfont. You come back on the byway and head W to the vedette. You can extend this ride down to Shrewton before

turning E and then head N when you get to Rolleston Camp (096 449). There's loads of options in this area.

Route B: Head E from the same area and skirt the ed of the plain towards Upavon. It's feasible to do this all road but as you approach Compton (132 519) you m have to drop onto the A345 for a couple of miles befo you pick up the byway again at Haxton (143 494) and then continue the loop round to the top edge of Larkh Camp, head W to Tilshead and turn N just before Westdown Camp to take you back to the car park.

Mapping OS Explorers 157, 143 & 130 (Landranger 184 Salisbury & the Plain, 173 a little northernmost ar

Mountain bike club Contact SPAM Biking (Salisbury Plain Area MTBing, www.spambiking.co.uk) for inform tion on club rides and links to events.

Bike shop Bikes and Boards, Sidmouth St, Devizes 01380 729621; Hayball Cycles, Winchester Street, Salisbury (tel 01722 411378); R Barnes, Westbury (tel 01373 822760)

Events Salisbury Plain Challenge, Solstice Challenge, Lavington Blast, Erlestoke national events, contact Spa Biking for information.

Tourist office Salisbury (tel 01722 412787)

SEVENOAKS
Kent Downs

(Weasel out a some good tracks on the Kent Downs east of Sevenoaks.
Otherwise, bridleways in the High Weald tend to be discontinuous, and are muddy in the wet.)

Where to ride
Self-navigating
The Plaxtol Two Step (figure-of-eight loop): this can be ridden as a figure-of-eight or two separate loops.
Highlights: Carter's Hill technical descent, Wilmot Hill views and fast descent to Ightham Mote, technical riding in Oldbury Woods (byway between 569 545 and 573 549).
Start at One Tree Hill car park (559 532, can also start Plaxtol village), W on road, descend Carter's Hill then up to One Tree Hill, to Ightham Mote, then Plaxtol, Branch, Mereworth Woods, Plaxtol, N to Oldbury Woods (good at Seal, Godden Green, One Tree Hill).

Mapping
OS Explorer 147 Sevenoaks and Tunbridge, 148 Maidstone and Medway Towns (Plaxtol and Mereworth Woods only) Landranger 188 Maidstone
Mountain bike club
Weald & Downland MTBers (will@wildside.uk.com, Richard@ wildside.uk.com)
Station Sevenoaks
Location Sevenoaks lies off the A21, from M25 J5
Bike shop Wild Side Cycles, 77 Camden Rd, central Tunbridge Wells (tel 01892 527069)
Where to eat Al fresco at the NT cafe at Ightham Mote (no entrance ticket necessary)

SHERWOOD PINES
Clipstone, Nottingham

(Forest-wide singletrack and and very long dual-descender course built by local bikers make Sherwood Pines a cool site. The riding is on well-drained sandy soil with smart ups and downs but no major hills. A regular national & local race venue, it's at the heart of ancient Sherwood Forest.

Where to ride
Singletrack end-to-end of the forest, linked by fire track on an excellent trail network that includes a training circuit. The highlight is the specially-built 1km **dual descender** (graded black) which features cross-overs, jumps and bends, also an unofficial jump/freeride area, and jungle project area (?). History corner: routes utilise the gradients of practice trenches built to train WW1 soldiers headed for the Somme. There are **three waymarked family routes** (including an adventurous 7km blue route), while Sustrans NCN 6 allows access
north and south into other woods with about 15000ha of land, so you can link into places like Clumber and Blidworth Woods without using major roads. **Mapping** OS Landranger 120. **Facilities** Good visitor centre with a cafe, providing refreshments. The Forestry office is on tel 01623 822477. Parking is £2 peak, £1 offpeak. **Bike facilities** Sherwood Pines Cycles (hire, tel 01623 822855). **Location** The forest park is off the B6030 east of Old Clipstone. **Where to stay** Center Parcs lies south and east of the forest. *YHA hostel* Sherwood Forest, Edwinstowe (meals, tel 0870 770 6026).

**A Lake District MTB classic:
a quick trip up the High Street**

The South Downs are blessed with beautiful long open climbs and descents

SOUTH DOWNS
East Hampshire and Sussex
(see also Friston Forest, QE Country Park, South Downs Way)

The beautiful 200m-high South Downs rear up out of the plains for 150km between Winchester in Hampshire to Eastbourne in East Sussex. Bridleway sections run throughout its length on or near the South Downs Way long-distance trail, and there are infinite self-navigable loops, from long to short, steep to shallow. As the broad chalkland ridge rolls through the English countryside, the views and sense of timelessness pervade. The river valleys of the Meon, Arun, Adur, Ouse and Cuckmere break the continuity of the ridgeline as they escape to the sea, creating long steady climbs and high-speed open descents, up to 2km long, to tire and inspire you. Singletrack is rare, but the commonplace deep rut-lines demand sharp eyes and skill especially on the descents. Enjoy the speed but don't crash, and you must slow right down to pass walkers. For information visit the South Downs site, www.vic.org.uk.

Where to ride

Guided and supported Saddle Skedaddle (weekends, 0191 265 1110, www.skedaddle.co.uk)

Self-navigating on 1300km of bridleways and byways. The best riding is (from west); around West Meon/East Meon; NW and S of Petersfield (QE Ctry Park/Harting Down); around West Dean/East Dean/Goodwood; Graffham (Graffham Down); above Amberley (Wepham Down); west of the Adur valley (Worthing/Steyning); E of the Adur valley - above Steyning, Findon, Fulking, Devil's Dyke, Saddlescombe, Worthing/Shoreham; downs between Brighton and Newhaven above Saltdean; downs N from Brighton - Ditchling Beacon to Lewes; E of the river Ouse to Alfriston; Friston Forest (see entry); W of Eastbourne (East Dean/Wilmington).

Prescribed routes *Trails by Rail* (six MTB circuits from stations; Devil's Dyke (17km, Portslade station), Falmer (4km, Falmer station), Lewes (27km, Lewes station), Saredown (14km, Portslade station), Shoreham (16km, Shoreham station), Newhaven ((26km, Newhaven stn))

Other recommendations For very easy riding, the *Downs Link rail trail* from South Downs at Bramber to North Downs at Guildford, and bridleway links.

'Camp Lane', the old coach road from Jevington to Firle, climb 150m to Firle Beacon and return on the South Downs Way (map ref TQ 516 038).

Mapping OS Landranger 185 Winchester, 197 Chichester, 198 Brighton, 199 Eastbourne & Hastings; Guidebook *Philip's Cycle Tours - Kent and Sussex* and *Hampshire and the Isle of Wight* (two-three mapped rides in each)

Stations-straight-to-Downs Southease, Glynde, Hassocks, Falmer, Amberley, Rowlands Castle, Petersfield, Shawford Down. Stations with a short ride through town; Seaford, Newhaven, Lewes, Portslade, Shoreham, Chichester, Petersfield.

The Hiker Biker Bus carries bikes free in summer in a trailer anticlockwise round the eastern downs (two hourly, Sun & Public Hols, July-Sept, adult/child £2/£1), from Lewes via Newhaven, Exceat, Eastbourne, Folkington and back to Lewes.

Good towns for eating & drinking Lewes, Hassocks, Steyning, Storrington, Arundel, Midhurst, Petersfield, Liss

Where to stay (see 'Guided and supported' riding); *YHA hostels* Alfriston (overlooks Cuckmere valley, meals, tel 0870 770 5666, alfriston@yha.org.uk), Arundel (meals, tel 0870 770 5676, arundel@yha.org.uk), Brighton (international, breakfast included, tel 0870 770 5724 brighton@yha.org.uk); Eastbourne (self-catering, breakfast on request, tel 0870 770 5806).

83 ▶ SOUTH DOWNS WAY
EAST HAMPSHIRE AND SUSSEX
(see Queen Elizabeth Country Park, South Downs)

The classic 158km South Downs Way ride can be done at a comfortable pace in three days, with more of a push in two, and if you like to suffer in one – as the South Downs Way Randonee had 'em doing a couple of times! Total climbing is around 3000m (that's 10,000 foot).

Riding part of the South Downs Way is great introduction to mountain biking. Riding the whole linear route is a worthy challenge for an experienced biker who likes to get into the rhythm.

Where to ride
The start point is Winchester Youth Hostel, the finish point is the western End of Eastbourne Promenade. The western part of the downs is the plainest, just rolling farmland. The central West Sussex Downs are dominated by a steep, often wooded scarp with views across the Weald below. But the East Sussex Downs are classic open grassland running down to the sea cliffs. Just 8km of bridleway splits off from the main Way, between Alfriston and Eastbourne, and in the Meon Valley. The highest point is Ditchling Beacon (248m), the lowest virtually at sea level in the river valleys that break the ridge in half a dozen places.

Nearest towns Eastbourne, Winchester and Alfriston are en route. Steyning is at 1km, Storrington (1km), Pulborough (13km), Midhurst (6km), Petersfield (6km), Newhaven (5km), Lewes (6km), Portsmouth (19km),
Alton (24km), Brighton (11km), Shoreham (6km), Worthing (6km)

Mapping and literature The South Downs Way National Trail Guide (Paul Millmore, Aurum Press (£12.99, Harvey route strip map (Harvey, tel 01786 841202, www.harveymaps.co.uk). OS Landrangers 185, 197, 198, 199

Where to stay Accommodation guide, £2.50, from the National Trail Officer (tel 01392 597618).

YHA hostels
Winchester (breakfast only, tel 0870 770 6092)
Arundel (meals, tel 0870 770 5676, arundel@yha.org.uk)
Truleigh Hill (meals, tel 0870 770 6078)
Brighton (international, breakfast included, tel 0870 77 5724 brighton@yha.org.uk)
Alfriston (overlooks Cuckmere valley, meals, tel 0870 770 5666, alfriston@yha.org.uk)
Eastbourne (self-catering, breakfast on request, tel 087 770 5806)

OUTH PENNINES AND THE
1ARY TOWNELEY LOOP
West Yorkshire/Lancashire

23

he raw, dramatic South Pennines lie north of the Peak District, south of the Yorkshire Dales, est of Halifax and east of Burnley. The high open moorland and deep-cut valleys have long been focus of MTB culture, stimulated by the density of bridleways, the ancient packhorse trails and roximity to Manchester and Leeds. Here you find the moors of Keighley, Heptonstall and aworth (traversed by the Pennine Way), the towns and villages of Hebden Bridge, Haworth ome to the Brontes) and Todmorden (home to *Singletrack* magazine). You can ride the trails that spired Emily Bronte's *Wuthering Heights*, and which do the same for Mark Alker, *Singletrack* ditor. Base town is Hebden Bridge.

here to ride

ebden Bridge, in Calderdale, is the most central and t starting point. Todmorden (8km west) is also the rt of a great ride. From both, all paths lead up the leysides, so expect considerable climbs. There's ational Trust parking at Hardcastle Crags in Hebden dge, and a car park in the centre of town.

lf-navigating routes

Hebden, climb N through Hardcastle Crags, N on to moors, either over to Haworth, or go W, over Gorple Road into Lancashire.

Hebden, climb N through Hardcastle Crags, E over 'Limers Gate', over High Brown Knoll, down to _uddenden Dean, back towards Pecket Well, and return

Hebden, S from behind station up to Kilnshaw Lane, round below Stoodley Pike, to Mankinholes (good oridleway), drop down to Todmorden.

From the valley between Todmorden and Hebden, up through Upper Eastwood to Great Rock (big rock by the side of the road), W then down to Windy Harbour, contour parallel to the route between Todmorden and Burnley, to Mount Cross (ancient cross marked on map). On road stay W to past windfarm, go offroad N to Cant Clough Reservoir, inks into bridleway to return over the moor to Hebden.

The Mary Towneley Loop

Swallowed whole, this tough 68km circular route on the Lancashire and Yorkshire borders is one big ride. Opened in 2002, it is the first part of the developmental Pennine Bridleway (see entry), due for completion 2008. It is signposted, but you're better off getting the free easy-to-order guide (see below).

From 20km north of Manchester, it crosses open moorland near Watergrove Reservoir and Rochdale, then follows an old packhorse route from Bottomley to Erringdon (views across the Calder Valley) and descends towards Hebden Bridge. Between Widdop and Hurstwood Reservoirs, it crosses open countryside on the ancient Gorple Road (views towards Burnley), then the Rossendale Valley to Waterfoot, climbing to another historic route, Rooley Moor Road near Rochdale (built with stone sets to provide work during the cotton famine in the 1860s).

The route is dedicated to the memory of Lady Mary Towneley, who conceived and campaigned over many years for a long-distance horse-riders route over the Pennines. She died in February 2001 after a long illness. Mountain bikers make up 45% of users.

Location To Hebden Bridge; **by car** (awkward) M62 J21, follow signs for Littleborough, then Todmorden; **by train** (far easier), from Manchester or Leeds (bikes carried without problem).

Where to eat and drink Todmorden - The Tenth
Muse cafe, Staff of Life inn (1.6km up from Tod on the
Burnley road, good-value B&B, see below); **Hebden** -
Station cafe (sausage butties, big mugs of tea, at the foot
of the descent off London Road), The Blue Pig working
mens club at Hardcastle Crags (locally famous with
MTBers, short on glamour, long on excellent beer, at the
start/finish of some of the best trails)
Bike shop Blazing Saddles, Market Street, Hebden
Bridge (showers!, route info, sales, repair, 01422
844435, www.blazingsaddles.co.uk)
Mountain bike club Blazing Saddles runs rides Sunday
and Thursday evening rides, all welcome (see above).
Mapping and literature Excellent *Mary Towneley
Loop free guide* from Countryside Agency Publications or
tourist offices (map, accommodation and services, tel
0870 120 6466, email countryside@twoten.press.net).

OS Explorer OL21 South Pennines (marked on the
latest edition); Landrangers 109 Manchester Bolton and
Warrington, 103 Blackburn and Burnley.
For the general South Pennines; Outdoor Leisure 21
(centred on the Hebden Bridge and Todmorden area),
Landranger 103 Blackburn, Burnley (just about covers
the area)
Tourist office Hebden Bridge (tel 01422 843831)
Where to stay
YHA hostels Haworth (meals, tel 0870 770 5858)
Mankinholes (self-catering only, tel 0870 770 5952);
B&Bs Staff of Life, Todmorden (good value, tel 01706
812929), Badger Fields Farm, Blackshawhead, Hebden
Bridge (tel 01422 845161), Poppyfields House, Slack
Top, Heptonstall (tel 01422 843636), Prospect End, 8
Prospect Terrace, Hebden Bridge (tel 01422 843586),
Robin Hood Inn, Pecket Well (tel 01422 842593).

84 ▶

SURREY HILLS EAST & REDLANDS TRAILS
(see also Surrey Hills West, North Downs, North Downs Wa

The trails of the eastern Surrey Hills are a mecca for London mountain bikers. Ride up to the
highest point in Surrey at Leith Hill (294m), and you're rarely alone - cyclists can easily outnumbe
walkers. The bridleway/byway network around the uplands of Coldharbour and Holmbury St
Mary is steep and wooded, and full of singletrack and doubletrack. Volunteer trail-builders have
been at work on the Redlands Trails around Coldharbour and the country pubs are nice.

Where to ride
Guided and supported Contact Lets Offroad (tel 020
8402 6652, www.letsoffroaduk.com) and Saddle
Skedaddle (tel 0191 265 1110, www.skedaddle.co.uk).
Self-navigating The riding area covers all points
between the A24 S of Dorking and the A281 S of
Guildford. For longer loops, link N to the North Downs
(see entry) via bdwys 1km and 2km W of Westcott.
Start points are Dorking, Westcott, the Landslip car park
(1km S Coldharbour, map ref 147 433) or Forestry
Enterprise entrances to Redlands (see below) and
Buryhill, Peaslake, and Holmbury St Mary.
Dedicated Redlands Trails Regurgitator, *Waggledance*
and *Summer Lightning* are short built trails meant as part
of longer self-navigating rides (start opposite the pub in
Coldharbour, map ref TQ 150 445), and designed to
draw MTBers from overcrowded bdwys particularly
Leith Hill). Contact the Redlands Trails volunteers on tel
01306 887923, www.redlandstrails.org).
Where to eat & drink Coldharbour - the Plough
(brews own, expensive food), Peaslake - the Hurtwood
Inn (a worthy host), Leith Hill Tower tea-kiosk, North
Downs - the Boxhill servery and caravan at Headley;

barn cafe at Bockets Farm (map ref 156 550).
Mapping and information *Redlands Trails* leaflet (£
available at www.redlandstrails.org or justridingalong.
com; OS Explorer 146 Dorking Box Hill and Reigate,
Landranger 187 Dorking Reigate; the area is owned/ru
by the Forestry Commission, the National Trust, Wott
Estate (Leith Hill to Wotton), Hurtwood Control (for
Holmbury and Hurtwood)
Location Dorking to Westcott - W on A25 signed for
Guildford; Dorking to Coldharbour - take Leith Hill
turning from one-way system. **Stations** Dorking,
Holmwood, Gomshall.
Bike shops Nirvana at Westcott (guiding and hire, te
01306 740300), Beyond Mountain Bikes at Cranleigh
(guiding, tel 01483 267676)
Where to stay (see 'Guided and supported') *Campi.*
Etherley Fm (foot of Leith Hill, tel 01306 621315,
groups welcome, map ref TQ 139432); *YHA hostel*
Holmbury St Mary - check it's not been closed (tel 08
770 5868); *B&B* Bulmer Farm, Holmbury St Mary (te
01306 730210)
Tourist offices Dorking (Mole Valley visitor centre, t
01306 879327), Guildford (tel 01483 444333)

SURREY HILLS WEST (DEVIL'S PUNCHBOWL) 81
see North Downs, NDs Way, Surrey Hills East-Redlands)

ag stunning riding on dramatic bridleway and byways around Surrey's highpoints. Owned by the lational Trust, the Devil's Punchbowl is a high blind combe with a very decent cafe at the rim. rom Gibbet Hill nearby, the second highest Surrey alp, you can see both the South and North owns, and descend to the valleys below. Locals can leave the car at home and travel there by ike on the Haslemere branch of the Surrey Cycleway. Londoners can take the train to Haslemere for a good warm-up climb to the Punchbowl!

here to ride
:ay on the bridleway/byways; the majority of the area is esignated SPA and SSSI for its rare heathland habitat 1d associated species.
elf-navigate the extensive bridleway/byways.
ood start points are the Devil's Punchbowl car park 1d cafe (A3 junction with the A287 Hindhead cross-)ads), and Haslemere station, down in the valley to the)uth (from where rides all start with a climb and finish ith a descent!).

Jggested routes
Punchbowl car park, north along then down the west Je of the Punchbowl, east past Ridgeway Farm, return) the east side.
Punchbowl car park, east 1km to Gibbet Hill (272m), op east and south into the valley, and return west and orth via lanes and trails.
South of Haslemere, gentler trails around Black Down 80m), the highest point in West Sussex (also NT).
Hindhead Also gentler west of Hindhead on Ludshott ommon.
Extend north to Rushmoor, Thursley. Tilford and stead, to the North Downs and North Downs Way 0km as the crow flies).

6) Extend south to Henley and Midhurst, to the South Downs and South Downs Way (18km as the crow flies).
Mapping and literature
OS Explorer 133, Landranger 186 Aldershot Guildford; *Surrey Cycleway* map free (tel 08456 009 009)
Location
Cycle via the Surrey Cycleway on the Haslemere link; by train ride up from Haslemere station (5km south by road, 3km offroad); by road from the A3, park at the NT car park by the cafe.
Bike shops
Liphook Cycles, Liphook (8km A3 southwest, tel 01428 727858)
Where to eat & drink
Devil's Punchbowl Cafe (tel 01428 606565), pubs and cafes in Haslemere
Where to stay
YHA hostel
Hindhead (self-catering only, tel 0870 770 5864) at the bottom of the Punch Bowl (car parking 1km away)
Tourist office
Guildford (14 Tunsgate, tel 01483 444333)
Info point at Haslemere Museum (tel 01428 645425)

62 **TEIGNBRIDGE TRIANGLE**
Southeast Devon
(see also Dartmoor, Haldon Forest)

Dartmoor may be far better known in Devon for mountain bike trails, but on the coastal countryside to the south is a labyrinth of bridlepaths and green lanes (unclassified white roads) worth exploring. The area lies inside a triangle formed by Newton Abbot, Shaldon (on the mouth of the Teign) and Torquay. Link the ways for interesting riding, which does get rough in places.

Mapping OS Landranger 202 (192), Explorer 110
Bike shops OnAbike in Queen St, Newton Abbot (tel 01626 334664), The Big Peaks, Ashburton (tel 01364

654080), Hot Pursuit, Totnes (tel 01803 865174)
Tourist office Newton Abbot (Courtney St, tel 0162 215667) **Station** Newton Abbot

41 **THETFORD FOREST PARK**
Suffolk-Norfolk
(see also Peddars Way, Tunstall Forest)

Thetford Forest (pictured above) lets East Anglia hold its head up high in mountain bike circles. A large patchwork of pine and heathland, it lies in the driest part of Britain and is known for volume of good forest single and doubletrack, and as a competition venue. Being sandy, the tracks drain well, so the forest stays rideable when the rest of England sinks into the mire. A great place to lure a mate with MTB potential to. Also excellent for families to play in while the riders ride.

Where to ride
Start from High Lodge forest centre. The toll road to the forest centre costs £3.50.
Dedicated routes
Black (16km difficult/technical) singletrack with technical and varied tracks, experience and skill needed.
Blue (10km easy/moderate) some sand and gradients;
Self-navigating On all surfaced tracks across the forest park, but do not stray onto neighbouring army land
Mapping and info OS Landranger 144, Explorer 229; Thetford Forest Park is run by the Forestry Commission (www.forestry.gov.uk/thetfordforestpark)
High Lodge Forest Centre (tel 01842 815434) Facilities include a good cafe and shop.

Bike shops and hire Bike Art Cycle Hire, at High Lodge (sales, repairs, tel 01842 810090, www.bike-art.com). **Mountain Bike Club** loads of friendly regulars but no organised local club at time of writing.
Location Off B1107 halfway Thetford-Brandon.
Where to stay *Camping* Thorpe Woodland C&C, Shadwell (6km E Thetford town, in season tel 01842 751 042, out of season tel 0131 314 6505); *Self-catering* Old School Cottage, Great Hockham (13km NE of Thetford town, tel 01953 498277); *Farm B&Bs* College Farm, Thompson (NE of forest, tel 01953 483318), Home Farm, Stow Bedon (off A1075 NE of forest, tel 01953 483592); *B&B* Colveston Manor, Mundford (N edge of forest, tel 01842 878218).

TROUGH OF BOWLAND
Lancashire
(see also Gisburn Forest)

12

The bridleways around the Trough of Bowland are a favourite with those in the know. Spectacular trails climb steep-sided hills to the highest hilltops, such as Ouster Rake, for the finest views. The area is part of the vast upland Forest of Bowland (although it has few trees), located inland from the Lancashire seaside towns. Dunsop Bridge is the start/finish village.

Where to ride

The beauty of the Trough is you can do several very different loops over a few days, then join some or all of them for rides which either last a few hours or become a day epics.

warning. Most routes cross at least one exposed hilltop. In the winter navigating the bridleways can be tricky. A map, compass and extra layers are a pre-requisite, regardless of the starting conditions.

Self-navigating

All routes start from Dunsop Bridge.

Ouster Rake Toughie (very spectacular, with a steep and very technical descent), go north along the Trough road, then take the bridleway east rising over the moor to Ouster Rake summit.

Short Loop Easier For a less technical but no less scenic route go south of the village on farm tracks, forested singletrack and open moorland, before a rollercoaster down the wide grassy hillside to the Trough road. Then you can go left for an attempt on Ouster Rake, or right back to the village.

Gisburn Forest lies 23km north with its waymarked and graded trails (see entry). Grab a local to show you

the hidden depths of the undiscovered options.

Location From M6 J31 go E on the B6243. After 7km join the B6244 and head into Longridge. From there follow signs for Whitewell, then Dunsop Bridge. By the time you've arrived, you'll understand how remote this place is. **Station** Clitheroe

Bike shop Pedal Power, Clitheroe (20km from the start, tel 01200 422066)

Mapping and literature

OS Landranger 103 Blackburn Burnley

Where to eat and drink

Dunsop Bridge is a summer-time tourist trap, yet has one cafe and few shops.

Newton, 5km east (on the final descent off the moor) has the fine Parkers Arms which welcomes mountain bikers. Or grab a meat and potato pie with brown sauce from the burger van (tea in proper mugs too).

Where to stay

YHA hostel

Slaidburn (self-catering only, tel 0870 770 6034)

B&B Wood End Farm, Dunsop Bridge (a working farm, and cheap depending on the season, tel 01200 448223)

Tourist office Clitheroe (tel 01200 442226)

Along the ancient road: the Ridgeway

Doctor's Gate: the Peak District

North Wales' other mountains: the Clwydians

43 ▶ TUNSTALL FOREST
Suffolk
(see also Thetford Forest)

Official singletrack *a la* Thetford is part of future plans at Tunstall Forest. Meanwhile you may pedal anywhere in this brackeny forest near Aldeburgh on the coast, on a significant amount of fu twisty singletrack that scoots between the forest roads, bucking over little banks and ditches. For the family, there's lots of easy riding in Rendlesham Forest, the next woodland south.

Location
Park at Sandygalls car park (from A12 Aldeburgh turning, go 4km E towards Aldeburgh, then S to Snape, through Blaxhall Common, then left on white road (direction Iken), go 2km and the car park's on the right. Or park anywhere in the spaces in the forest (but please don't block the forest gates – at the end of the day the foresters can't get home!)
Mapping and literature OS Landranger 156,

Explorer 212; ride leaflet on the Rendlesham Forest family riding from the forestry office (tel 01394 450164) but none for Tunstall Forest.
Where to stay
YHA hostel Blaxhall (meals, tel 0870 770 5702)
Farm B&B Moat House Farm, Carlton (1km N of Saxmundham, tel 01728 602228)
Farm B&B and self-catering High House Farm, Cransford (15km NW of forest, tel 01728 663461).

47 ▶ WARWICKSHIRE

Warwickshire has 555km of bridleways, which you can link together using lanes to make up easy-moderate rural farmland routes with some mellow hills.

Where to ride
Start points include Kenilworth (north) Ratley and Middle Tysoe for Edge Hill (S & Oxfordshire) Upper and Lower Brailes/Whichford and Stourton (south/Oxfordshire).
Mapping and literature
OS Explorer 221 Coventry and Warwick
Guidebook *Mountain Bike Guide – West Midlands* (Dave Taylor, The Ernest Press www.ernest-press.co.uk)

Website www.warwickshire.gov.uk/ countryside.
Bike shop Mike Vaughan Cycles, Kenilworth (tel 019? 853944), Broadribbs, Leamington Spa (tel 01926 421428) **Stations** Warwick, Leamington Spa
Where to eat and drink
Kenilworth has cafes and pubs
Where to stay Lots of B&Bs in Kenilworth, Warwoc Leamington Spa and Stratford
Tourist office Warwick (tel 01926 492212).

WESSEX RIDGEWAY
Dorset-Wiltshire
(see also Blandford Forum, Cranborne Chase, Dorset Coast)

73

long and wonderful 30km section of the Wessex Ridgeway trail in Dorset is bridleway, between aiden Newton (on the A356 10km northwest of Dorchester) and Iwerne Courtney, north of landford Forum. The trail follows the steep curves of downland and is well off the beaten track. ne high number of connecting bridleways make any number of wonderful downland loops ossible. One highlight is Hambledon Hill 6km north of Blandford Forum.

here to ride
lf-navigating The bridleway section of trail runs for
)km. Use any of these as start/finish points, SW-NE; via
aiden Newton, Sydling St Nicholas, Cerne Abbas,
ton Pancras, Melcombe Bingham, Woolland, Ibberton,
keford Hill (see Blandford Forum Freeride Park),
illingstone to Hambledon Hill and Iwerne Courtney.
apping and literature
5 Landranger 194 Dorchester and Weymouth

Where to stay see also Blandford Forum
B&Bs
Badger Hill, Cerne Abbas (tel 01300 341698)
The Poacher's Inn, Piddletrenthide (tel 01300 341698)
Manor House Farm, Ibberton (tel 01258 817349)
Station Maiden Newton
Tourist offices
Dorchester (tel 01305 267992)
Blandford Forum (tel 01258 454770).

WHARNCLIFFE WOODS, SOUTH YORKS

24

harncliffe's contours have earned it a radical name with downhillers, but at time of writing the e's hardcore riding was undergoing a safety review. The woods lie at the very eastern edge of e Peak District (just on the OL1 Explorer map) within easy reach of Sheffield, and riding there s been developed so far with the help of world-beating downhiller Steve Peat.

here to ride
rt from the car park (see below).
time of writing, following collisions between bikers
d horses, the black route is undergoing a safe and
stainable redesign. Meanwhile, easy riders can use the
nily route, and the Trans-Pennine Trail which runs
oss the north of the site.
cation
harncliffe lies 8km north of central Sheffield, just
side the Peak District, bounded to the west by the
102 and to the east by the A61.
ach the wood from the car park on the Woodhead

road running northwards through the village of
Grenoside. Map ref SK 321 950
Mapping and literature
OS Landranger 110, Explorer OL1 Peak District – Dark
Park (latest edition)
Mountain bike club
Sports & social club Spice South Yorkshire does runs in
the woods, see www.spicesyorks.com.

9 ▶ WHINLATTER FOREST PARK
Lake District

Ride waymarked routes and an MTB trail-orienteering course on steep terrain with wonderful views in England's only mountain forest. Siskin's Tearoom at the visitor centre does meals, while nearby Keswick has ample choice of accommodation, cafes, pubs and outdoor gear shops.

Where to ride
The *Forest Park guide* map (from the visitor centre) shows cycling routes and numbered forest road junctions so you can create your own route.
The waymarked routes and orienteering course are colour-coded.

Waymarked routes
Purple route (12km easy/moderate), has a small single-track section, 250m climbing and 5km of descent mostly on forest roads, with fabulous views at the top.
Orange route (9km) 150m of climbing, amazing views
MTB orienteering course (7km, easy gradient) starts at Noble Knott in the forest
Mapping OS Landranger 89 West Cumbria, Explorer OL4 The English Lakes - Northwest
Location
From Keswick take the A66 northwest towards Cockermouth. At Braithwaite turn west onto the B5292 for Lorton. Follow the Visitor Centre sign posts.
Visitor centre The visitor centre is open daily from 11am-4pm in winter, and 10am–5pm in summer. Parking is pay and display, with a small charge for the orienteering course.

Bike shops
Keswick Mountain Bikes (hire, repairs, parts, tel 017687 75202)
Lakeland Pedlar cycle shop and cafe, Keswick (tel 017687 75752)
Mountain Bike Clubs For ride buddies visit Lakeland Pedlar or Keswick Mountain Bikes (above)

Sustrans routes
NCN 71 Coast to Coast route runs through the forest
Stations Penrith (40km east, West Coast mainline)

Where to eat
Siskins cafe at the visitor centre
Swinside Inn, Newlands Valley (3.5km from Whinlatter, real ales, good pub food including vegetarian, tel 0176 78253)
Plentiful pubs and cafes in Keswick town centre

Where to stay
Keswick tourist office has listings and does bookings. See also www.dokeswick.com.

Camping
Scotgate Caravan Park, Braithwaite (3km from the forest tel 017687 78343);
Whin Fell Hall Farm, Lorton (6km west of the forest, tel 01900 85260).

YHA hostel
Keswick (6.5km from forest, meals, tel 0870 7705894 6.5km from Whinlatter Forest Visitor Centre)

B&Bs
Brierholme, Bank Street, Keswick (tel 017687 72938, facilities include lock-up cycle storage and owners with extensive local knowledge);
Swinside Inn, Newlands Valley (tel 017687 78253);
Powter Howe, Thornthwaite, Keswick (cycle storage, tel 017687 78415).
Hotels The Cottage in the Wood, Whinlatter Forest, Braithwaite (tel 017687 78409, cycle storage)

Tourist offices
Keswick (tel 017687 72645)
Whinlatter Forest visitor centre (tel 017687 78469)
Cockermouth (tel 01900 822634).

WOODBURY COMMON
East Devon

ast Devon may not be famous for mountains but it has many rideable bridleways, green lanes
nd commons, with testing climbs, fast descents and good singletrack.
here are trails to suit everyone, from beginner to expert, with a Devon cream tea never far
way. Arm yourself with the OS Explorer map and get down there.

Where to ride
oodbury Common is the site of the local race series,
hich comes and goes, see www.svcc.org.uk, the local
d Valley club website.

Self-navigating
he terrain is very varied, from woodland to ancient
bblebeds, joining many towns and villages and never
ry busy. The commons remain rideable all year as
ey have very good drainage, the hills are a bit muddier
winter. There are great views from Woodbury
ommon (a hill fort, treat with respect) across Lyme
y, Dartmoor and the Exe valley. Excellent singletrack at
ngly Dell on Woodbury Common.

start/finish towns, these all have easy off-road access;
dmouth, Exmouth, Ottery St Mary, Budleigh Salterton

Dedicated routes (routes pack from East Devon
uncil tel 01395 517557)

cton and Woodbury Common (8km, challenging),
rough heath and woodland, rough tracks and some
ad; start at the Four Firs car park (map ref 032864), SE
und bottom Bicton Common, bottom of Hayes
ood, nearly to East Budleigh, N road back round.

mouth Off-Road (15km, challenging), steep climbs &
scents; start Peak Hill car park (map ref 108873), N
wards Bulverton Hill, E tracks to road, N, to near Fire
acon Hill, SW zigzag track past, S road to Bowd, NW
ad/track near Harpford Wood, W S road via
rthmostown, road back to Mutters Moor, SW then E.

utters Moor (5km mainly flat), a very attractive short
ute; start at Mutters Moor car park (map ref 108 874),
main bridleway, pass heathland, re-enter woodland,
k right signed bdwy, descend, cross golf course then

left up stony track, at top left, continue, right fork, cntu
1.5km, round left, back to major track, right to return.
Fire Beacon Hill (8km level), superb views and a fast
descent then climb; start White Cross (map ref 116914),
SW road, track right to Fire Beacon Hill reserve, left
across heath, down the zigzag, N on the road to a cross-
roads, right, then right again back to White Cross.
Colaton Raleigh (7km), starting at Woodbury Castle car
park (map ref 032876) head all the way round Colaton
Raleigh Common on track all the way

Location Woodbury Common lies between Exeter
and Sidmouth, on the B3179.
Stations Exeter, Honiton, Exmouth
Mapping OS Landranger 192, Explorer 115
Facilities None, but see tourist offices (below). The
land is owned and cared for by Clinton Devon Estates
(tel 01392 443881) and the Forestry Commission.
Mountain Bike Club Sid Valley CC has keen MTB
members (Richard Mallett, tel 01404 815338, see
www.svcc.org.uk for advice and contact with locals)
Bike shops The Bike Shed, 163 Fore St, Exeter
(tel 01392 426191);
Knobblies, Exmouth (hire, tel 01395 270182)
Bike shop Where to stay
Holiday Parks Ladram Bay Holiday Centre (tel 01395
568398), Pooh Cottage Holiday Park (1.5km away, tel
01395 442354), St John's Caravan and Camping Park
(3km east, tel 01395 263170); *Farmhouse B&B*
Holbrook Farm, Clyst Honiton (tel 01392 367000)
Tourist offices
Exmouth (tel 01395 222299), Budleigh Salterton (tel
01395 445275), Sidmouth (tel 01395 516441).

46 ▶ WYE VALLEY
Gloucestershire-Monmouthshire

It's not technical, but it's very lovely.

The twisting, steeply-wooded Wye Valley is carved by the River Wye en route to the Severn Estuary at Chepstow. In the valley bottom lie the superb Tintern Abbey and pretty villages.

By linking lanes and bridleway sections of the Offa's Dyke path, you can do a splendid easy ride along the river from Tintern Parva, just north of Tintern Abbey, to Redbrook and back.

The mapped route appears in *Philip's Cycle Tours - Around Gloucester & Hereford* (£8.99)

Tourist office Tintern (in old railway carriages, 1.5km north of abbey off B road, tel 01291 689566)

36 ▶ WYRE FOREST
Worcestershire

Bikers get a free run in the North Kinlet MTB area, the northernmost part of the Wyre Forest. Which is pretty lucky, as the forest is one of the most ecologically important in the country as well as being officially designated for family cycling (as there is so much good off-roading westward in the Shropshire Hills, see entry). In addition to the freeride area, there is a sound degree of handsome sloping bridleways plus easy riding on the main stoned roads – but don't ride anywhere else. The ranger writes, 'the Forestry Commission owns half the forest. The rest has many different landowners, including English Nature who have different policies to our own. In most cases there is no access to these areas, but the boundaries are not always clear!'

Where to ride
North Kinlet MTB area occupies the land (around 50m height difference) that lies north of the B4199 (section Buttonoak to Buttonoak Bridge), meaning Blackgraves Copse, Postensplain and Coldwell Copse.
Self-navigating Valley bridleway W-E 5km following Dowle Brook between the W edge near Far Forest and Bewdley, also N-S all the way from the B4194 to the visitor centre, on the S edge of the forest at Callow Hill. You may also ride anywhere on the stoned forest roads.
Family trails Two waymarked trails follow the stoned/clay roads from the visitor centre.
Where to eat and drink Cafe at the Wyre Forest

Visitor Centre (tel 01299 266944), pubs at Buttonoak (near freeride area), Callow Hill (near visitor centre) and Buckridge (SW of forest), also in Bewdley
Location Wyre Forest is NW neighbour to Bewdley. For the freeride area, park on B4199 4km NW of Bewdley either at the Buttonoak or the Earnwood Copse car parks. The visitor centre lies on the S edge of the forest at Callow Hill (on A456 6km W of Bewdley)
Mapping and literature OS Landranger 138, Explorer 218; family cycle route map from visitor centre
Bike shop Smith Cycles, Kidderminster (3 New Road, tel 01562 823721)
Tourist office Bewdley (tel 01299 404740).

YORKSHIRE DALES

(see also Howgills, Nidderdale)

The Yorkshire Dales ranks one of the top-five places to go mountain biking, aided by the four-sheet series of Harvey maps which colour-grade the rights of way according to difficulty. This is beautiful high open moorland with absolutely masses of bike-legal riding featuring dozens of long climbs and descents, and trails that traverse, contour and fall. The upland is wild but not alpine, and falls away into frequent valleys, so you get a dramatic experience with a measure of the demands of remote mountain riding. The dales towns and villages are picturesque and well set up for visitors, with cyclists' cafes and pubs, and accommodation for all tastes and budgets.

Many trails have a history as well as being great to ride, being a mixture of Roman byways, monastic highways, mining tracks and drovers roads.

Thus many are on gradients that keep you in the saddle rather than off and pushing!

Where to ride

Guided and supported Contact Saddle Skedaddle (tel 0191 265 1110, www.skedaddle.co.uk)

Self-navigating (this is scratching the surface) Use bridleways, by-ways (BOATS) and the extensive green lane network. You can design circuits that go up and down dales, and from dale to dale via the moorland tops. You can also use the Settle-Carlisle railway for linear routes (see below)

North – around Arkengarthdale, Melbecks Moor, around upper Swaledale, around Wensleydale, Castle Bolton, Wether Fell (bases are Aysgarth, Fremington, Hinton, Hawes, Leyburn, Muker and Reeth).

East – Pateley Bridge (see **Nidderdale** entry for the main entry).

South – Mastiles Lane and Malham Moor, Wharfedale, the Whernsides (bases are Grassington, Malham and Settle, see also Nidderdale).

West – Dentdale, Littondale, Langstrothdale, the Cam High Road towards Foxup and Pen-y-Ghent (694m) (bases are Ingleton, Hawes and Horton-in-Ribblesdale).

Waymarked route The Yorkshire Dales Cycleway is a set, circuitous 210km on-road route starting and finishing in Skipton, divided into six day sections of 30-40km. The route links Skipton, Malham, Ingleton, Hawes, Grinton and Kettlewell.

Mapping

Harvey Maps *Walking & Cycling: Dales - North, South, East and West* (1:40,000, waterproof, trails colour-graded for MTBing, £6.95, tel 01786 841202, www.harveymaps.co.uk);

OS Explorers OL2 Yorkshire Dales (northern & central), OL30 Yorkshire Dales (southern & western), 298 (Nidderdale, Fountains Abbey, Ripon & Pately Bridge), OL19 (Howgill Fells & Upper Eden Valley);

OS Landrangers 91 Appleby-in-Westmorland, 92 Barnard Castle, 98 Wensleydale & Upper Wharfedale, 99 Northallerton & Ripon.

Literature

Guidebooks: *Philip's Cycle Routes – The Yorkshire Dales* (£8.99, 20 mapped routes); *Mountain Bike Route Guide - Yorkshire Dales* (Tim Woodcock, Dalesman MTB Guides, £7.99, 22 mapped routes); **Webroutes**: see www.mtbroutes.com for downloadable routes for Malham-Suler-Foxup, West Cam-Cam High Rd

Bike Shops Settle Cycles, Settle (tel 01729 822216), Eric Burgess Cycles, Skipton (01756 794 386), JD Bicycle Workshop, Nelson Road, Ilkley (tel 01943 816101), Arthur Caygill Cycles, Borough Road, Gallowfields Trading Estate, Richmond (tel 01748 825469). [CONT]

Bike hire Dales Mountain Biking, West Hagg, Fremington (tel 01748 884356)

Mountain Bike Clubs
Blackburn & District MTB (tel 01200 445859, affiliated to On Yer Bike, Blackburn, tel 01254 662440) arranges rides to a number of nearby locations; Chevin MBC, Leeds (tel 01943 462105); Otley Women's MTB Group (tel 01943 465051)

Sustrans The Pennine Cycleway NCN 68 runs through the National Park from Gargrave in the south to Sedbergh.

Leeds-Settle-Carlisle railway This runs through the western dales (stations at Skipton, Gargrave, Long Preston, Hellifield, Settle, Horton, Ribblehead, Dent, Garsdale, see www.settle-carlisle.co.uk) for great linear rides where, if you play your cards right, you can have the wind at your back all day. Check conditions of bike carriage in advance as they vary. Skipton and Ilkley have excellent train services from Leeds and Bradford (bike-carrying capacity, no need to book, but avoid rush hour from Leeds).

Where to stay
Tourist offices have lists of local accommodation. Below is a selection. See more on the following;
www.stilwell.co.uk, www.dalesaccommodation.com and www.dalenet.co.uk.

Camping Bainbridge Ings, Hawes (tel 01969 667354, www.bainbridge-ings.co.uk),
Gordale Scar Camping (tel 01729 830333)

Bunkhouses
Barden Tower, Wharfedale (tel 01756 720616), Dub-Cote, Pen-y-Ghent (tel 01729 860238), Catholes, Sedbergh (tel 015396 20334),
Halton Gill, Littondale (tel 01756 770241),
Hill Top Farm, Malham (tel 01729 830320, www.malhamdale.com), the Barnstead, Ingleton (tel 015242 413386)

YHA hostels There are 12; Aysgarth Falls, Dentdale,, Ellingstring, Grinton Lodge, Hawes, Ingleton, Keld, Kettlewell, Kirkby Stephen, Linton, Malham, Stainforth, book in advance in season (tel 0870 770 8868, www.yha.org.uk)

B&Bs/Hotels The New Inn, Appletreewick, Wharfedale (tel 01756 720252).

Pubs Most towns and villages have hostelries. Here are three favourites;
The New Inn, Appletreewick (the Dales MTB pub, although the owner's tenure was in doubt at time of writing, excellent food and beer, tel 01756 720252).
Hill Inn (6km north of Keld on the county border, map ref NY896067, tel 01833 628246)
lies at the bottom of several routes, and has a good atmosphere.
The George, Hubberholme (tel 01756 760223) for good filling fayre and Yorkshire ales.

Cycling cafes
Gargrave - the Dalesman
(walls jam-packed with pictures of cyclists past and present, tel 01756 749250).
Settle - the Naked Man, the Settle Down.
Ingleton - Bernie's
(popular with cavers, cyclists and walkers).
Horton-in-Ribblesdale - the Pen-y-Ghent
(reasonably-priced food and drink, 'book-a-bed-ahead' tel 01729 860333).

Tourist offices
Aysgarth Falls (tel 01969 663424),
Hawes (tel 01969 667450), Leyburn (tel 01969 623069), Reeth (tel 01748 884059),
Kirkby Stephen (tel 017683 71199), Pateley Bridge (tel 01423 711147), Sedbergh (tel 015396 20125), Settle (tel 01729 825192), Skipton (tel 01756 792809), Grassington (tel 01 756 752774), Yorkshire Dales National Park Centre, Grassington (tel 01756 752748

YORKSHIRE WOLDS AND SPURN HEAD   ◀ 20

he South Downs of the north of England. Sounds odd, but that is exactly what the Yorkshire
'olds are. Situated to the east of York, and immediately north of the Humber between Goole
₁d Hull, this broad agricultural area is the last gasp of the great chalk belt that traverses England
₂fore it dives into the North Sea beyond out reach. Same close-cropped grass, same dry valleys,
₃ surface water worth speaking of, artesian wells at every farm and the occasional shard of flint
your tyre! This isn't mountain country, the transmission masts can be found about the 250m
₄ntour, but there is enough hard work to entertain the toughest and many of the downhills can
₅ very slippery when wet due to the generous covering of grass!

here to ride

₁f-navigating

₁e Wolds is an area you need to work at, both naviga-
₂nally and often in the riding: this is the worst place in
₃gland for bridleways turning into footpaths as they
₄ss parish boundaries!

₁ny of the bridleways see little use, many of the direc-
₂al arrows are hidden in undergrowth, disguised by
₃gradation or licked to death by cattle, but those on the
₄lds Way or the Minster Way are well-signposted,
₅y reassuring when following something that snakes
₆ng a dry valley bottom.

₁e of the greatest trail densities is found around Warter
₂ld (map ref SE 885 523), Huggate Head (SE 890
₃) and Huggate Wold (at 855 565); with an additional
₄ch in Welton Wold (SE 980 301).

₁er places worth visiting are Thixendale Wold (SE 840
₂ and 830 608) – keeping an eye out for bits of the
₃lds Way, look for blue 'patches' on the map –
₄thorpe Wold (SE 940 565 and 960 579), Mowthorpe
₅ld (at SE 892 680), Thirkleby Wold (929 681) and
₆th of Wetwang (at 943 613).

₁way of a change, the very low level bridleways
₂und Hotham Carrs (SE 850 329) might provide
₃ne amusement.

Spurn Head

And for something completely different, but also unique
ride the Spurn, a constantly changing thin spit of land
running 6km roughly SSW from the hamlet of Kilnsea
(TA 417 159) to Spurn Head (397 107), where you find
the Humber Pilots Station.

The road is not exactly 'as map'. It has changed many
times, as the North Sea has eroded the seaward side of
the spit, and when you get to the end you might be
amazed to find that people actually live out there! The
road, designated a bridleway, varies from broken tarmac
to sand. Allow at least three hours.

Bike shops Freetown Cycles, 70 Prospect St, Hull (tel
01482 589066), Minster Cycles, Beverley (tel 01482
867950), Bells Cycles, Driffield (tel 01377 253070)
Mapping and literature OS Landrangers 100, 101,
106, 107, 113; Explorers 291, 292 293, 294, 295;
Guidebook: *Mountain Bike Guide – Mid Yorkshire,*
Ryedale & the Wolds (Dennis Liversidge, the Ernest
Press, tel 0141 637 5492, www.ernest-press.co.uk)
Where to eat Cafe at Bell Mills Garden Centre,
Skerne Rd, Driffield (tel 01377 250912)
Where to stay B&B Number One Woodlands,
Beverley (tel 01482 862752);
Laburnum Cottage, Millington (tel 01759 303055)
Tourist offices Beverley (open year round, tel 01482
867430), Humber Bridge (tel 01482 640852).

Go with the flow on the classic Karrimor trail at Coed y Brenin, north Wales

wderdale Beck in the Howgills

Gliding through the trees at Glentress

NDEX OF PLACES

ACKNOWLEDGEMENTS

A large cast of mountain bikers and others helped out with this book;

WRITING CREDITS

Mark Alker (*Singletrack* magazine, singletrack-world.com) contributed the South Pennines (Mary Towneley loop) and Trough of Bowland entries.

Catriona Cooke of the British Horse Society for her piece in the introduction.

Katie Dixon compiled the entries for the Isle of Wight, Yorkshire Dales, Machynlleth, the Berwyns and Lake Vyrnwy, Deers Leap Park, Haldon Forest, Friston Forest/Cuckmere, Jack Mytton Way, Gisburn, Fochabers and Craigvinean Forest.

Kieran Foster wrote the entries for Co Durham, Nidderdale, the North Pennines, and provided info on the Cross-Border route (Newcastleton-Kielder)

Ben Haworth (benhaworth.frankencrank.com) wrote the entry for the Howgills and helped with Cader Idris.

Horace at Hobo for the Sirhowy and South Beacons entry.

Katie Jarvis of the Forestry Commission at Grizedale wrote the Broughton Moor/Walna Scar Road entry.

Colin Palmer provided information on IMBA.

Clive Powell (clivepowell-mtb.co.uk) for info on Rhayader and the Elan Valley, also the Brecon Beacons.

Derek Purdy (tel 01670 518708) wrote the entries for the Central Highlands, the Islands, Cairngorm and Monadliath Mountains (including Aviemore, the Corrieyairack Pass, Glen Livet), the Great Glen, the Peak District (Dark and White Peak), the Cheviots, North York Moors and the Yorkshire Wolds.

Neil Simpson contributed to the Rivington and South Pennines entries.

Andy Stephenson (of Bike Treks, Ambleside, tel 015394 31245) wrote the main entry for the Lake District.

Steve Thomas (imageadventure.co.uk, tel 01691 860536) wrote the entries for the Berwyns and Lake Vyrnwy.

RESEARCH CREDITS

Thanks to the following for providing information, including many rangers and staff of the Forestry Commission.
Thanks also to the Singletrack forum (singeltrackworld.com) for pointers regarding classic rides.

James Anderson-Bickley (FC West Argyll), Jeremy Atkinson (Radnor), Anna Baness (Dartmoor Nat Pk), Carl Bartlett (FC Scotland), Steve Bennett (Clent Hills, Kinver Edge, Wyre Forest), Paul Brandon (Hawick Cycles - Chaik), Chris Bray (FC Sherwood Pines, Wharncliffe), Dan Cadle (FC Galloway), Pete Carty (NT Long Mynd), Richard Castle (Epping MBC), Michael Clark (Sevenoaks), Martin Colledge (FC Gisburn), Marcus Craythorne (Thetford), Dafydd Davis (Wales), Brian Duff (FC Inverness), Pam Eastwood (FC Forest of Bere), Rachel Evans (FC SE England-Alice Holt), Emma Felkin (FC Brechfa, Canaston), Robin Fuller (FC Scotland, Dalbeattie, Mabie and Ae), Peter Fullerton (FC Tay), Jim Gaffney (Clwydian Range), Helen Gamble (Lincolnshire Wolds AONB), Hayden Garlick (Preselis), Andy Gattaker (South Downs), Emma Guy (Glentress), Bridgette Hall (FC Haldon), Kevin Haldane (West Argyll, Crinan Cycles), Jim Hardcastle (Mendips AONB), Paul Harris (Oxfords CC - Ironstone Hills), Paddy Harrop (FC), Paul Hawkins (Exmoor Nat Pk), Sally Haynes (Corp of London - Epping), Simon Hough (FC Delamere), John Ireland (FC Lochaber), Paul Jackson (Howardian Hills AONB), Kav Kavanagh (Salisbury Plain), David Keegan (Cairngorms - Bothy Bikes tel 01479 810111), Keith Bikes and Hikes (Brecon Beacons bikesandhikes.co.uk), Robin Kennedy (FC Scotland), Pippa Kirkham (FC North York Moors, Hamsterley, Kielder), Mike Johnson (Leicester), Adrian Jones (FC Whinlatter), Joss Joslin (Ridgeway) Graeme Layzell (FC Cwm Carn), Tim Lidstone-Scott (Peddars Way), James Littlewood (Chilterns AONB), Richard Mallett (Sid Valley CC - Woodbury Common), Robert Mayhew (FC Kielder), Nigel McDonald (Shropshire Hills), Jason McLean (FC Cannock), Rebecca Milbourn (Surrey Hills East-Redlands), Peter Mitchell (FC Trossachs), Dennis Moir (FC Shropshire), Matt Moseley (Warwickshire CC), Richard Morgan (Mid Wales Brecon Beacons, Radnor, Builth Wells, Rhayader, Llanwrtyd Wells), Mark Mortimer (FC Coed y Brenin), Nick Murfin (FC Afan), Lindsay Pearce (Pearce Cycles), Richard Pearce (FC Dalby), Grant Portsmouth (Pompy's Cycles tel 01643 704077, Combe Sydenham), Lindsay Robertson (Nevis Range), Justin Rowe (Blandford Freeride Park), Chris Saunders (Deer's Leap Park), Leo Scheltinga (FC Gwydyr-Betws), Tim Slade (Isle of Wight CC), Mark Shimizdu (Trossachs Backpackers), Paul Smedley (FC Nant yr Arian), Richard Smith (Sevenoaks - Wildside Cycles), John Stafford (FC Friston Forest), Janie Steele (FC Lorne), Swinnerton Cycles (tel 01782 747782, Cannock) Ian Warby (Aston Hill, Chilterns), Tony Watson (Teignbridge), Chris Weedon (FC Ashton Court, Bristol), Sandy White (FC Galloway), Phil Whitfield (FC Moray/Fochabers).

PHOTO CREDITS

Simon Barnes (bogtrotters.org): p82 Walna S route, p108 Parkamoor, p138 Dark Peak, p1 White Peak, p152-153 High St, p161 Bowla

Steve Behr/Stockfile (stockfile.co.uk): p12 Afi p104 Exmoor, p143 Penshurst.

Steve Bennett (stratobiker.blokes.org.uk): p8 Bringewood, p111 Hopton trio.

Chipps Chippendale (singletrackworld.com) Coed Y Brenin, p9 Lakes, p10 Coed y Bren p14-15 Berwyns, p27 Marin Trail/Gwydyr Forest; p30 Machynlleth, p31 Nant yr Arian; p59 Glentress; p60-61 Slab/Dalbeattie Fores p68 Mabie Forest; p92-93 Nr Penrith/Lake District, p105 Forest of Dean, p112 S Penni p113 Quantocks summer and winter, p142 Pennines, p144 Quantocks, p157 S Pennine p160 Thetford.

Clwydians (ridetheclwyds.com): p21, p163 Clwydian range

Robert Hamilton-Smith: p26 Gower Penins

Ben Haworth (benhaworth.frankencrank.co p2 Howgills, p22 Coed y Brenin, p25-25 B Y Coed, p38-39 Marin Trail/Gwydyr Forest, p59 Glentress, p115 Howgills, p126 Long Mynd, p174 (Deliverance Glentress), p172 Coed Y Brenin, p173 Howgills.

Horace Hobo (hobo-backpackers.co.uk): p Outside Hobo Backpackers.

Ian Linton (ianlinton.co.uk); p50-51 all shots downhilling at Innerleithen and Ae Forest.

Bob Love (Scottish-downhill.co.uk): p42 Ae Forest.

Andy McCandlish (www.object4.com): p43 Ardgartan; p45 Rothiemurchus; p46 Cairngorms, p47 Central Highlands (left - heading down to Kinlochleven); p53 Dalbe p56 Glen Trool/Galloway Forest Park; p60-Slab/Dalbeattie Forest, 155 South Downs.

Steve Makin: p37 Snowdon, p99 Delamere Forest, p100 Long Mynd, Delamere Forest p154 South Downs, p162 (bottom) Peak District.

Nevis Range: p40, p55, p71 Fort William.

Neil Simpson: p47 Central Highlands, p13 North York Moors, p169 Yorkshire Dales.